Beyond Privatization:
The Tools of Government Action

LESTER M. SALAMON, Editor
assisted by Michael S. Lund

Beyond Privatization: The Tools of Government Action

THE URBAN INSTITUTE PRESS
Washington, D. C.

THE URBAN INSTITUTE PRESS
2100 M Street, N. W.
Washington, D. C. 20037

Library of Congress Cataloging in Publication Data
Beyond Privatization: The Tools of Government Action / edited by Lester M.
   Salamon ; assisted by Michael S. Lund.
       p.   *284*
     Includes bibliographies.
1. Government spending policy—United States. 2. Administrative agencies—
United States. 3. Grants-in-aid—United States. 4. Loans—United States—
Government guaranty. 5. Tax expenditures—United States. 6. Corporations,
Government—United States.
I. Salamon, Lester M.   II. Lund, Michael S.
HJ7539.B48 1988   338.973—dc19   88-27948
ISBN 0-87766-454-4
ISBN 0-87766-455-2 (casebound)

Printed in the United States of America

Distributed in the United States and Canada by
University Press of America 4720 Boston Way Lanham, MD 20706

THE URBAN INSTITUTE is a nonprofit policy research and educational organization established in Washington, D.C., in 1968. Its staff investigates the social and economic problems confronting the nation and government policies and programs designed to alleviate such problems. The Institute disseminates significant findings of its research through the publications program of its Press. The Institute has two goals for work in each of its research areas: to help shape thinking about societal problems and efforts to solve them, and to improve government decisions and performance by providing better information and analytic tools.

Through work that ranges from broad conceptual studies to administrative and technical assistance, Institute researchers contribute to the stock of knowledge available to public officials and private individuals and groups concerned with formulating and implementing more efficient and effective government policy.

Conclusions or opinions expressed in Institute publications are those of the authors and do not necessarily reflect the views of other staff members, officers or trustees of the Institute, advisory groups, or any organizations that provide financial support to the Institute.

ACKNOWLEDGMENTS

This is a book of exploration. It explores a new approach to the study of government operations, one that places at the center of analytical attention the numerous instruments or tools that governments use to carry out their objectives.

Like any work of exploration, this one required a leap of faith. Fortunately, a number of people were willing to take that leap with me, and, in doing so they helped make this book possible. Most importantly, I want to express my appreciation to the authors of the chapters that comprise this book. Many of them approached the "tools framework" that is explored here with a healthy degree of skepticism. Yet they were willing to put the approach to the test in their own areas of expertise and to submit to the discipline required to explore a new approach within a common analytical framework.

In addition to the authors, a number of other people made useful contributions to the development of the tools concept through their participation in a conference held on the topic in 1984, from which the papers in this book are drawn. Foremost among these were: David Beam, Jonathan Bruel, Robert Coakley, Erwin Hargove, Regina Herzlinger, Robert Newton, Harvey Sapolsky, and Kent Weaver.

In addition, I want to express my appreciation to Michael Lund and Alan Abramson, who helped me refine my thinking about the tools notion, often by questioning my assumptions or identifying thorny conceptual problems that I had not yet addressed. Dr. Lund also assisted in the organization of the conference from which this volume is drawn and in reviewing early drafts of many of the chapters.

A special thanks also goes to Janet Sale for transforming the various manuscripts into an integrated typescript and for doing so amidst other pressing responsibilities; and to Jacquelyn Perry for keeping the disparate pieces of this project in order.

Finally, to my wife, Lynda, and my sons, Noah and Matthew, I owe my deepest thanks for their love and support, and for the many distractions that help keep my thinking fresh and my work in useful perspective.

Support for the conference and related work from which this book is drawn was provided by the Alfred P. Sloan Foundation, the National Science Foundation, and The Urban Institute. To all of these organizations I am also deeply grateful. Naturally, however, they do not bear any responsibility for the result. That responsibility is mine alone.

Lester M. Salamon

CONTENTS

Text Tables

New ideas are a rarity in the social sciences. Most new approaches turn out, on closer inspection, to be rehashes of concepts developed at an earlier time and then lost from view.

It is this fact that makes *Beyond Privatization* such an important book. For here a group of scholars have begun to explore systematically a distinctively new approach to the study of public policy—an approach that identifies a new unit of analysis for policy research: namely, the different instruments or tools that the public sector uses to carry out its objectives.

This approach grows out of a very productive body of work that Dr. Lester Salamon carried out at The Urban Institute in the early 1980s. Salamon's argument is that a veritable technological revolution has taken place in the public sector in recent decades as a result of a rapid proliferation of new tools of government action. Each of these tools, he argues, has its own characteristics and its own consequences for program operations. Many of the problems attributed to the poor management of public programs may consequently really be a product of the choice of tool that is made. Under these circumstances, it becomes critically important to examine the characteristic properties and operating features of these different tools.

For several years, Salamon and a research team he assembled at The Urban Institute explored one of the least understood of these tools of government action—government's use of private nonprofit organizations to carry out public objectives. Their work, reported in over 40 monographs, books, and articles, revealed that in the human service field more government-funded services are delivered through nonprofit organizations than through government agencies. The American "welfare state," in short, is not run by the state at all, but by a host of nongovernmental "third parties."

In this volume, the net is thrown more broadly to encompass a wide range of different tools—loan guarantees, regulation, government corporations, grants, tax subsidies, and direct government. While several of these "tools" have been examined individually before, this is the first work that examines a substantial number of them in one place and within a common analytical framework. One of the significant conclusions is to confirm Salamon's contention that a widespread pattern of "third-party government" has emerged in this country with significant implications for how we think about the public sector. Beyond this, the result is a very encouraging start on a field of inquiry that seems likely to contribute to our understanding not only of how public programs work, but also of how they should be designed.

William Gorham
President

Part One

Introduction

Chapter One

THE CHANGING TOOLS OF GOVERNMENT ACTION: AN OVERVIEW

Lester M. Salamon

The enterprise of government has recently found itself under unusually severe attack in the United States. Popular frustration with the cost of government activities and disappointment with the effectiveness of many government programs, coupled with new "public choice" economic theories suggesting the inherent inefficiency of the public sector, produced a broad-gauged backlash against activist government during the 1980s. The result was the generation of political support for a significant reduction in government expenditures and widespread calls for the transfer of governmental responsibilities to the private sector or to lower levels of government.

What has so far been overlooked in the resulting debate over the proper role of government in modern America is the extent to which existing government programs already embody many of the key features of "privatization" and decentralization that conservative critics of government have recently been advocating. While popular rhetoric conveys the image that federal programs are run wholly by federal bureaucrats, in reality most are not. To the contrary, they make heavy use of precisely the private sector and state and local authorities that recent advocates of privatization and decentralization tend to favor. This is so thanks to a basic transformation that has occurred over the past 50 years or more in the underlying structure of the public sector in this country—a transformation that has attracted little attention but that lies at the heart of many of the challenges facing modern government.

What is involved in this transformation is not simply an expansion in the scope or range of government action. Even more important has been a massive proliferation in its basic forms—in the instruments or tools the public sector uses to carry out its activities.[1] These tools now include much more than direct service delivery by government bureaucrats. They also include project grants,

3

formula grants, direct loans, loan guarantees, interest subsidies, social regulation, contracting out, tax expenditures, vouchers, government corporations, franchises, price supports, entry restrictions, and many more. Indeed, a veritable technological revolution has taken place in the operation of the public sector in this country, characterized by a widespread expansion of the basic instruments used to carry out the public's business.

The purpose of this book is to lay a foundation for understanding this technological revolution and assessing its implications for the operation of the public sector. In particular, the book identifies the main rudiments of a "tools approach" to the analysis of public policy and analyzes six tools of public action now in widespread use.

To set the stage for this analysis, the present chapter outlines more fully the changes that have occurred in the tools of public action in recent decades and the challenges these pose for both the theory and practice of public management.

THE NEW TOOLS OF GOVERNMENT ACTION

A crucial starting point for this discussion must be the concept of a tool or instrument of public action itself. Underlying this concept is the notion that the multitude of individual government programs actually embody a limited array of mechanisms or arrangements that define how the programs work. One type of mechanism, for example, is the grant-in-aid, which essentially involves the provision of resources from higher levels of government to lower ones to encourage certain objectives. The federal Aid to Families with Dependent Children (AFDC) Program, for example, involves federal grants to state governments to finance payments by the state to female-headed families with children that have incomes below a state-prescribed level. Several hundred federal programs embody this grant-in-aid "technology," and these programs operate in fields as diverse as transportation and health. Other programs utilize direct service delivery by federal agencies, federal guarantees of loans made by private banks, or voucher payments such as food stamps or Medicare that allow eligible individuals to pay for certain specific commodities with some cash substitute.

Because many of the newer forms of government action do not appear as outlays in the federal budget, the technological revolution that has occurred in the public sector has attracted far less at-

Table 1.1 FEDERAL LOAN AND LOAN GUARANTEE PROGRAMS, FISCAL YEAR
1987 (billion dollars)

	Disbursements or guarantees	Outstanding amount
Loan guarantees	151.7	507.0
Direct loans	35.2	234.2
Total	186.9	741.2

Source: U.S. Office of Management and Budget, Budget of the U.S. Government Fiscal
Year 1989, Special Analysis (Washington, D.C.: OMB, 1988), F-16 and F-21.

tention than its counterparts in the worlds of science and industry.
Yet it is every bit as profound and certainly every bit as substantial.
Indeed, the scale of some of the newer tools of public action is
often quite staggering. Take federal *loan guarantees*, for example.
In fiscal year 1987 alone, the federal government extended $152 bil-
lion in new loan guarantees and had $507 billion in loan guaran-
tees outstanding (see table 1.1). In the same year, the federal
government extended $35 billion in *direct loans* and had $234 billion in direct loans outstanding. To put this into context, the total
amount of both direct loans and loan guarantees outstanding as of
1986 was thus more than two-thirds the size of the regular federal
budget for that year.[2]

A similar situation is also apparent with many other tools. Despite passage of the 1986 Tax Simplification Act, for example, the
federal government still made available an estimated $322 billion
in *tax expenditures* in fiscal year 1988 (see table 1.2). Such "expenditures" represent exceptions from the regular operation of the
income tax intended to encourage various types of activity (for example, investment in low income housing).

Federal *grants-in-aid* to state and local government, another instrument of government action, totaled $108 billion in fiscal year
1986. Such grants were a favored mechanism of government program growth during the 1960s and 1970s, as shown in table 1.3.
Their growth slowed during the Reagan era; however, grants still
represent close to 20 percent of all federal domestic spending.[3]

Similar data could also be presented on the many other types of
instruments, such as regulation, insurance, government corporations, and contracting out. Each of these has also become a major
system of action involving substantial resources, activities, and
personnel. What is more, each has expanded not only in scale, but
also in scope. Grants-in-aid are thus used for business promotion

as well as for social welfare. Loan guarantees are used for housing and also for higher education. This means that it is now necessary to view every substantive field of government action not simply as a collection of numerous programs, but also as an assemblage of wholly different types of tools. The 200 business assistance programs identified in the *Catalogue of Federal Domestic Assistance* as of 1980, for example, contained 14 separate forms of government action—including 5 formula grant programs, 23 direct loan programs, 29 guaranteed loan programs, 38 specialized or advisory services, and numerous others. And the *Catalogue* does not even

Table 1.2 TAX SUBSIDIES, 1970–88 (billion dollars)

Policy area	1970	1979	FY 1988 (estimated)
Agriculture	0.9	1.2	0.7
Commerce and transportation	14.1	42.4	79.7
Defense and international	0.3	3.7	4.8
Education and employment	1.4	12.6	22.8
Energy and natural resources	2.0	5.5	4.6
Health	3.2	15.5	36.1
Housing	8.7	24.3	50.6
Other	9.4	51.9	122.4
Overall order of magnitude[a]	40.0	157.1	321.7

Sources: U.S. Congress, Joint Economic Committee, *Federal Subsidy Programs* (Washington, D.C., 1974), 5; U.S. Office of Management and Budget, *Budget of the United States Government, Fiscal Year 1981, Special Analyses* (Washington, D.C.: OMB, 1980) 230–34; 1988 estimates from Joint Committee on Taxation, *Estimates of Federal Tax Expenditures for Fiscal Years 1988–1992* (JCS-3-87), February 27, 1987.
a. Figures shown here are intended to be suggestive only of orders of magnitude. Tax expenditures cannot properly be added together because of interactive effects not reflected in the individual figures.

Table 1.3 FEDERAL GRANT-IN-AID EXPENDITURES

	Fiscal year			Percent change	
	1950	1980	1987	1960–80	1980–87
Grants-in-aid (billion dollars)	2.3	91.5	108.4	+3,878	+18
Total domestic spending (billion dollars)	19.8	392.7	573.5	+1,883	+46
Grants as percentage of domestic spending	11.6%	23.3%	18.9%	—	—

Source: U.S. Office of Management and Budget, *Special Analysis, Budget of the United States Government, Fiscal Year 1988* (Washington, D.C. 1987), H-22.

Table 1.4 FEDERAL BUSINESS ASSISTANCE AND HEALTH PROGRAMS,
BY TYPE OF ASSISTANCE, 1980

Type of assistance	Number of Business and Commerce		Number of Health	
	Programs	Agencies	Programs	Agencies
Formula grants	5	3	26	8
Project grants	40	18	198	21
Direct payments specified use	8	4	5	2
Direct payments unrestricted	1	1	5	2
Direct loans	23	6	6	3
Guaranteed loans	29	6	11	4
Insurance	8	6	n.a.	n.a.
Sales, exchange of property	1	1	4	3
Use of property	2	2	3	3
Specialized services	17	8	16	6
Advisory services	21	9	17	9
Dissemination of information	25	5	21	9
Training	6	4	11	7
Investigation of complaints	7	6	2	1

Source: Computed from U.S. Office of Management and Budget, *Catalogue of Federal Domestic Assistance*, 1980.
n.a. Not applicable.

cover regulatory programs and government corporations (see table 1.4). Similarly, the 300 health-related programs listed in the *Catalogue of Federal Domestic Assistance* embody 13 different tools of public action.

THE CHALLENGE TO THEORY AND PRACTICE

This dramatic expansion in the technology of public action has important implications for recent critiques of modern government. It also poses serious challenges to public management and to traditional theories of public administration. The reason is twofold.

The Political Economies of Alternative Tools

In the first place, both the recent critics of government and the standard public administration theories take as given that government programs have essentially the same basic structure, involving the provision of some good or service by a set of public servants/ bureaucrats. It is this premise that makes it possible for advocates of the "public choice" school to posit general laws about the under-lying propensities of the public sector.

The fact that various government programs embody significantly different instruments of public action, however, opens this premise to serious question. What makes the use of different instruments so significant is that each instrument has its own distinctive proce-dures, its own network of organizational relationships, its own skill requirements—in short, its own "political economy." The operation of a loan guarantee program, for example, involves dealings with commercial banks; judgments about creditworthiness and equity participation; and procedures for secondary market sales, loan pro-cessing, default management, and the like. Such considerations have little in common with the operating requirements of, say, a social regulatory program. Whereas loan guarantee programs re-quire the skills and outlook of a banker, social regulatory programs more often need those of a lawyer and scientist. This is so because they require the specification of scientifically validated standards (for example, for air or water pollution) and the translation of such standards into legally enforceable rules.

In other words, each distinctive form of government action is really a complex system of action with its own personality, actors, and dynamics. Because of this, different instruments can be ex-pected to impart their own distinctive twists to the operation of public programs. What this suggests is the need for a body of theory that focuses not only on the distinction between the public and private sectors, but that also takes account of the distinctive features of the various technologies that the public sector uses to carry out its purposes. In short, it suggests the need for a tools ap-proach that shifts the unit of analysis in policy analysis from indi-vidual programs or policies to the generic tools or instruments of public action.[4]

The Rise of "Third-Party Government"

Not only has the recent critique of government failed to take ac-count of the distinctive characteristics of the various tools of gov-ernment action now in widespread use, it has also failed to recognize one of the most important features of some of the newer forms of action—that they put government in the position of oper-ating by remote control, relying on other entities to deliver the services that government has authorized. The federal government in particular does increasingly little itself, at least in the domestic sphere. Instead it operates through other entities—states, cities, counties, banks, industrial corporations, hospitals, nonprofit organizations, and a host of other nonfederal third parties. Indeed, we have created an elaborate system of third-party government,[5] in which government establishes priorities and generates funds but leaves the actual delivery of services and the operation of public programs to a variety of nonfederal third parties.

What is involved here is not simply contracting out for the purchase of clearly specified goods and services—a time-honored, traditional form of government action. The distinctive feature of third-party government is the sharing of a far more basic governmental function: the exercise of *discretion* over the use of public authority and the spending of public funds. The central reality of many of the newer tools of government action is that they vest a major share—perhaps even the lion's share—of the discretionary authority involved in the operation of public programs into the hands of one or another nonfederal, often nonpublic, third-party implementor.

This point is clearly evident in the operation of federal grants-in-aid, perhaps the principal vehicle for federal social program expansion from the 1930s through the 1970s. Grants-in-aid are essentially payments by the federal government to state and local governments to support state and local action that advances a federal objective. By its very nature, therefore, the grant-in-aid mechanism makes the pursuit of federal objectives dependent on the good offices of a host of relatively independent state and local governments. These are the governments that receive federal grants to carry out the federal purposes. Although the federal government imposes restrictions, state and local governments retain a considerable amount of discretion. Indeed, most recent studies of grant-in-aid implementation have come to the same conclusion V. O. Key reached in the 1950s: despite the complaints about federal intrusion, grant programs tend to do more to "liberate" state and local governments than to restrict them.[6] As Morton Grodzins explained in the 1960s, "the influence of the federal government in state and local operations, made possible by its purse power, and exercised through grants-in-aid, is more than balanced by the political power of the peripheral units. . . . Politics here are stronger than the purse."[7]

A similar situation exists, moreover, with some of the other mechanisms of third-party government. For example, under the federal student loan program, applicants go not to a bureaucrat in the Department of Education for their loans but to a local commercial bank, which actually extends the loan that the federal government then guarantees. It is therefore up to the bank in significant measure to determine how the application guidelines are applied in practice. Even regulatory programs vest considerable responsibility in the regulated industries, which must take the actions needed to meet the regulatory objectives and often generate the data needed to confirm this.

This heavy reliance on third parties to carry out public objectives has, in fact, become virtually the standard pattern of federal operation in the domestic sphere. This is clearly evident in recent trends in government spending and employment. While federal expenditures increased 12-fold in actual dollars and 4-fold in inflation-adjusted dollars between 1950 and 1978, federal employment barely increased by 50 percent. And even this understates the transformation that occurred, since some of the most rapidly growing forms of public action—such as regulation and loan guarantees—never show up in these budget figures. Quite clearly, by adopting the mechanisms of third-party government, the federal government has found a way to achieve an impressive surge of productivity, expanding its activities massively without expanding its work force correspondingly. It has done so by enlisting other institutions in its activities, though at the cost of sharing with them a significant portion of the responsibility for defining and achieving public objectives.

IMPLICATIONS FOR PRIVATIZATION

This widespread pattern of third-party government makes recent debates over the proper roles of government and the private sector, if not irrelevant, at least largely moot. What becomes clear is that the typical domestic government program involves not government takeover of some private function, as conservative critics seem to fear, but a complex pattern of sharing between the two. To be sure, the resulting relationships are not without their tensions and strains, but it is still inappropriate to view them as wholly governmental when in fact they compel government to share key elements of its discretionary authority with private and other public bodies.

Despite its strains, moreover, this form of government action has much to recommend it. Most important, it utilizes government for what it does best—raising resources and setting societal priorities through a democratic political process—while utilizing the private sector for what it does best—organizing the production of goods and services. In the process it reconciles the traditional American hostility to government with recent American fondness for the services that modern society has increasingly required government to provide.

For advocates of privatization, however, this widespread and historically rooted practice of third-party government poses something of a problem. To the extent that privatization implies the sharing of governmental functions between the public and private sectors, it is already firmly entrenched in the federal program structure, and has been for decades. Many of the very governmental programs that have attracted the most severe conservative critiques—such as Urban Development Action Grants and employment and training— have embodied such shared authority most starkly. What this demonstrates is the importance of going beyond simplistic stereotypes about the structure of public programs and examining more carefully the actual technologies being used.

IMPLICATIONS FOR THE THEORY OF PUBLIC ADMINISTRATION

Not only do the proliferation of new tools of public action and the prevalence of third-party government pose problems for advocates of privatization, they also raise serious questions about the adequacy of traditional theories of public administration. For all its advantages, third-party government creates serious problems of management and accountability for which standard public administration theory fails to prepare us. This is so because, as noted, third-party government places significant shares of the authority for running federal programs into the hands of nonfederal, often nonpublic, institutions over which federal managers have imperfect control at best. Thus the task facing the federal manager is even more difficult than Norton Long suggested in his seminal essay, "Power and Administration," almost four decades ago. Power in the American administrative state, Long observed, does not simply flow down the chain of command from the top. Rather, each agency must actively pursue it on its own, reaching out to key legislators and private groups and thus bringing the power to act into the agency "from the sides."[8]

The third-party government concept outlined here suggests that even when federal managers succeed in bringing the power to act into their agencies "from the sides," they are constantly in danger of seeing it seep out "through the bottom" as substantial shares of authority are parceled out to the private and other nonfederal partners on which federal agencies increasingly rely. In fact, reliance on such indirect tools of action is often a prerequisite for generating the political support needed to start a program in the first place. In other words, federal managers are often forced to accept, for reasons of political expediency, forms of government action that complicate program management and create serious problems of accountability.[9]

Unfortunately, traditional public administration theories provide little help in coming to terms with these problems. Traditional public administration draws sharp lines between the public and private sectors and among levels of government, and it emphasizes hierarchic patterns of authority. The new tools of government action we have been discussing, however, involve a blurring of sector lines and a sharing of authority. It is no wonder, then, that these forms of government action should involve immense confusion and contradiction over who should perform what roles and in what fashion. In a sense, the public management problem has spilled beyond the borders of the public agency. It no longer involves simply the running of a public agency and the management of public employees. It also involves the manipulation of a complex network of players and institutions over which the public manager has only imperfect control, yet on which he or she must depend to operate an agency's programs.

Public administration research and theory, with its stress on personnel management and agency budgeting, has far too little to say about this. Indeed, there is frequently a failure to recognize what is at stake. This may explain how the Office of Management and Budget's 1986 report, *Management of the United States Government*, could include an endorsement of *both* privatization and the conclusion of the President's Council on Integrity and Efficiency that "holding managers more directly accountable for the efficient administration of their programs and operations is the single most effective means of preventing waste and deterring fraud."[10] The problem, of course, is that the two are in significant conflict: the more federal program managers are required to share program authority with nonfederal actors, the more difficult it is to hold them accountable for the results. Nor is there much help available from some of the newer public administration theories, which emphasize informal rather than formal relationships in bureaucracies.[11]

\

These theories, too, still take the public agency as the basic unit of analysis and thus overlook the extent to which the public management problem has fundamentally changed.

To come to terms with these new forms of public action, therefore, new theories and concepts will be needed. Instead of command and control, such theories will have to emphasize *bargaining* and *persuasion*. Instead of the clarification of directives, they will have to stress the manipulation of *incentives*.

To formulate such theory, however, it is necessary to begin with a clearer understanding of the basic operating characteristics of the major tools of government action now in widespread use. Fortunately, some work along these lines has already been done, at least with respect to a handful of major tools. For example, extensive studies on grants-in-aid have been conducted by the U.S. Advisory Commission on Intergovernmental Relations and others.[12] Similar work was done during the 1970s on regulation, though focusing chiefly on the economic aspects of this tool.[13] By contrast, however, numerous tools have received very little attention—such as insurance, loan guarantees, direct loans, and others. What is more, the work to date has tended to focus on one tool and, frequently, one program at a time, with little effort at explicit comparison and little opportunity to examine a variety of tools within the same framework. Thus each study has pursued a slightly different topic with a slightly different purpose, making it difficult to build the kind of analytical framework and coherent understanding that are needed.

TOWARD A TOOLS APPROACH: THE PURPOSE AND STRUCTURE OF THIS BOOK

The purpose of this book is to help fill the resulting gap—to take at least an initial step toward assembling what is known about some of the major tools of public action and developing a more coherent framework for comparing and contrasting these different instruments. The book is a set of essays, commissioned for this book, on a number of widely used tools. Each essay is on a particular tool, written by an expert on that tool. But all the essays address a common set of questions: What is the nature of the tool? How widespread is its use and what accounts for the pattern of usage that is apparent? How does the tool really work—what are the major tasks that must be carried out and who is responsible for them? How do these operating features affect the impact of the tool or the substance of the policy it is supposed to promote? These essays grew out of a conference convened in mid–1984 in Washington, D. C. to explore the feasibility of the tools approach as a paradigm for the analysis of public policy. Also included is a revised version of the concept paper used to help frame the discussion at this conference, which details more fully some of the basic analytics of the tools approach.

What emerges from this effort is a first test of the tools framework and a wealth of insights into some of the major instruments of action the public sector uses. The remainder of chapter 1 summarizes some of these insights and the conclusions that result.

The Tools Approach: Basic Analytics

The starting point for this discussion, naturally enough, must be the tools approach itself. As Lester Salamon and Michael Lund point out in chapter 2, three basic premises underlie this approach: first, that it is really possible to discern a limited number of tools of action among the welter of individual government programs; second, that each of these tools has its own dynamics and operating characteristics; and third, that these characteristics have more or less predictable implications for the way the programs that embody the tool function.

Translating these theoretical observations into operational terms, however, proves not to be simple. In practice, each tool has multiple characteristics which can be combined in a variety of different forms in particular programs. It is therefore difficult to determine what the "pure" form of a particular tool really is and which characteristics are critical in differentiating it from another tool. The analysis of the tools must therefore begin with a set of underlying tool dimensions in terms of which different tools can be compared and contrasted. Chapter 2 illustrates this by examining a number of such potentially pivotal dimensions. These include such features as the nature of the activity that the tool embodies (for example, providing payments, providing goods or services, offering legal rights and protections, or imposing restrictions), the structure of the delivery system (direct vs. indirect), and the degree of automaticity. Such characteristics can be expected to affect both the manageability of public programs and the ease with which they will generate political support. For example, indirect programs are likely to be more difficult to manage (because operational responsibility is widely dispersed), but they are likely to attract greater political support (because interested parties can be given a role in program implementation).

Direct Government

Many of these hypotheses find at least partial support in the subsequent chapters. In chapter 3, for example, Christopher Leman challenges some of the traditional criticisms of direct government service delivery, which he terms "the forgotten fundamental." As Leman shows, this tool has hardly been a growth area of the federal government for a long period. Indeed, though accounting for the bulk of federal employment, the agencies of direct government at the federal level are not very large in comparative terms. Thus, the Internal Revenue Service (IRS), which ranks second among U.S. government domestic agencies, would rank twenty-fifth among U.S. corporations; and the Federal Bureau of Investigation (FBI), another direct government agency, has fewer employees than the New York City Police Department.

What has limited the growth of direct government as an instrument of public action has been a set of popular beliefs about its inefficiency, unresponsiveness, and ineffectiveness. But the charges against direct government turn out to be at best unproved and at worst grossly incorrect. In fact, the agencies of direct government have a substantial record of success, whether measured in terms of effectiveness, efficiency, innovativeness, political feasibility, or responsiveness. What is more, these successes are related to the inherent characteristics of this tool—the fact that it internalizes transactions which indirect government must negotiate across institutional boundaries, maintains solid in-house expertise, minimizes legalism, and provides a more stable framework for bargaining with external interests. The rare successes of indirect government, Leman asserts, are stories "of talented individuals improvising against enormous odds." The more frequent successes of direct government, by contrast, hinge less on unique individuals than on "an organization's subunits negotiating with one another according to established processes." Far from being ineffective, the one great problem that agencies of direct government encounter is overeffectiveness—carrying assigned goals to excess and allowing the agency to become an end in itself.

Grants-in-Aid

Analysis of some of the more indirect tools of government lends credence to these conclusions. Perhaps the most important of these indirect tools, at least during much of the past 50 years, has been the grant-in-aid to state and local governments. One reason for this is that the grant-in-aid instrument made it possible to overcome longstanding political and ideological opposition to an activist federal government. Through grants-in-aid, the federal government could become involved in a wide array of program fields without displacing the role of the states. Rather, these grants allowed the federal government to function less as a substitute for state and local action than as a subsidizer and stimulator of it.

As a consequence, Donald Haider notes in chapter 4, the grant-in-aid tool has probably attracted greater attention than almost any other instrument in the federal tool chest. Of central concern has been the pivotal question of the relative degree of influence of federal, as opposed to state and local, governments in the operation of grant-in-aid programs. In fact, at least three broad types of grant programs have emerged as a product of this debate. Traditional grant programs were categorical grants, in which the federal government provides financial support for some clearly defined categorical purpose but leaves considerable discretion to state and local governments to work out the details of how that support will operate. To target aid more precisely and increase federal control, federal authorities in the 1960s turned to project grants, which require state and local governments to apply to federal authorities for support for particular projects, and thus vest a greater degree of control in federal agency hands. Finally, as state and local opposition to federal controls increased in the 1970s, block grants and general revenue sharing were developed, both delivering aid to state and local authorities for broad categories of functions and therefore tilting the balance of authority toward the state and local side.

Differences among grants make it difficult to evaluate the grant tool per se. This is particularly true in view of the fact that federal authorities have superimposed a variety of regulatory programs in such fields as equal opportunity and environmental protection on top of the basic grant-in-aid instrument. Grants also have a variety of other problems as a tool of government action. For example, political pressures in the design of grant funding formulas considerably limit the ability of grants to even out economic disparities among regions, thus undermining one of major rationales for their use. In the second place, the sheer complexity of the grant device—the fact that grant programs are implemented through a highly indirect administrative mechanism—means that grants are difficult to use for complex programmatic objectives. Thus, although the grant-in-aid tool has been reasonably effective in promoting physical development activities (for example, construction of the federal highway system), it has performed less effectively in programs designed to stimulate human capital development or overcome poverty. On the other hand, grants seem to have contributed positively to the political and administrative evolution of state and local governments, helping to transform these governments into effective laboratories for policy development and implementation.

Loan Guarantees

Where grants-in-aid deliver federally sponsored financial assistance through state and local governments, another tool—the loan guarantee—delivers such aid through private banks. Through loan guarantees the U.S. government essentially pledges to cover any defaults that private financial institutions experience on loans to certain classes of borrowers (for example, students) or for certain purposes (for example, home purchase in low-income neighborhoods or economic development in rural areas). In this way guarantees are supposed to overcome imperfections in the market thought to inhibit the flow of credit to these borrowers or activities.

Whereas grants-in-aid were the principal vehicle for federal domestic-program growth in the 1950s and 1960s, loan guarantees became the principal growth vehicle in the 1970s. As Lund points out in chapter 5, this is so in substantial part because loan guarantees do not appear in the regular budget and thus seem to involve no real cost to the public. The growing budgetary pressures of the late 1960s and 1970s, therefore, made loan guarantees an increasingly popular mechanism for government action, and their use spread into a variety of new fields.

In fact, however, loan guarantees often involve greater costs and are more difficult to manage than is widely recognized. For one thing, although lender participation is assumed, it is by no means automatic. Beyond this, the more complex and risky the objectives sought through loan guarantees, the more complex and difficult to manage the programs have had to become to accommodate them.

Insufficient lender participation, delayed and faulty loan approval, inattentive portfolio management, problems of coordination with other forms of assistance, and difficulties in reaching very far down the income distribution because of the expectation of repayment have all marred loan guarantee performance as a consequence. At the same time, the loan guarantee has proved its value in a number of spheres—such as mortgage finance and overseas credit—where market imperfections clearly existed and where federal involvement through loan guarantees could make a significant difference at relatively little public cost. As with other tools, therefore, the key is to fit the characteristics of the tool to the nature of the task.

Tax Expenditures

Like loan guarantees, tax expenditures also rely on the private sector to deliver federal financial assistance for certain public purposes. But where loan guarantees rely on the banking system and the "full faith and credit" of the U.S. government, tax expenditures rely on the tax system and the administrative facilities of the IRS.

Tax expenditures are provisions in the tax laws that provide deductions or exemptions from income taxation for certain kinds of activities. Because they are disguised on the revenue side of the federal budget and do not show up as outlays, tax expenditures, too, have recently been immensely popular as a form of government action; and many of them survived the reform of the tax code in 1986. But as Paul McDaniel notes in chapter 6, tax expenditures are not as simple as they may seem. For one thing, tax laws are inherently complex and must be interpreted through regulations and ultimately enforced through administrative procedures. Because tax regulations are developed and administered by the IRS, which brings to the task an essentially tax orientation rather than a program orientation, programmatic goals can easily be subverted and opportunities for program coordination lost as the IRS seeks to maximize its revenue collections rather than the substantive goals of the tax expenditure "program." What is more, taxpayers themselves often bring the same orientation to the programs, reducing the efficiency of the tool since windfall benefits go to some taxpayers. Finally, tax expenditures have an upside-down effect, since by nature they deliver larger benefits to upper income taxpayers, who have larger tax obligations, than to lower income taxpayers.

Many of these difficulties are the result of poor design, however, not the inherent characteristics of the tax-expenditure tool. As McDaniel notes, for example, the upside-down character of tax expenditures could be remedied by creating refundable tax credits. Similarly, the problem of inadequate budgetary and programmatic control over tax expenditures could be remedied by giving the same Congressional committees jurisdiction over tax expenditures and direct programs in a particular field, setting budgetary totals for both, and allowing agencies to choose whether the funds should be provided in the form of direct outlays or tax expenditures. In short, just as the perceived advantages of tax expenditures may be more limited than they appear, so too the perceived problems may be more easily remedied than they seem.

Regulation

Where grants-in-aid, loan guarantees, and tax expenditures all function by delivering essentially financial benefits, regulatory programs function by imposing restrictions. This has led, naturally enough, to the assumption that the management of regulation is a cut-and-dried affair consisting of the specification of rules and the enforcement of adherence to them.

As Eugene Bardach makes clear in chapter 7, however, such a rigid view of regulation is a prescription for disaster. Rarely is there clear consensus about the outcomes desired from a regulation, or about the relationship between a given activity or input and the desired regulatory outcome. Furthermore, the cost of achieving what regulatory programs call for is frequently ignored, causing great difficulty when the programs are enforced blindly. In practice, therefore, regulatory programs, too, involve the management of difficult tradeoffs. Judgments have to be made about where to target scarce enforcement resources, about whether to insist on perfect compliance or settle for reasonable outcomes achieved through bargaining, and about the degree of discretion to leave in the hands of compliance officers as opposed to the courts. The management of a regulatory program is therefore every bit as challenging as the management of a grant-in-aid or loan guarantee, except that in the case of regulatory programs the basic statutory language is often less accommodating to the management judgments that must be made. This has placed regulatory managers in an almost no-win situation between the legal demands of the law and the realities of regulatory enforcement. To cope with this, Bardach recommends limiting regulation to situations of clear market breakdown, periodic review of alternatives to regulation, and greater recognition of the basic operational requirements that regulation entails.

Government Corporations

If direct government represents one pole of a continuum of government instruments, then the government corporation, the final tool considered here, represents the opposite pole. Whereas all the other instruments we have considered vest ultimate authority over government programs in the hands of a government agency, even when this authority is shared with other actors, the government corporation tool takes authority completely out of the hands of the existing governmental apparatus and vests it instead in a separately incorporated entity.

Initially developed to accommodate federal involvement in commercial-type activities, government corporations have become popular in recent years as a way to escape some of the budgetary and personnel controls that apply to regular government departments. The result is a wide assortment of different institutions functioning as government corporations. Indeed, Lloyd Musolf suggests in chapter 8 that the government corporation may be less a single tool than a catch-all category established to meet a variety of essentially political needs. In the process, however, important governmental functions have been placed outside the reach of traditional governmental budgetary and other controls. This can contribute to short-term efficiencies, but it can also pose a significant long-term threat to accountability and democratic control. Under these circumstances, resort to the government corporation tool should be pursued with caution.

CONCLUSIONS

The past several decades have been a period of considerable inventiveness in the technology of government action in this country, and the recent calls for privatization make it clear that such inventiveness is by no means at an end. Major efforts are underway to improve the effectiveness of public action, to conserve public resources, to promote cooperation between government and the private sector, and to find new ways to pursue public purposes.

The chapters in this book illustrate forcefully that such efforts do not by any means eliminate the problems of public management, even when they involve reliance on the private sector to help carry out public objectives. To the contrary, some of the newer, indirect forms of government action involve even more difficult management challenges than direct government itself. Slogans such as privatization, appealing though they may be, disguise as much as they reveal. To make sense of what is being proposed, it is necessary to look behind the slogans at the actual operational realities of the new approaches being suggested.

The tools approach explored here represents a call to do just this, to develop a coherent body of knowledge about the characteristics of the alternative tools of government action. Although the chapters in this book reveal how difficult it is to identify unequivocally the crucial, defining characteristics of the various tools, and to link these to actual program outcomes, they also reveal how fruitful such an attempt can be. Problems with the operation of environmental protection or student loan programs turn out, from this perspective, to be due not so much to errors of administration as to inherent limitations in the respective tools they embody. Aside from their theoretical value, such insights can be extremely useful in designing public programs and in equipping managers to operate them effectively.

For the tools approach to achieve the promise it seems to hold, however, a great deal of additional work will be needed. Efforts must be made to examine other tools—such as procurement and insurance and vouchers—as well as to refine the links between tool characteristics and program outputs. This book thus represents not the end of work in this field but a beginning; its objective is to open a field for further scrutiny. If it succeeds in sensitizing scholars and practitioners to the existence of different tools of public action and to the need for greater attention to these tools in both research and practice, the book will have served its purpose well.

Notes

1. For an earlier and fuller development of this argument, see Lester M. Salamon, "The Rise of Third-Party Government," *The Washington Post*, June 29, 1980; Lester M.

Salamon, "Rethinking Public Management: Third-Party Government and the Changing Forms of Government Action," *Public Policy* 29, no. 3 (Summer 1981): 255–75.

2. U.S. Office of Management and Budget (OMB), *Special Analysis, Budget of the United States Government, Fiscal Year 1989* (Washington, D.C.: OMB, 1988), F–16 and F–21.

3. *Budget of the United States Government, Fiscal Year 1989, Special Analysis,* H–20.

4. This suggestion is developed more fully in Salamon, "Rethinking Public Management," 1981, 256.

5. See Salamon, "The Rise of Third-Party Government," 1980; Salamon, "Rethinking Implementation: Third-Party Government and the Changing Forms of Public Action," Paper delivered at the American Political Science Association Convention, Washington, D.C., September 3, 1980, published as "Rethinking Public Management," 1981. See also: Frederick C. Mosher, "The Changing Responsibilities and Tactics of the Federal Government," *Public Administration Review* 40 (1980): 541–48.

6. V.O. Key, *American State Politics: An Introduction* (New York: Alfred A. Knopf, 1956), 4.

7. Morton Grodzins, "Centralization and Decentralization in the American Federal System," in Robert A. Goldwin, ed., *A Nation of States: Essays on the American Federal System* (Chicago: Rand McNally, 1963), 9.

8. Norton Long, "Power and Administration," *Public Administration Review* 9 (1949): 257–67.

9. For further elaboration of this "public management paradox," see Salamon, "Rethinking Public Management," 1981, 272.

10. U.S. Office of Management and Budget, *Management of the United States Government, Fiscal Year 1987* (Washington, D.C., 1986), 13.

11. For a summary, see, for example, Vincent Ostrom, *The Intellectual Crisis in American Public Administration* (University, Ala.: University of Alabama Press, 1962).

12. See, for example, U.S. Advisory Commission on Intergovernmental Relations, *Categorical Grants: Their Role and Design* (Washington, D.C., 1977); U.S. Advisory Commission on Intergovernmental Relations, *Federal Grants: Their Effects on State-Local Expenditures, Employment Levels, and Wage Rates* (Washington, D.C., 1981); U.S. Advisory Commission on Intergovernmental Relations, *Federal Grants: The Dynamics of Growth* (Washington, D.C., 1980).

13. One exception is Eugene Bardach and Robert A. Kagan, *Going By the Book: The Problem of Regulatory Unreasonableness* (Philadelphia: Temple University Press, 1982). More generally, see U.S. Congress, Senate Committee on Governmental Affairs, *Study on Federal Regulation*, 95th Congress, 2d sess. (1977); Nicholas Ashford, *A Crisis in the Workplace: Occupational Injury and Disease* (Cambridge, Mass.: MIT Press, 1976); Richard Zeckhauser, "Government Comes to the Workplace: An Assessment of OSHA," *The Public Interest* 49 (Fall 1977).

Chapter Two

THE TOOLS APPROACH: BASIC ANALYTICS

Lester M. Salamon and Michael S. Lund

Chairman Blanchard: Have you made any conclusions as to where governmental loans are an effective policy instrument and where they are not? Where loan guarantees are an effective policy instrument and where they are not? How they work, in what instances they work well and where they don't, and where they can be effective and where they aren't? Because we are looking at these in relation to other tools that the government has to operate. . . . Have there been any studies on . . . federal use of direct spending versus loans versus loan guarantees versus the tax code, and then the various types of tax preferences and their effectiveness in different instances?
Dr. Rivlin: Let me see if my colleagues know of any such study . . . .
Mr. Shillingburg: We are unaware of any such literature, Mr. Chairman.[1]

In the 1981 article that forms the immediate backdrop for this book, Lester Salamon argued that the field of public management analysis was fast approaching a dead end and that a basic change was needed in the unit of analysis used to focus thinking and research in the field:

Rather than focusing on individual programs, as is now done, or even collections of programs grouped according to major "purpose," as is frequently proposed, the suggestion here is that we should concentrate instead on the generic tools of government action, on the "techniques" of social intervention that come to be used, in varying combinations, in particular public programs.[2]

Inviting though this suggestion is, however, it raises a number of critical questions. What exactly is a "tool" of government action? How can tools be distinguished from one another? What are the central characteristics of different tools? How do these characteristics affect program operations? How does the "tools approach" differ from other approaches to the analysis of public policy?

It is the purpose of this chapter to begin answering these questions, to identify the basic analytics of the tools approach, and thus to lay the foundation for converting the tools paradigm from an interesting idea into a concrete field of inquiry. To do so, the chapter first puts the tools approach into context by comparing it to other major approaches to the study of governmental action. It then examines the basic analytical dimensions of the tools approach. It ends by exploring some hypotheses that suggest how the tools approach can be used in practice.

THE CONTEXT: EXISTING PARADIGMS

The tools approach grew originally out of dissatisfaction with the research paradigms dominant in the fields of public administration, policy analysis/program evaluation, and American politics. As a first step to clarifying the tools approach, it is therefore useful to outline these other paradigms and show how the tools approach differs from them. Broadly speaking, four such prior approaches to the analysis of government action can be distinguished.

Classical Public Administration

Much of the early analysis of public policy had its origins in traditional public administration, which dominated serious study of the functioning of government prior to the 1960s. The central unit of analysis in this body of literature is the governmental agency—its organization, its housekeeping functions and, more recently, its external relationships. The central concern has been how to equip the public agency with the resources and systems it needs to operate smoothly and efficiently. Accordingly, research and analysis focused on such issues as recruitment and management of personnel, financial management and accounting, requisites of agency leadership, purchasing and deployment of materiel, agency "ethos," and the legal prerogatives and authority relationships of different governmental units.[3]

Although the fields of organizational theory and management science apply more rigorous behavioral and quantitative methods to the study of both governmental and nongovernmental organizations, they retained the focus on the agency—and later its relations with its "environment" or other organizations—as the unit of analysis.

Policy Analysis

As the scope, roles, and complexity of government activity have expanded over the past two and a half decades, interest in governmental dynamics has changed increasingly from a focus on government's "inputs" to a concern about government's "outputs" (policies) and, further, to the societal effects of these policies. One manifestation of this new concern has been a shift in policy research from the agency toward the *individual governmental program* as the unit of analysis. A program, in this sense, is a particular combination of authority, organizations, resources, and personnel assembled to achieve specific public purposes. Usually the name of a particular program, as well as its legislation and sponsoring agency, is based on the program's imputed social purposes (for example, Medicare and Occupational Health and Safety), not on the method through which the program operates.

By and large, the growth fields of the 1970s—policy analysis and evaluation—have pursued this program focus. Of central concern in this program-oriented research has been the question of how effective individual programs really are in achieving their societal objectives and what changes in program design or operation might enhance their effectiveness. Accordingly, scholars of public policy developed subject area specialties based on the particular programs or the arrays of programs aimed at various societal problems, such as poverty, ill health, poor housing, or environmental degradation.

Although the program focus has preserved a substantial degree of concreteness in policy research, it has not lent itself easily to theory building or broader analytical development. Individual programs have been well described and analyzed, but since every program is sui generis, little progress was made in developing broader observations and testable propositions regarding what general properties of policies lead to what sorts of consequences.

A second limitation of the conceptualization and categorization of governmental activity in terms of programs or groups of programs is the tendency to identify program goals with established program means. This discourages the search for alternative methods to reach the same public objectives. Linking the pursuit of substantive goals to the use of methods that have been adopted by historical accident reinforces the assumption that conventional techniques are the only way. It is clearly possible, however, that several different modes of intervention may be available to achieve the same goals. This has, in fact, been one of the major criticisms that advocates of privatization and other market-oriented interventions have made against traditional public policy.[4]

Implementation Research

One offshoot of the policy research spawned in the 1960s was research on policy implementation. It, too, was a response to the expansion of governmental activity. But it differed from the more rationalistic, cost-benefit variety of policy analysis in its central emphasis on the implementation sequence; that is, the institutional mechanisms and political processes that transform given laws and program designs conceived in Congress and Washington agencies into actual operation in the field. Program evaluations of social programs had uncovered considerable evidence that the impacts intended by federal policymakers were frequently not achieved; and research on policy implementation suggested that at least some of the reasons for this widespread failure lay in actual program execution, not solely in initial program design.

Implementation research focuses on processes, institutional arrangements, and actor behaviors that are relevant to the ways tools function and perform. With a few exceptions, however, this research field has relied on case studies of particular programs and thus has lacked a systematic effort to develop propositions that link general properties of the technologies embodied in programs with actual outcomes.[5] In other words, it suffers from some of the same limitations as other program-focused analysis.

Political Science

At the opposite extreme from the agency and program foci of public administration and policy analysis have been the efforts within the political science profession to formulate broader theoretical constructs to group individual programs or policies. Examples here are Lowi's fourfold division of policy spheres (distributive, redistributive, regulatory, and constitutive) and Wilson's division of policy spheres into majoritarian, interest group, client, and entrepreneurial.[6]

Though quite suggestive, this more theoretical approach has two main shortcomings. First, while it has been more fruitful in generating theory, it has not yielded a set of concepts sufficiently concrete to be tested empirically at any but the most abstract level. The attributes of the policies identified are so broadly defined they are hard to operationalize. Because the categories are "ideal types," it is difficult to know what the categories refer to in observable governmental activities; interpretive differences can therefore easily arise. This is especially true regarding categories like Lowi's and Wilson's, which are based on the perceptions people have of a policy's consequences, not on either a policy's observable operations or its actual societal consequences. In sum, although suggestive and perceptive regarding possible broad patterns, the conceptual clarity of these typologies is low; and measurement of them has been extremely difficult.

Second, the dominant concern of these typologies has been to demonstrate how, in Lowi's words, "policies determine politics." That is, the dependent variables in this analysis deal with the ways political actors respond to given policy types, or the institutional arenas in which the types are formulated. With a few exceptions, however, there has been no effort to use these broad policy typologies as the keys for describing or predicting the administrative processes and consequences attending different policies or the objectively determinable societal consequences of policies. As a result, the broad typologies have little directly to offer legislators or administrators faced with trying to make responsible choices among specific alternative methods for achieving public goals.

Summary

This brief overview of existing paradigms in policy research indicates that categorization and explanation of purposeful government action remain surprisingly underdeveloped. What one survey of the policy field concluded in 1976 continues to have relevance today: "We are not even sure of what it is we want to explain or what our dependent variables should be. . . . We need much better descriptions of what governments actually do."[7]

THE TOOLS APPROACH

The tools of government action framework under consideration here is conceived as a middle range alternative to the existing efforts at theory building in the policy field. It seeks to combine the concrete concern with procedures and organizational dynamics of public administration, the sensitivity to policy process and substantive outcomes of policy analysis, and the theoretical aspirations of political science typologies.

The central premise of the tools paradigm is that it is possible to discern in the multitude of governmental programs, each with its own special purposes and operating details, a limited number of distinctive devices or means by which the programs operate. Furthermore, it assumes that each of these devices has a characteristic set of basic features and an associated array of likely consequences wherever it is applied. While hardly determining policy outcomes by itself, the choice of a tool is thus assumed to impart a certain "spin" to program operations that increases the likelihood of particular results.

This notion finds support in the suggestions of Rivlin and others that it is necessary to examine carefully the "alternative means" to carry out government policy,[8] in the argument of recent implementation research that programs embody certain "dispositions" or "potentialities" that shape the implementation process,[9] in a limited number of inquiries into alternative instruments that suggest they pose characteristic problems or dilemmas for their managers,[10] and in the search by policymakers for more efficient and effective means to pursue public objectives.

Although these bodies of literature suggest that a tools approach would have considerable promise for both theory building and improved policy effectiveness, however, they stop short of developing this approach explicitly. To take the next steps, several different types of work are needed. These include

□ *definitional and descriptive work* to clarify what is meant by a policy tool, identify some of the major tools now in use, and describe how these tools operate;
□ *analytical work* to identify the major underlying dimensions in terms of which different tools can be sorted and compared, identify the kinds of impacts likely to flow from the use of different tools, and specify the features of the tools likely to produce these consequences; and
□ *prescriptive work* to suggest the kinds of tools most appropriate for particular policy purposes and the improvements in the operation of certain tools that will make them function more effectively.

It is to these tasks that we now turn.

A Working Definition: Identifying the Domain of the Tools Approach

To make headway in the analysis of policy tools, it is important to clarify at the outset what a tool is and how it differs from related concepts in the policy field. For the sake of simplicity, therefore, we define a "policy tool" as a method through which government seeks a policy objective. This definition distinguishes a policy tool from several other common conceptions of governmental action: program, policy, administrative tool, and function.

☐ A tool resembles an individual *program* in that it is a concrete mechanism for achieving a policy goal that is normally specified in legislation or regulations and manifested in identifiable organizations. But a tool differs from a particular program in that it refers to the underlying methodology or approach used in a program or part of a program—not to the particular application of goals, resources, organizations, funding levels, administering agency, activities, and target groups or problems that constitute that program. In this sense a tool is more general than a program, and a particular tool can be used in a number of different programs.

☐ A tool differs from a *policy* in that a policy is a collection of programs aimed at achieving a particular set of outcomes in a particular field of government activity (for example, health, housing, and transportation). A policy can thus embody many programs that utilize a variety of tools.

☐ A policy tool differs from an *administrative tool* in that administrative tools are devices that government agencies utilize to serve themselves and thus enable them to carry out their missions. They include such devices as personnel recruitment, civil service rules, procurement of items for the agency's own use, internal management procedures, budgeting, and the like. Policy tools, by contrast, are the means the agency uses to impact on the society.

☐ A policy tool is also different from the broader *functions* or ends sometimes attributed to government—such things as stabilization and economic management. These latter functions frequently embrace multiple policies, which in turn can encompass many different programs, each of which embodies a particular type of tool or technology.

The domain of tools research thus lies midway between the level of individual programs and the level of broad policies or governmental functions. As such, it provides a basis for theory building that is more concrete than groupings of policies, yet more theoretical than case studies of individual programs.

Classification of Tools

If tools are the distinguishable means by which programs operate, what are the major such tools in existence? Unfortunately, the answer to this important question is not as simple as it might seem. This is so for several different reasons.

□ There is no single set of clearly defined tools simply waiting in a federal toolshed to be inventoried. What exists are thousands of programs that can be roughly grouped into certain differing approaches. But the task of ferreting out the features of the various programs that make it possible to group them in terms of the tool they embody has yet to be done. Indeed, some programs embody more than one tool, and some embodiments of a tool differ from others. As a result, there is no single authoritative list of tools. Rather, a great many different lists of policy tools exist in both official government documents and related scholarly literature. Table 2.1 portrays 10 different tool-related classification schemes among the many we have identified in our effort to flesh out the various tools. Although these schemes have many points of similarity, they also differ significantly in their coverage and in how they group forms of government action. *The Catalogue of Federal Domestic Assistance* (CFDA), for example, distinguishes project grants from formula grants whereas the Office of Management and Budget's (OMB) *Managing Federal Assistance* groups formula and project grants together and distinguishes grants as a class from cooperative agreements.

□ No single tool typology is available because a tool embodies several different features, and different typologies select different features as the basis for their groupings. Each scheme thus highlights certain tool differences, or dimensions, as of primary significance in the scheme's own descriptive, predictive, or prescriptive purposes; other dimensions tend to be disregarded. A corollary is that tools are distinguishable along not one dimension but several.

The difference between the CFDA grouping and the OMB grouping identified above, for example, hinges on the fact that the CFDA system singles out the *method of determining eligibility* for grants as an important basis for distinguishing different tools, whereas the OMB scheme places more emphasis on the *degree of federal in-*

volvement as the basis for classification (a grant involves limited federal involvement and a cooperative agreement, more). In addition, the first scheme is aimed mainly at description; the second has a prescriptive purpose. In predictive typologies, which try to link tool characteristics to the outcomes of government action, the classification schemes will elevate or prioritize certain tool dimensions above others because these dimensions are deemed to have greater explanatory power. It follows that no one classification scheme is likely to encompass the whole range of variations among tools. The choice of typology is thus influenced by the type of purpose sought.

□ To confound the direct application of these schemes further, official and scholarly usage of particular tool-related terms is vague or inconsistent. Sometimes "guaranteed loans" mean something different from "insured loans" in official documents and sometimes the terms are used interchangeably. Tool terms used in academic sources, such as incentive, subsidy, regulation, are usually no more helpful. They, too, are often defined imprecisely, and the scope of governmental action they encompass is sometimes quite broad.

□ To make matters still worse, even if one can find a clear, consistent definition of tax expenditure, or grant, or regulation, particular programs that are given that label may not operate in fact the way the terms used to describe them would suggest.

Generic labels used for classes of governmental programs, such as insurance, often seem to be used honorifically, to *legitimate* these programs rather than to *describe* them accurately. Similarly, some grant programs are actually operated as if they were procurement arrangements, with detailed specification of desirable products. So widespread is this phenomenon, in fact, that the Congress enacted the Grants and Cooperative Agreement Act of 1977 to sort out the meanings of these various types of assistance, and create a guidance system to monitor program operations and ensure their consistency with prevailing definitions of how particular instruments should function. In practice, however, this guidance system has had only limited effect.

Taken together, these findings suggest certain conclusions that should guide future tools research:

□ Tools differ from one another along a number of dimensions.
□ Which of these dimensions are most important depends on the types of tool-related consequences that are of interest. To go from a

Table 2.1 10 EXISTING CLASSIFICATION SCHEMES OF GOVERNMENT TOOLS

Catalog of Federal Domestic Assistance[a] (1982)	Office of Management and Budget[b] (1980)	Mosher[c] (1980)	Bryson[d] (1983)	Chelf[e] (1981)	MacRae[f] (1980)	Salamon[g] (1981)	Herzlinger[h] (1979)	Weaver[i] (1980)	Rivlin[j] (1977)
Formula grants	Grants	Grants	Formula grants	Expenditures	Direct monetary transaction—subsidy	Grants-in-aid	Grants	Subsidy	Federal grants for human services
Project grants	Cooperative agreements	Income support	Intergovernmental agreements	Grants	Regulation	Interest subsidies	Direct payments to individuals	Loans	Revenue sharing
Direct payments—unrestricted	Direct payment	Loans	Categorical grants	Welfare	Monitoring and enforcement	Loans	Loans to producers	Loan guarantees	Vouchers for specific services
Direct payments—restricted	Direct payment to individuals	Loan guarantees	Vouchers	Loans	Direct monetary transactions—taxes	Loan guarantees	Loan guarantees	Regulation	Social insurance
Direct loans	Vouchers	Regulation	Subsidy	Legal sanctions	Production and delivery of goods	Insurance	Insurance	Tax incentives	"Neat" cash transfers
Loan guarantees	Subsidies	Contracts	Insurance	Self-regulation	Meta-policy	Economic regulation	Contracts with producers	Contract out	Institution changing
Insurance	Prizes	Direct service	Regulation	Inspection and testing	Delivery of services	Social regulation	Government services	State-owned enterprise	
Sale, exchange of property	Loans with and without subsidy	Quasi-government organizations	Tax incentives	Taxation		Tax expenditures		Indicative planning	
Use of property facilities	Loans with various types of forgiveness		Contract or purchase of service	Service contracts		Government corporations		Jawboning	
Provision of specialized services	Loan guarantees		Franchise	Government ownership and operation				Government agencies	
Advisory	Insurance			Publicity and investigation					
	Regulation			Certificates					
	Procurement contracts			Licenses					
				Franchises					

services
and coun-
seling
Dissemina-
tion of
technical
information
Training
Investigation
of com-
plaints
Federal em-
ployment
Property
manage-
ment

Direct fed-
eral action
Fees

a. U.S. Office of Management and Budget, *Catalog of Federal Domestic Assistance* (Washington, D.C., 1981).

b. U.S. Office of Management and Budget, *Managing Federal Assistance in the 1980's* (Washington, D.C., 1980).

c. Frederick Mosher, "The Changing Responsibilities and Tactics of the Federal Government," *Public Administration Review* (November/December, 1980): 541–48.

d. John Bryson, et al., "Toward a New Theory of Policy Intervention." Paper presented at American Society for Public Administration, Annual Meeting, 1983.

e. Carl P. Chelf, *Public Policymaking in America: Difficult Choices, Limited Solutions* (Santa Monica, Calif.: Goodyear Publishing Company, Inc., 1981).

f. Duncan MacRae, Jr., "Policy Analysis Methods and Governmental Functions," in Stuart Nagel, ed., *Improving Policy Analysis* (Beverly Hills, Calif.: Sage Publications, 1980).

g. Lester Salamon, "Rethinking Public Management: Third-Party Government and the Changing Forms of Government Action," *Public Policy* (Summer, 1981): 255–75.

h. Regina Herzlinger and Nancy Kane, *A Managerial Analysis of Federal Income Distribution Mechanisms* (Cambridge. Mass.: Ballinger, 1979).

i. Kent Weaver, "Choosing Instruments for State Intervention: Public Enterprise and Passenger Trains in Canada," unpublished manuscript, 1980.

j. Alice M. Rivlin, "Social Policy: Alternate Strategies for the Federal Government," in Robert Haveman and Julius Margolis, eds., *Public Expenditure and Policy Analysis*, 2d ed. (Chicago: Rand McNally College Publishing, 1977).

list of characteristics of tools to an analytical typology, therefore, it is necessary to give some thought to the range of impacts to be examined.

□ Some of the "nominal" categories now used to differentiate tools (for example, grants, loans, loan guarantees, regulation) may contain programs that differ from each other along certain relevant dimensions more than they differ from programs that seem to embody another nominal category of tool. For example, in terms of the actual amount of federal outlays, some loans may be more like grants than they are like other loans.

□ Great care must be taken to verify that a program which is supposed to embody a particular tool actually embodies the crucial features of the tool.

Dimensions of Tools

Given these considerations, what are some of the crucial characteristics in terms of which tools can be differentiated from each other? What dimensions or features of programs seem most promising as a basis for developing a typology of tools and generating testable hypotheses about them? No single answer to these questions is possible, but a number of tool dimensions seem especially important.

THE NATURE OF THE ACTIVITY IN WHICH GOVERNMENT IS ENGAGED

Perhaps the most basic tool characteristic concerns the nature of the activity a program involves. What is of interest here is not the goal government is seeking (for example, equal opportunity or improved housing), but the basic type of stimulus government uses to get some desired result. This is important not only because it determines the kind of transaction the program entails and, therefore, some of its basic operating characteristics, but also because it affects the character of the personnel likely to be involved.

Among the types of activity government might undertake are the following:

Providing payments to individuals
Making grants to other organizations
Providing services or goods
Guaranteeing loans or other financial obligations
Restricting or penalizing specified activities

Making loans
Imposing charges
Taxing
Granting exemptions from regular tax liabilities
Guaranteeing prices or markets for products
Distributing information
Purchasing
Granting preferential treatment

For analytical purposes, it is possible to collapse these types of action into four broad categories, as follows:

1. *Outright money payments,* either to provide benefits to ultimate beneficiaries of government aid, or to induce others to supply such benefits. Included here are payments to individuals, grants-in-aid to state and local governments, and procurement.
2. *Provision of goods or services, including information.*
3. *Legal protections,* such as monopolies, guarantees, or exemptions from requirements, which seek to shelter some activity from risk, to reduce its costs, or to stimulate it. Included here are loan guarantees, price supports, and tax exemptions.
4. *Restrictions/penalties,* which compel someone to do something or refrain from doing something. This includes regulation, criminal laws, and the like.

Table 2.2 provides an illustrative list of federal programs grouped in these terms.

STRUCTURE OF THE DELIVERY SYSTEM

A policy tool not only embodies a particular type of activity or combination of activities; it also involves a delivery mechanism. To some extent, the delivery system is dictated by the nature of the activity. Loan guarantees, for example, are normally delivered through private financial institutions because they rely on private capital. But the connection between the type of activity and the nature of the delivery system is far from simple. Many types of activities can be handled through more than one type of delivery system.

The nature of the delivery system is important because it affects the complexity of the implementation process, the degree of control that can be exercised over program operations, and the nature

Table 2.2 FEDERAL PROGRAMS GROUPED IN TERMS OF TYPE OF
GOVERNMENT ACTIVITY

Type of activity	Illustrative programs
Money payment	Social Security Military procurement Title I education grants
Provision of goods or services	Forest Service Public Health Service
Legal protection or guarantees	Tax subsidies Small business set-aside FHA loan guarantees
Prohibition or restriction	Clean Air Act Occupational safety and health regulations

of the pressures built into the program administration by the involvement of different types of organizations with different outlooks and purposes. It is also likely to affect the level of political support for a program, since tools that provide a meaningful role for affected organizations are more likely to win the support of these organizations than tools that do not.

At the federal level, a wide assortment of delivery systems exists. These systems involve roles for at least the following kinds of organizations:

Executive branch agencies
Quasi-independent federal agencies
State governments
Local governments
Special districts (e.g., school districts)
Banks
Insurance companies
Industrial corporations
Other for-profit businesses
Hospitals
Universities
Research institutes
Other voluntary, nonprofit organizations

For analytical purposes, the various delivery mechanisms can be divided into two broad groups: *direct*—essentially involving federal agencies alone; or *indirect*—essentially involving nonfederal actors in the operation of the program in a fairly substantial way.

The indirect mechanisms can in turn be divided into three groups depending on whether the nonfederal actors are: *other public agencies,* such as state and local governments; *for-profit businesses;* or *private nonprofit organizations.*

Table 2.3 provides an illustrative list of federal programs grouped in terms of the delivery system.

THE DEGREE OF CENTRALIZATION

A third dimension of tools is the degree of centralization of control they entail. This dimension is partly embodied in the nature of the delivery system that is used because indirect mechanisms are likely to be less centralized than direct ones. Within the categories of direct and indirect tools, however, important variations exist in the degree of centralization or decentralization of decision making. Thus, some direct, federally operated programs are highly centralized in their operations and others are considerably more decentralized, leaving substantial discretion to field staff. Similarly, some indirect tools involve a higher degree of central control by federal agencies than others. For example, categorical grants-in-aid involve a greater degree of federal direction than do block grants even though both are indirect tools relying on other public agencies.

Table 2.3 FEDERAL PROGRAMS GROUPED IN TERMS OF TYPE OF DELIVERY SYSTEM

Type of delivery system	Illustrative program
Direct	Forest Service
	Social Security
Indirect	
Other public	Urban Mass Transit Administration grants
	Community development block grants
Private business	Federal Housing Administration loan guarantees
Private nonprofit	Social service purchase-of-service contracts
	Medicare
	Research grants to private universities

DEGREE OF AUTOMATICITY

A fourth dimension for distinguishing among tools is the degree to which they require detailed administrative action. Some tools are relatively automatic in their operation, making use of market relationships or other routinized and nondiscretionary actions. Others require continuous, detailed administrative activity to operate, including things like periodic verification of eligibility, individual review of applications, and detailed judgments about purposes.

Examples of the first category of tools would include tax incentives and effluent charges to control water pollution. Both of these are, to a significant extent, self-administered.[11] Examples of the second category would include social regulatory programs and needs-tested income assistance programs. Both of these require almost case-by-case administrative decision making.

The distinction between administered and automatic mechanisms is particularly relevant to the recent debate over privatization. Advocates of privatization generally favor tools that utilize essentially automatic, non-administered processes, preferably the private market.[12] Opponents fear that such mechanisms will lead to inequitable or ineffective results.

OTHERS

The four criteria discussed above do not exhaust the useful distinctions that can be drawn among policy tools. For example, tools can also be distinguished in terms of whether or not they involve on-budget expenditures, and whether or not they impart benefits as a matter of right or on the basis of a competition.

Even with the four tool criteria we have singled out, however, it is possible to develop a useful framework in terms of which different tools can be compared and contrasted. This is apparent in table 2.4, which differentiates some of the "nominal" tool categories such as project grants, formula grants, loan guarantees, and regulation in terms of these four dimensions. As this table makes clear, various tools are alike along some dimensions but differ along others. Thus, project grants, formula grants, and direct loans all involve outright money payments; but loans utilize a direct delivery system; and grants involve an indirect one.

Configured in a slightly different way, these same four dimensions can be used to classify every program in the federal program inventory. This is evident in table 2.5, which illustrates how vari-

Table 2.4 ILLUSTRATIVE DEPICTION OF FEDERAL TOOLS IN TERMS OF
FOUR MAJOR DIMENSIONS

	Tool				
Dimension	Project grant	Formula grant	Loan guarantee	Direct loans	Regulation
Nature of activity	Money payment	Money payment	Legal protection	Money payment	Restriction
Delivery system	Indirect— other public or nonprofit	Indirect— other public	Indirect— private	Direct	Typically direct
Degree of centralization	High	Moderate	Moderate	Moderate	High
Degree of automaticity	Low	Moderate	Low	Low	Low

ous programs can be sorted using this framework. Thus, Social Security is an example of a program that provides a money payment through a direct federal delivery system that is relatively centralized and automatic in its operation. Federal crop allotments, by contrast, involve legal guarantees that are administered indirectly through local nonprofit entities (Agricultural Stabilization and Conservation Service committees) in a fairly decentralized fashion and with little automaticity. To be sure, some cells of this framework are more difficult to fill than others, but overall the framework provides a useful basis for beginning to distinguish programs in terms of the tool characteristics they embody.

Consequences of Tools

Suggestive though the above categories for differentiating policy tools may be, the ultimate payoff from research on policy tools must be to establish a link between the choice of tool and the actual operations of programs. But what facets of program operations are of most interest?

The answer to this question for tools research must be a little different from that for policy analysis generally. In policy analysis, programs are evaluated in terms of their success or failure in alleviating specified societal problems. The key question is whether the public sector has devised a range of activities that can indeed help solve the problem. The consequences that are of interest in tools research are, in a sense, one step removed from these ultimate policy impacts—though in no sense irrelevant to them. The key

Table 2.5 A FRAMEWORK FOR DEPICTING FEDERAL PROGRAMS IN TERMS OF KEY TOOL CHARACTERISTICS

Nature of activity	Degree of automaticity	Delivery system and degree of centralization				
		Direct		Public	Indirect	
		Centralized	Decentralized		For-profit	Nonprofit
Money payment	High	Social Security	Pell grants	Revenue sharing	Naval petroleum	
	Low	Needs-tested income assistance (SSI)	SBA loans Reclamation grants	AFDC	Military procurement	Nonprofit housing grants
Provision of goods or service	High	Medicare		Medicaid	Social Service purchase of services	Social Service purchase of services
	Low	Food stamps	Forest Service			
Legal protection or guarantee	High					Charitable deduction
	Low	Chrysler loan guarantee			FHA Loan guarantee	Crop allotments
Prohibition, restriction, penalty	High	FDA		Clean Air Act		
	Low					

question in tools research is not whether the theory embodied in a program is correct, but whether the program utilizes a mechanism that allows that theory to be tested. In other words, it is more the impact of the tool on the functioning of the program than the impact of the program on the underlying societal problem that is of principal concern. For example, in the area of employment policy, the question in tools research is not whether the best way to overcome long-term unemployment is to stimulate general economic growth or provide the unemployed with a public service job or training, but whether, having selected one of these, it makes a difference how the program substance is delivered and what form government involvement takes (for example, direct training, a tax incentive to compensate employers for the training, a grant to state and local governments to encourage them to provide training, or payments to the unemployed themselves to allow them to purchase training).

But which of the many potential consequences of the use of different tools are most important? For our purposes, five such consequences are especially worth exploring:

□ *administrative feasibility*—the degree of ease or difficulty involved in establishing and operating a program
□ *effectiveness*—the success a program has in producing the outputs and, to a lesser extent, the outcomes it was seeking. This, in turn, has two distinct aspects (1) *supply effectiveness*—the level of output the program achieves in a specified time period; and (2) *targeting effectiveness*—the program's success in producing the desired benefits or prohibitions for the intended target group.
□ *political support*—the ability to attract the support of key actors with a stake in the program area
□ *efficiency*—the relationship between the program's outputs and its costs, both the costs to the sponsoring government and the costs to society more generally
□ *equity*—the program's impact on the distribution of resources in the society.

These are not, of course, wholly independent criteria. Trade-offs are likely to be involved in the choice of tools. The features that make a tool desirable in terms of one set of criteria are likely to make it problematic in terms of another. For example, direct tools may be the easiest to manage but they may also have the greatest difficulty in achieving "supply effectiveness" because of start-up problems and government personnel limits. Understanding these trade-offs between tool characteristics and tool consequences thus becomes the central analytical challenge of the tools field.

PUTTING THE TOOLS APPROACH TO WORK: SOME SUGGESTIVE HYPOTHESES[13]

To make headway on this challenge, it is useful to show how the framework developed above can be used to generate hypotheses about the relationships between the tool characteristics we have identified and the various program consequences of interest. Although it will not be possible to subject these hypotheses to rigorous empirical testing, the hypotheses themselves are still needed to guide future empirical work and to serve as a framework for accumulating knowledge. The intent here is thus to be suggestive rather than exhaustive; the discussion focuses on only some of the tool characteristics and on only some of the potential consequences.

In particular, we concentrate here on the impacts that each of the various tool characteristics are likely to have in terms of just two tool consequences—administrative feasibility and political support. What emerges from this analysis is the suggestion of an important paradox that may lie at the heart of some of the disappointment with public program operations in recent years.

The Nature of the Activity

A first set of hypotheses considers the effects flowing from the nature of the activity that a tool involves. As noted above, tools differ markedly along this dimension. Some provide cash payments, others provide goods and services, others involve protections and guarantees, and still others impose restrictions.

This feature of a public program can have significant implications both for its administrative feasibility and for its political attractiveness. In fact, existing literature as well as conventional beliefs suggest at least two sets of hypotheses relating the nature of the activity that a tool involves and the administrative and political consequences that result. One of these has to do with the distinction between cash payments and the provision of goods or services (in-kind aid), and the other with the distinction between more visible and less visible forms of action.

CASH VS. IN-KIND AID

Important differences exist between programs that take the form of outright cash payments and those that provide in-kind aid, such as commodities and services. Cash-type programs reserve far more choice to recipients and are typically easier to administer since government does not have to handle the actual production of the goods or services recipients ultimately receive. Even when they provide benefits in the form of vouchers instead of actual goods or services, in-kind programs constrain recipient choices, thus making the benefits to the recipient worth less than the costs to the government.

Although, they are administratively more cumbersome, however, in-kind forms of assistance have a number of advantages. For one thing, they are likely to have a higher degree of target effectiveness: expenditures are more likely to go for the purposes intended since the expenditures are used to purchase only those items. This can lead to inefficiencies in the purchase of these items, of course, since more will be purchased than a purely market choice would provide, but at least the leakage to other purposes is minimized. Partly for this reason, in-kind forms of assistance are more likely to win the support of affected producer groups, who can easily see the relationship between the government expenditure and the commodity or service of interest to them. This is particularly true where the government relies on the existing producers to provide the good or service. In this way producer groups can often be added to client groups as advocates for the program, creating a powerful political coalition. This may explain why in the welfare field, for example, in-kind assistance programs such as food stamps, Medicaid, subsidized housing, and social services have outpaced the growth of cash assistance by several orders of magnitude despite the widespread acknowledgment that the poor would be better off with the cash. What this suggests is the following:

Hypothesis 1 (the Cash vs. In-Kind Dimension): Tools that involve cash payments are generally easier to administer and more likely to have superior supply effectiveness than those that involve in-kind benefits; but they are less likely to attract political support.

THE VISIBILITY/INVISIBILITY DIMENSION

A second feature of different types of assistance has to do with the degree of visibility they have in standard government decision-making arenas. Some forms of action, such as cash payments and direct provision of goods and services, are highly visible in government accounts and records. To operate them, personnel must be hired and outlays made. By contrast, other forms of activity, such as guarantees, tax expenditures, and regulations, operate much less visibly. Authority is exercised, but it does not show up as clearly in the government's financial ledgers.

From the point of view of management control and accountability, visibility is a highly desirable feature of a tool. It makes it possible for managers to trace the flow of funds and authority and to ascertain results. Visibility can also be expected to contribute to target effectiveness. Certainly at a time of budget stringency, visibility in standard budget accounts is likely to reduce the chances of program growth. Because of this, however, visibility is not likely to be a politically attractive attribute of a tool from the point of view of potential recipients. Those with political clout may therefore prefer to receive their benefits through the less visible routes. This may help to explain the finding by Boulding and Pfaff that the less visible federal subsidies delivered most of their benefits to the better off whereas assistance to the poor tended to come in more visible forms.[14] What this suggests is the following hypothesis:

Hypothesis 2 (The Visibility/Invisibility Dimension): The more visible a tool, the easier to manage but the more difficult to enact.

The Delivery System

Beyond the consequences that flow from the nature of the activity a tool involves, other consequences are likely to flow from the structure of the delivery system that is utilized. At issue here, as noted above, is the extent to which the tool involves direct vs. indirect government action; and, if indirect, the nature of the third-party agents carrying out the government's purposes.

Direct forms of action have the great advantage of concentrating decision making in government agencies and thus guaranteeing a higher likelihood of administrative accountability and control. At the same time, however, because they require the creation of administrative structures to carry out programs, they may have a lower degree of supply effectiveness than indirect programs, which can make use of already existing private or other public structures.

This feature of indirect programs, moreover, translates into powerful political advantages. Since the success of federal programs frequently depends on access to a resource under some third party's control, delivering a degree of authority to this third party is often the only way to get the program the resources it needs. This is especially true where there is hostility among key producer and provider groups (including state and local governments) to federal competition in their fields. The price of political acquiescence in the establishment of a federal role, therefore, is frequently the acceptance by the federal government of a form of action that cuts these third parties into a meaningful piece of the federal action.

Counterbalancing the political advantages of indirect devices, however, are a number of administrative disadvantages—their cumbersomeness and the risk they pose to the fulfillment of public objectives. Pressman and Wildavsky demonstrate convincingly, for example, that federal efforts to encourage economic development and employment in Oakland, California were frustrated by a form of action that dispersed critical responsibilities among a large number of federal and nonfederal actors, each of whom had its own priorities and perspectives that had to be reconciled at each of several dozen decision points that stood between program conception and completion.[15] Similarly, Chase found that the most serious problems in implementing three social service programs in New York City all involved "some player or players in the implementation process whom the program manager does not control but whose cooperation or assistance is required."[16] And Berman differentiates between the "macro- implementation" of a program and its "micro-implementation," to emphasize the looseness of the tie between the adoption of a policy and its actual operation by a largely autonomous local agent.[17]

What is important about the use of indirect forms of action is not simply the administrative complexity of the resulting program structure, however. Of equal or greater importance is the incongruence that can arise between the goals of the federal government— as articulated, however imperfectly, in legislation, report language, or regulations—and the goals of the nonfederal implementing agents. This is clearly the case when the agent is a for-profit corporation. But it is also true of state and local governments since different interests, different priorities, and different concerns find effective expression at different levels of government. Proposals to turn more decision-making power over to states and localities thus involve more than questions of administrative efficiency; they also involve questions of program purpose and substance.

What these considerations suggest is the following:

Hypothesis 3 (The Direct/Indirect Dimension): Indirect tools of government action are far more difficult to administer but far easier to enact.

The Degree of Automaticity

Another of the tool dimensions identified above that has potential consequences for program performance is the extent to which they rely on automatic, as opposed to administered, processes.

An automatic process is one that utilizes existing structures and relationships—such as the tax structure or the price system—and requires a minimum of administrative decision making. A tax credit available to any firms investing in new plant or equipment, for example, would represent a largely automatic tool. A similar sum made available through grants on the basis of separately reviewed applications would represent a more highly administered tool.

Generally speaking, automatic tools are operationally more efficient since they involve less administrative oversight and transaction cost. They are also less disruptive of ongoing social processes, such as the price system and the market.

Despite these hypothesized advantages, however, instruments that rely upon essentially automatic processes have significant drawbacks. For one thing, there is far less certainty that they will achieve the results intended, especially when they are attached to processes with far different purposes. A program that seeks to promote worker safety by levying higher disability insurance charges on companies with poor safety records rather than by imposing detailed safety regulations, for example, may continuously be in the position of doing too little too late. In addition, while promoting administrative efficiency, such tools sacrifice "target efficiency," the effective targeting of program benefits. A tax credit program aimed at encouraging additional productive investment in plant and equipment, for example, may end up delivering substantial benefits to firms that would have made these investments anyway, or freeing resources for forms of investment that are nonproductive. Those most concerned about the achievement of program objectives and the targeting of program resources may consequently be wary of tools that lack sufficient controls. These considerations suggest the following:

> *Hypothesis 4 (The Automatic/Administered Dimension): The more automatic the tool the easier to administer, but the lower the target effectiveness and the greater the difficulty in attracting political support.*

Summary

The hypotheses identified above by no means exhaust the range of insights that the tools framework opens up. What is more, these hypotheses must still be subjected to empirical scrutiny. To the extent they hold up under such scrutiny, however, they suggest an important paradox that may explain some of the problems that public programs now encounter. In particular, many of the features that seem most likely to make programs easier to implement and operate—such as reliance on cash payments, visibility, direct delivery, and automaticity—also make them less likely to attract political support. By contrast, the features that seem most likely to generate political support also create serious administrative burdens. In other words, we seem most likely to be able to enact precisely the types of tools that are most difficult to manage. To the extent this is true, it suggests that current public sector problems may result less from deficiencies on the part of public managers than from shortcomings in our political process coupled with inattention to the characteristics of the tools that public managers are required to use.

CONCLUSION

The tools framework outlined here thus calls for a shift in the basic unit of analysis in policy research and public management from the government agency or program to the generic tools or instruments the public sector utilizes. As this chapter makes clear, the identification of such tools is not a simple matter. Various tools share many characteristics and individual programs often combine these characteristics in complicated and confusing ways. Nevertheless, it is possible to sort out some of these complexities and generate testable hypotheses about the relationships between key characteristics of tools and the consequences that flow from them.

The framework developed in this chapter is hardly the only form that a tools framework can take. Other crucial characteristics of tools can doubtless be identified. What is more, additional hypotheses can be generated to link the characteristics of tools to the consequences they have for program operations. Nevertheless, the framework developed here can still serve as a guide to the assembly of the empirical data that will be needed to put the tools concept to work. Against the backdrop of this framework, therefore, we can turn now to an explicit treatment of some of the major policy tools.

Notes

1. U.S. Congress, House Committee on Banking, Finance and Urban Affairs, Subcommittee on Economic Stabilization, *Hearings on Federal Credit Practice*, 97th Cong., 2d sess., 1981, 11.

2. Lester M. Salamon, "Rethinking Public Management: Third-Party Government and the Changing Forms of Government Action," *Public Policy* 29, no. 3 (Summer 1981), 256.

3. Among the classic works within this tradition are Philip Selznick, *TVA and the Grass Roots: A Study in the Sociology of Formal Organization* (Berkeley: University of California Press, 1949); Herbert Kaufman, *The Forest Ranger: A Study in Administrative Behavior* (Baltimore, Md.: Johns Hopkins University Press, 1960); Chester Barnard, *Functions of the Executive* (Cambridge, Mass.: Harvard University Press, 1968).

4. See, for example, Charles Schultze, *The Public Use of Private Interest* (Washington, D.C.: Brookings Institution, 1977); E.S. Savas, *Privatization: The Key to Better Government* (Chatham, N.J.: Chatham House, 1987).

5. See, for example, Jeffrey Pressman and Aaron Wildavsky, *Implementation: How Great Expectations in Washington Are Dashed in Oakland* (Berkeley: University of California Press, 1973). For a broader view of implementation research which nevertheless says little about alternative public "technologies" see Erwin Hargrove, *The Missing Link: The Study of Implementation* (Washington, D.C.: Urban Institute Press, 1976).

6. Theodore Lowi, "Public Policy, Case Studies, and Political Theory," *World Politics*, 17 (July 1964): 677–715; James Q. Wilson, *American Government: Institutions and Policies*, 2d ed. (Lexington, Mass.: D.C. Heath and Co., 1983).

7. Richard Simeon, "Studying Public Policy," *Canadian Journal of Political Science*, December 1976, 548.

8. Alice Rivlin, "Social Policy: Alternate Strategies for the Federal Government," in Robert Haveman and Julius Margolis, eds., *Public Expenditure and Policy Analysis,* 2d. ed. (Chicago: Rand McNally College Publishing, 1977).

9. G. Majone and A. Wildavsky, "Implementation As Evolution," *Policy Studies Review Annual 2,* 1978.

10. Eugene Bardach, "Implementation Study and the Study of Implements," Paper presented at the 1980 Annual Meeting of the American Political Science Association, Washington, D.C., August 1980. Regina Herzlinger and Nancy Kane, *A Managerial Analysis of Federal Income Distribution Mechanisms* (Cambridge, Mass.: Ballinger, 1979).

11. For example, unlike water pollution regulations, which require detailed rules on hundreds of types of effluents and continuous enforcement, effluent charges allow as much dumping as firms can afford and thus achieve control through the simple expedient of raising charges until they either cover the costs of clean-up or induce less dumping.

12. For an effective statement of this perspective in the context of social regulation, see Charles Schultze, *The Public Use of Private Interest* (Washington, D.C.: Brookings Institution, 1977).

13. The discussion here draws heavily on Salamon, "Rethinking Public Management," 1981: 266–72.

14. K. E. Boulding and M. Pfaff, *Redistribution to the Rich and the Poor: The Grants Economics of Income Distribution* (Belmont, Calif.: Wadsworth Publishing Co., 1972): 2–4.

15. Pressman and Wildavsky, *Implementation.*

16. G. Chase, "Implementing a Human Services Program: How Hard Will It Be?" *Public Policy 27,* no. 4 (Fall 1979): 385–435.

17. P. Berman, "The Study of Macro and Micro Implementation of Social Policy," *Public Policy 26,* no. 2 (Spring 1978), 157.

Part Two

The Tools

Chapter Three

THE FORGOTTEN FUNDAMENTAL: SUCCESSES AND EXCESSES OF DIRECT GOVERNMENT

Christopher K. Leman

Conventional wisdom among politicians and academics alike now has it that government cannot be counted on. With little real evidence, all public agencies stand accused of being ineffective, inefficient, and uncreative, and of being unresponsive and oppressive besides.[1] It is hardly news that government can fail, but the axiom that failure is inevitable contradicts the extensive if little noticed success of many agencies in doing just what we ask of them. Description is a fundamental prerequisite for theory. This chapter seeks a theory of what will be called here "direct government," by building from the ground up, through a close examination of actual experience.[2]

REDISCOVERING DIRECT GOVERNMENT

Recent social science research on government performance—much of it cited in other chapters of this book—has generally focused on cases of indirect government (regulation, grant-making, and so on). This attention to indirect government arose partly because, with the proliferation in recent decades of agencies that regulate or financially aid other organizations, programs of indirect government are the most numerous in the federal government; and partly because these programs have some of the most far-reaching and controversial federal impacts. Meanwhile, much less research has been conducted recently on programs of direct government, in which federal agencies themselves supply goods and services. In fact, although various lists of federal regulatory, grant-making, and loan guarantee programs have long existed, no similar list of direct government activities has been available; an appendix to this chapter therefore catalogs these activities. Another reason for the shortage of research on direct government is that few new agencies of this type have been founded in recent years; generally those in existence antedate the founding of most of the agencies of indirect government. In fact, prior to the 1960s, the great bulk of social science research on the performance of the federal government focused on the agencies of direct government.[3]

The research on direct government that characterized earlier eras of social science was considerably more upbeat than is the more recent research on indirect government, where failure is more often emphasized. This difference in tone is no accident. Many direct government activities have, by one measure or another, been more successful than many of those carried out indirectly. This overall success is another reason for the relative shortage of research on direct government: we take its achievements for granted. Research on governmental failure is not very helpful in understanding the conditions for success, however, if the failures apply to indirect government and the successes to direct government.

DEFINITION OF DIRECT GOVERNMENT

Direct government is defined here as the delivery of a good or service by federal employees, funded by appropriations from the federal treasury. This definition excludes government programs funded from receipts not channeled through the Treasury, but it includes parts of some programs such as Old Age, Survivors, and Disability Insurance which are funded in part by Treasury receipts that by law are automatically made available for agency spending.[4] Direct government is also defined here to include instances where a federal agency is reimbursed for activities carried out on behalf of others. For example, two-fifths of the budget of the National Bureau of Standards and nearly one-third of the budget of the Geological Survey come not from appropriations made directly to the agency but as reimbursements by other federal agencies, state or local agencies, and other organizations.[5]

It should be noted that several important federal programs satisfy only part of this definition but are discussed here because they operate much like direct government. Thus, the Smithsonian Institution is technically not an executive agency but a federal "establishment" whose governing board includes the vice president, members of Congress, and private citizens appointed by Congress, and is chaired by the chief justice of the Supreme Court. Although the Smithsonian has endowment funds and other nonfederal income, more than two-thirds of its employees are funded by federal appropriations and are part of the federal civil service.[6] The Tennessee Valley Authority, which is in some respects a government corporation funded from its own receipts, also receives appropriations to carry out some federal programs directly, for which it is officially designated as a federal agency. The U.S. Postal Service is another example. Until 1971 what was then known as the Department of the Post Office fully met the above definition of direct government. Now, however, it is an independent federal establishment whose governing board is appointed by the president but whose employees are not part of the federal civil service. Although the Postal Service now charges for some services—such as the congressional franking privilege—that once were provided without charge, it still provides a number of congressionally mandated free services—such as low rates for nonprofit groups—for which it receives an annual appropriation.

The notion of a policy tool is understood here generically to include a means of supplying goods and services to users not only external to government but also internal to government, as overhead support of external tasks. Direct government obviously involves significant internal administrative effort; indirect government does too, but less obviously. Although policy tools vary in their internal administrative demands, not a single indirect program of government among the many identified in other chapters in this book is entirely self-executing. Whether external goods and services are being supplied directly or by more indirect tools, the additional choice—which tool is to supply internal overhead needs—remains. For example, direct, regulatory, tax, and financial aid agencies alike need offices, supplies, and services for their employees; although many of these needs are supplied directly (such as by federal ownership of facilities and federal employment of support staff), the indirect tool of procurement is also widely used (such as in leasing office space, purchasing equipment, and contracting for maintenance).[7] However, direct and indirect government alike rely on direct supply in their internal management of funds and personnel, and for information.[8] For example, the collection of income taxes by the Internal Revenue Service (IRS) and the payment of individual benefits by the Social Security Administration are largely done directly by these agencies rather than indirectly by relying on other organizations. Almost 10 percent of the workload of the Social Security Administration is, in fact, carried out on behalf of other agencies.[9] Technical information produced directly by agencies like the Bureau of the Census, Geological Survey, National Bureau of Standards, and National Weather Service is depended on heavily by many other agencies in their own missions.

References in this chapter to "the agencies of direct government" apply to federal agencies insofar as they carry out direct functions; this usage is not meant to obscure the fact that these same agencies may often exercise tools of indirect government, especially procurement. Many agencies are involved simultaneously in direct and indirect government in their external activities. Sometimes the same functions are exercised both directly and indirectly, even in competition with one another, as when the National Institutes of Health directly operate the world's largest complex of biomedical research laboratories while also indirectly funding, by contracts and grants, a larger research effort outside the federal government. More often, direct and indirect tools are complementary, as when regulatory agencies directly conduct research for use in their indirect duties. Programs in the Department of Energy, the military services, and the National Aeronautics and Space Administration (NASA) that directly test nuclear bombs, organize for war, and operate space missions, respectively, rely heavily on contractors to supply the hardware. The indirect tool of procurement is often closely associated in practice with the tool of direct government; many agencies face constant "make- or-buy" decisions, and usually operate through a combination of direct government and procurement. For this reason, and because this book does not discuss procurement separately, it is discussed at several points in this chapter.

INCIDENCE OF DIRECT GOVERNMENT

The agencies of federal direct government are a forgotten fundamental of public policy. These agencies may not be as new or as numerous as most agencies of indirect government, but they are among the oldest and most diverse; some, such as the Bureau of the Mint, the Customs Service, the National Bureau of Standards, and the armed services, derive their authority from specific mentions in the U.S. Constitution itself, their origins dating back to the earliest years of the republic. Along with the direct activities of state and local governments, direct federal action led the nation's early development. For example, the U.S. Army conducted much of the exploration of the continent and built harbors, waterways, and roads. One reason more agencies of direct government have not been founded recently is that the nation has turned repeatedly to existing agencies to carry out new functions. Even today the Army (via the Corps of Engineers) operates civilian dams, locks, waterways, and harbors; the Navy (via the Naval Observatory) keeps the official time; and the Department of the Treasury (via the Secret Service) protects the president.[10]

Today, direct government activities account for a large share of federal employment. Agencies whose functions are primarily direct include many of those with the most civilian employees, such as the Public Health Service, Forest Service, Federal Aviation Administration, Veterans Administration (VA), Social Security Administration, Internal Revenue Service, and General Services Administration. Recent reductions in spending for indirect government have increased the relative prominence of direct government to a level it had not known for decades. The agencies of direct government account for a large share of the spending that the Office of Management and Budget classifies as relatively controllable.

Domestic federal functions currently being carried out via direct government can be classified into 10 categories (see appendix to this chapter): facilitating commerce; managing public lands; constructing public works and managing real property; research, testing, and statistics; technical assistance and libraries; law and justice; health care, social services, and direct cash benefits; education and training; marketing; and supporting internal overhead needs. Specifically, the federal government owns and operates many schools, libraries, laboratories, hospitals, road systems, shipyards, airport control towers, ocean navigation systems, correctional facilities, parks, fish hatcheries, monuments, museums, historic sites, places for the performing arts, a botanical garden, and a zoo. Many of these activities are carried on separately by more than one agency.

Federal employees manufacture the nation's currency, maintain and merchandise a common system of weights and measures, forecast the weather, chart the seas, survey and map the land, view and visit the heavens, investigate transportation and construction disasters, control river flows, pilot ships, deliver mail, deliver babies, fight epidemics, fight fires, fight crime, mediate labor disputes, and market various products and services. In addition, the federal government owns about one-third of the nation's land area (738 million acres), including 21 agencies with more than 10,000 acres each, and 5 with more than 50 million acres each. Direct activities that serve the internal administrative needs of the federal government include realty, purchasing, publishing, transportation, communications, financial services, legal services, and policy analysis. Three of the seven uniformed services of the U.S. government are involved primarily in domestic functions. Research is the most widespread of all direct federal activities. A recent survey found 388 federal laboratories with a total employment of more than 220,000.[11]

The focus of this book, and therefore of this chapter, is largely on federal domestic programs. If policy tools are viewed generically, however, it is important to remember that most of the country's experience with the direct approach has been outside the federal domestic sector. National defense and foreign policy are major instances of direct government; the Department of Defense employs nearly half the federal work force and owns about three-quarters of all federal building space. State and local agencies—whose collective employment dwarfs that of the federal government—are and always have been the dominant providers of roads, law enforcement, justice and corrections, fire protection, libraries, education, parks and recreation, public health, and social services.[12] And of course, the greatest providers of goods and services—and the biggest employers overall—are business or nonprofit institutions such as hospitals, factories, retailers, wholesalers, banks, cooperatives, associations, churches, and families. Since the great majority of organizations, whether governmental or nongovernmental, provides goods and services directly rather than regulating or financially aiding other organizations, the federal agencies of direct government are probably more typical of other U.S. organizations than are those that are engaged in indirect government.

Although many of the federal agencies of direct government are relatively large employers when compared with other federal agencies, most are exceeded in size by various state, local, business, and nonprofit organizations. Only the Postal Service (in most ways not an agency of direct government as defined here) has more employees than does General Motors, the largest nonfederal employer; the next largest federal domestic agency, the IRS, would rank only 25th among U.S. corporations in number of employees, and hundreds of other corporations are larger than most of the other agencies of direct government.[13] Many direct federal agencies are also smaller than parallel state and local agencies; for example, the New York City Police Department has more employees than does the Federal Bureau of Investigation (FBI), and at least three state corrections systems have more inmates and employees than does the federal Bureau of Prisons.

Direct government is more widely used, especially for commercial activities, in many other countries than it is in the United States. Although this chapter suggests that direct government is sometimes preferable to indirect government, the argument is emphatically not that government should preempt activities that are now the province of the market. Although in some cases a good argument could be made for doing so, the market has many strengths which in other cases could justify eliminating the government presence, whether it be direct or indirect. However, this chapter does not attempt to establish the proper dividing line between public authority and the market. The question is: Once government action has been decided on, how does the performance of direct government compare with that of the various tools of indirect government?

A MODEL OF DIRECT GOVERNMENT AND CRITERIA FOR ITS EVALUATION

Direct and indirect government alike make use of bureaucracy, but whereas indirect government generally has some self-executing features, bureaucracy is fundamental to direct government programs. The great sociologist Max Weber originated an influential portrayal of bureaucracy as a hierarchy of routine tasks that is insulated against external pressures. This monolithic view was perhaps accurate as a description of the Prussian military, which Weber regarded as emblematic of bureaucracy; but it can be very misleading without a recognition of the internal occupational differentiation and external political influence typical of U.S. bureaucracies.[14]

The bureaucracies that administer direct government programs have four distinctive features.[15] These features are briefly described here; later sections elaborate on them and explore their implications. One distinctive feature of direct government is an ability to *internalize transactions*. As emphasized in the other chapters of this book, indirect government depends greatly on the cooperation of other organizations and on entrepreneurs inside and outside of government who can piece together needed bargains. The vertical integration that characterizes direct government brings many of the key decisions into a single agency. A second distinctive feature of direct government is the *management of experts and information*. While the agencies of indirect government generally rely more on outside experts and sources of information, the agencies of direct government typically employ a relatively wide range of occupational specialties, and generate large amounts of technical information. A third distinctive feature of direct government is that administrative processes and organizational culture combine to *minimize legalism*—the externally imposed rules and administrative procedures that have marked indirect government in recent years. Laws are carried out more by an internal managerial approach than by formal "regulation" imposed by other agencies or the courts. A fourth feature of direct government is that it establishes a more stable framework than is usually found with indirect government for *bargaining with external interests*. Depending on how this framework is used, a direct government program can be either very open to political demands or highly resistant to them.

This chapter applies six criteria to evaluate the performance of direct government. *Effectiveness* is the ability of a program to reach an assigned objective. *Oppressiveness* is infringement on civil liberties. *Efficiency* includes both minimization of cost in reaching an objective (cost-effectiveness) and maximization of broader social welfare (economic efficiency). *Innovation* is the origination or adoption of new technologies, policies, or management techniques. *Political feasibility* is the ability of a program to attain the support sufficient for its adoption and maintenance. *Political responsiveness* is the degree to which a program's management is accountable to various interests and is adjusted to their desires.

Effectiveness

Effectiveness, the ability to reach an assigned objective,[16] is easiest to determine for agencies with a relatively clear mission and measurable performance—as with the Bureau of the Mint in manufacturing coins and the National Archives and Records Service in preserving historic documents and storing current ones. In other cases, the mission is clear but how to achieve it is subject to interpretation, as with the Secret Service in protecting the president.[17] In still other cases, the mission itself is indeterminate: how the Bureau of Prisons should manage inmates and how the Forest Service should manage wildlands have long been a subject for debate and change.[18] The "mission" of still other agencies is to grapple with problems that have no certainty of ever being solved, and for which no clear standard of success has been agreed on. Unenviably, the Office of Civilian Radioactive Waste Management has custody of lethal waste for which no safe method of permanent disposal has yet been devised. Reversing the growth of illegal immigration is the daunting assignment of the Immigration and Naturalization Service, which may not be able to complete this task even with large increases in funds and personnel. Effectiveness will be difficult to determine in such cases.

Important components of effectiveness include capacity, administrative discretion, and influence and control. In building effectiveness, direct government's relative lack of reliance on other organizations has the advantage that capacity is often most successfully developed within a single organization; it has the disadvantage that any public agency has limitations which are difficult to remedy without resort to outside help.

CAPACITY

Resources, skills, and information are essential for effectiveness, and large organizations are noted for having this capacity. The massive mobilization of equipment and people needed for the moon landings and exploration of deep space could hardly have been managed except by a large agency like NASA. A special need in management, public or private, is to mobilize diverse occupational specialities and to integrate their respective points of views.[19] The agencies of direct government generally have a wide range of specialists, offering them diverse responsibilities, geographic locations, and opportunities for advancement. Some state and local agencies and commercial or nonprofit organizations that operate as arms of indirect government show similar strengths, but others fall short, failing to employ enough skilled personnel or to procure them from elsewhere. Economies of scale in federal data collection are also important. The information and skills of the federal statistical and research agencies are widely relied on throughout American society.[20] Even the private weather forecasting companies that have proliferated in recent years rely heavily on information they receive for a nominal fee by tapping directly into the computer data banks of the National Weather Service.

Capacity can decline if adequate resources are not devoted to maintaining it. Budget cuts in the federal statistical agencies have begun to compromise the accuracy and timeliness of their products.[21] Also in recent years, lags in federal pay behind the private sector have made it increasingly difficult to recruit and retain federal scientists, engineers, lawyers, and other specialists.[22] Congress is considering and (as of August 1988) is likely to pass legislation to allow federal managers greater latitude to pay at the market rate. Personnel limitations can also reduce capacity. Although the workload of the IRS in the past decade has increased by half, its work force has grown less than 3 percent. Whereas 5 percent of all income tax returns were audited in the 1960s, this proportion is now barely over 1 percent. As a result, taxpayers are not as fearful of being caught, and cheating is on the increase. Contracting out is one way to continue government functions in the face of personnel limitations, but some functions of agencies like the IRS are too sensitive for this to be much of an option.

Direct government has commonly been instituted when alternative means of securing the same public purposes are unavailable, as in federal schooling and health care for the residents of Indian reservations and overseas military bases. Some people are alive today only because the Centers for Disease Control develop and manufacture drugs for health problems that are too rare to attract commercial involvement. Violent inmates that state prisons cannot handle have traditionally been transferred to the custody of the federal Bureau of Prisons, where they therefore are numerous enough to be grouped in a specially equipped facility. In other cases, the nation is committed to providing service everywhere, whether or not nonfederal alternatives may be available. National coverage is not easy; the offices of the FBI, U.S. Marshals Service, U.S. Attorneys, and the district courts, are spread more thinly in sparsely than in densely populated areas, even though lawbreaking (such as drug offenses on the federal lands) has greatly increased in the former. Users who must travel long distances to the 172 hospitals of the Veterans Administration may prefer indirect aid (which the VA also offers in extreme cases) that allows them to choose from among non-VA hospitals located nearer their homes.

The capacity of direct government is not easily developed. The personnel practices and skills that make an agency effective often depend upon a charismatic, demanding founder like Gifford Pinchot at the Forest Service, Hugh Hammond Bennett at the Soil Conservation Service, or J. Edgar Hoover at the FBI.[23] Although such unusual leadership is not as crucial after the founding period, continuity remains important. The chief administrators of such agencies as the Bureau of Prisons, the Forest Service, and the National Bureau of Standards have typically served for periods of a decade or more. Although these chiefs originated as career employees of their agencies, it is possible for a political appointee to have similar tenure: the director of the Bureau of the Mint is an outside political appointee, yet some have had lengthy tenures, with one serving for 20 years. Turnover in leadership can hamper an agency's effectiveness, as in the recent experience of the General Services Administration and the Immigration and Naturalization Service.[24]

The difficulties of founding a direct agency are a major reason why new direct tasks have often been assigned to existing agencies, but this approach has risks. Drawing in part on analogies with the private sector, some have argued that the most successful agencies concentrate on a single, well-defined mission.[25] Highly focused agencies like the Bureau of the Mint, the National Weather Service, the National Bureau of Standards, and the FBI do seem to be among the most successful in achieving their official missions. In contrast, the Immigration and Naturalization Service has been torn by conflicting needs to combat illegal immigration and to welcome and assist legitimate immigrants.[26] Fixation on a single mission also presents the dilemma of what to do when that mission is achieved; the Bureau of Reclamation's traditional role of water diversion in the West makes less sense now that, as a result of its dam construction, much of the water there is now spoken for. The very real organizational problems in NASA's shuttle program that culminated in the Challenger disaster were partially rooted in pressures to turn an agency well-suited for development and demonstration projects into the operator of a routine transportation system.[27]

When existing agencies have trouble expanding their capacity quickly, they may contract out some activities to another federal agency that has the capacity to undertake them. In addition to agencies like the National Bureau of Standards and the Geological Survey, whose very mission in part is to conduct activities for others, there are many ad hoc instances, as with the cooperative agreement under which the Forest Service manages at Department of Energy expense about 150,000 acres of timberlands on the Savannah River Reservation. Another alternative is for federal agencies to pool their resources, as with the central command provided by the Interagency Fire Center and the cooperative efforts of the Federal Laboratory Consortium for Technology Transfer.[28] Of course, a massive or rapid expansion of federal capacity is more commonly secured indirectly; regulatory actions, grants, loan guarantees, and procurement contracts can produce quick results. For example, procurement allows a federal agency to rely on organizations that already exist and—in theory, at least—to choose the one that can best achieve the objective. The agencies of direct government often supplement their efforts with procurement.

As bureaucracies grow they can become unmanageable, and direct government sometimes enhances its own effectiveness by leaving some tasks to indirect government. Procurement is used selectively as a means of "load-shedding," as for example, by the federal land management agencies, which have long contracted out such routine tasks as road maintenance and tree planting without appreciably diminishing their capacity to deliver goods and services.[29] In fact, some of the greatest successes in procurement have come from agencies whose major responsibilities with direct government give them the capacity to manage contractors very closely. Agency managers know what they want from the contractor, and they integrate procurement results into their overall direct operation. But procurement is no panacea. Indirect government imposes on the responsible agencies its own administrative load, in the need to deal with more outside organizations. The outside organizations relied on may themselves lack the needed capacity, and may not operate well under time pressure.[30] Contractors will be cooperative only insofar as their interests allow; indirect government retains the disadvantage that some of the greatest needs of federal managers will be for capacity that an outside organization has no desire to provide.

ADMINISTRATIVE DISCRETION

The effectiveness of direct government in delivering goods and services is also enhanced by discretion in how to implement external rules. Some purposes are most effectively carried out when they are integrated into the overall management process, using organizational procedures that are difficult to specify in laws and regulations.[31] Harold Seidman points out that in many indirect programs "federal administrators are concerned not with the results but with the enforcement of grant and contract provisions and applicable federal regulations. [They] are converted from 'doers' to paymasters and auditors."[32] The National Environmental Policy Act of 1969 has generally been implemented more successfully by the agencies of direct government (for example, the Army Corps of Engineers, the Soil Conservation Service, and the Forest Service) than by agencies engaged in regulation, grant-making, or other indirect activities.[33] The discretion often exercised by the agencies of direct government is especially useful in reconciling the frequent conflicts between external rules. Direct and indirect government alike exercise discretion, but keeping it within a particular agency reduces the possibility of litigation that often arises when transfers of authority are made from the federal government to other organizations. Although there is increased risk of illegality, at best the minimization of legalism may allow an agency to implement the spirit of the laws more effectively than can legalism itself.

INFLUENCE AND CONTROL

Research on indirect government reported in other chapters of this book shows that the need to gain the cooperation of other organizations introduces potentially impassable roadblocks, requiring time and compromise that can frustrate the original purposes of federal intervention.[34] By not depending as much on other organizations, direct government internalizes many of these transactions and reduces their cost. Negotiations still occur among an agency's hierarchical levels, geographic and functional divisions, or occupational specialities, but managers have more opportunity for informal influence, and more authority to exert formal control.[35] Thus the in-house printing done by the Government Printing Office (GPO) is generally more prompt and more accurate than the printing that the GPO contracts out to businesses.[36] Direct government has been assigned such critical tasks as controlling river flow through the nation's dams.[37] The general freedom of government from liability lawsuits is a decisive advantage over nongovernmental organizations for risky activities of this sort.

Direct government's advantages in control can be seen in the greater success in attaining the official objectives of the Endangered Species Act on federal lands than elsewhere.[38] On nonfederal lands, the federal government (through the Fish and Wildlife Service) is a regulator. Given the complexity of joint action, it is not surprising that enforcement of the Act is very uneven on nonfederal lands, especially private ones.[39] In contrast to this often adversarial nature of indirect government is the more cooperative arrangement under which each federal land agency is responsible for enforcement of the Act on its own lands.[40]

The agencies of direct government vary in how effectively they exert the influence and control that are at their disposal. Some— such as the Immigration and Naturalization Service and the General Services Administration—have been poorly managed.[41] Those—like the National Park Service—that are moderately well managed often have considerable room for improvement.[42] And even those—like the IRS and NASA—that have been regarded as among the best managed, have suffered prominent lapses at times. For example, in 1985 the IRS destroyed income tax returns, sent incorrect delinquency notices, and allowed the accumulation of large backlogs of unprocessed returns; and in 1986 NASA suffered the dramatic loss of the space shuttle Challenger.[43] But when direct government is aimless, incompetent, or corrupt, these problems are more readily subject to correction than when similar problems arise with indirect government, where federal managers are often helpless to correct the matter. Social programs that are not directly managed by federal civil servants have considerably more fraud and waste than those that are.[44] A combination of influence and control has made the land management agencies among the least scandal-prone in government, comparing well in this respect with most state and local agencies and commercial and nonprofit organizations. Business ethics are comparatively weaker, judging from recent scandals in the financial world over check-kiting and insider trading.

Direct government depends less than does indirect government on external entrepreneurs ("fixers") and internal leaders. The occasional successes of indirect government are stories of talented individuals improvising against enormous odds.[45] The more frequent successes of direct government hinge less on unique individuals than on an organization's subunits negotiating with one another according to established processes.[46] Since it is widely agreed that government suffers from a shortage of leaders and entrepreneurs, it is of no small consequence that in ongoing operations the direct federal programs have found a partial organizational substitute for them.

Federal personnel management is subject to many rules and to the provisions of union agreements, and indirect government is sometimes a way to get around the rigidity that can result. However, the most effective agencies of direct government have been successful in taking these requirements in stride and managing for results; the managers are able to hire, promote, discipline, and fire personnel to their satisfaction, and do not envy their counterparts in state and local governments or commercial and nonprofit organizations. In labor relations, they even have an advantage over these counterparts in that federal employees are prohibited from bargaining over wages or from striking for any reason.

Oppressiveness

The very effectiveness of the agencies of direct government poses the risk that they will trespass on the liberties of the citizenry. At various times the law enforcement agencies, the IRS, and other agencies have badly abused their power. Watergate constituted an ominous abuse of direct presidential government; although the FBI and CIA refused White House pressure to engage in the break-in, and helped unravel the coverup, prior to Watergate they had inflicted their own abuses. For example, the FBI under J. Edgar Hoover used confidential information from files to intimidate congressional critics and wiretapped and attempted to blackmail Martin Luther King, Jr.[47] Earlier the Army helped wage the Indian Wars that wrested the continent from its original inhabitants. Abroad the horrors of police states, censorship, political prisoners, torture, and genocide have been the work of direct government. In recent years, however, U.S. direct government is perhaps most striking for its lack of oppressiveness. Its greatest threat to citizens is probably from accidental rather than deliberate interference.

Some of the worst abuses of civil liberties in the United States have been inflicted not by the federal government but by state or local governments, businesses, unions, or other organizations. Serious injustices have occurred in private credit checks, debt collection, investigation, and professional practice.[48] The Jim Crow system of racial discrimination emerged and persisted under state and local government, and its ending depended on such direct actions as President Eisenhower's dispatch of the U.S. Army to Little Rock in 1957, the FBI's undercover campaign against violence by white supremacists in the 1960s, and the direct administration of some local schools by federal district judges in the 1970s.[49] Although the Bill of Rights was added to the U.S. Constitution by the states as a check on the federal government, its subsequent use has actually been directed mainly at state and local abuses. It was not until 1965 that the U.S. Supreme Court found any direct federal action to be in violation of the First Amendment.[50]

In certain cases, the protection of constitutional rights is better achieved by an agency than by legalism and the courts. Twenty years before the Supreme Court's Miranda decision called upon law enforcement officers to advise arrested persons of their constitutional rights before questioning them, this practice was official policy in the FBI, where even today protections for the constitutional rights of those in custody exceed those of many state and local agencies.[51] Federal prisons have long avoided the inhumane practices in many state prison systems that have been found unconstitutional by the federal courts.[52] Certainly the courts should not leave the protection of constitutional rights to bureaucratic discretion; but when agency leaders choose to, they can enhance these rights more effectively than could the courts alone.

Efficiency

Two different standards of efficiency are used here. One is *cost-effectiveness*—the ability to achieve a given level of benefit at a minimum cost. The other is *economic efficiency*—the contribution to overall social welfare.[53] Government is widely regarded as not being very cost-effective and as not contributing much to economic efficiency. Comparisons are difficult, however, because U.S. governmental and nongovernmental organizations are usually not involved in the same kinds of activities. State-owned enterprises are more common in virtually every other country, including the western democracies; in the United States, enterprise has generally been left to the private sector.[54] At their best (examples being the British Broadcasting Corporation, Volvo, and Petrocanada), foreign enterprises that are partly or wholly government-owned are arguably as cost-effective as their private competitors. But a probably more numerous group (such as Soviet collective farms, and the British–French Concorde project) are considered classic examples of inefficiency.[55]

Comparisons of the cost-effectiveness of government and commercial organizations must consider their respective goals. For example, Job Corps centers that are administered by commercial contractors are cheaper per enrollee than those administered by the federal agencies, but this difference is almost entirely attributable to the government-run centers' smaller size, which is congressionally mandated.[56] Government performance should be compared not to an idealization of the private sector, but to how it would work given the inevitable role of indirect government. Any politically realistic scenario for transferring federal timberlands to private ownership, for example, would involve extensive protections for amenities by covenants on the transfer and by subsequent regulation, greatly reducing the commercial windfall from a change in ownership.[57]

Some U.S. federal agencies are well known for their cost-effectiveness. An observation of the late Arthur Okun for the most part holds still: "It is my impression that check-writing and check-collecting agencies like the Social Security Administration and the Internal Revenue Service are paragons of efficiency."[58] In fact, increases in the IRS budget often repay themselves many times over in increased revenues to the Treasury. Such agencies are disciplined by the need to deal with a very large proportion of the U.S. public; errors and slowness are politically risky. The cost-effectiveness of other agencies, such as the National Bureau of Standards, the National Weather Service, and the Bureau of the Census is encouraged by constant contact with their commercial customers.[59] The auctioning of minerals and timber from the public lands introduces into the land management agencies a certain consciousness of markets. Among arguably the least cost-effective of federal agencies are those—like the General Services Administration and the armed services—that have a monopoly and supply few goods and services to outside customers. However, such an impact is not inevitable; the straightforward financial criteria used to measure the success of the Financial Management Service in its governmentwide overhead functions seem to have strongly disciplined even this crucial but virtually unknown agency.[60]

Cost-effectiveness is promoted by targeting the effort where it will produce the greatest benefits. Other direct federal activities have been founded to give aid to a specific geographic area; the tools of indirect government are more likely to apply to all in a particular category regardless of geography.[61] Historic economic boosts were provided the West by the Bureau of Reclamation and the South by the Tennessee Valley Authority (in some respects a government corporation).[62] Pressures to spread the effort evenly can in some circumstances thwart these targeting efforts. The Soil Conservation Service has long deployed its technical assistance efforts rather broadly across the country, despite the fact that the problem of soil erosion was never evenly distributed and has shifted over time.[63]

Even if a program is carried out cost-effectively, it may not contribute to overall economic efficiency. Well before its recent problems, NASA's space shuttle program was criticized by some economists for discouraging private sector development of expendable launch vehicles that could achieve many of the same purposes more cheaply.[64] Even if water projects are managed cost-effectively (which many of them probably are), there are still too many of them. National economic efficiency would be better promoted if some had never been built.[65] On the other hand, some current practices of direct government may serve economic efficiency even if the monetary gains to the Treasury could be greater. Federal research and information-gathering play a central role in the private economy that could never be fully captured in a system of user charges. Although the land management agencies earn revenues from commercial development, they also place emphasis on public goods such as scenery, water quality, and wildlife that would tend not to be protected by market forces.

Innovation

Innovation is a concept widely recognized in organization theory, economics, and technology.[66] The variety of participants that reduces the effectiveness of indirect government probably encourages more experimentation than is typical for direct government. When direct government turned Washington, D.C.'s Union Station into the deserted, leaking National Visitors Center, a series of procurement contracts were relied on to transform it into a bustling mall of shops and offices.[67] Even so, the disparity between direct and indirect government has been exaggerated. State and local governments, businesses, and nonprofit groups that are the chosen instruments of federal indirect government have not always produced the innovations that were expected of them. Some lack the capacity that would help them play a creative role; others are hampered by the federal impact itself, especially by the legalism of federal grant-making or regulation.

Direct government, on the other hand, has on occasion innovated dramatically. The military services contributed many of the scientific discoveries and engineering advances of the 19th century. The Forest Service virtually created the American forestry profession, and by the 1920s had introduced the country to both industrial forestry and the preservation of wilderness areas. The Fish and Wildlife Service helped originate the ecological approach to environmental quality that is now widely accepted inside and outside government.[68] Engineering innovations from federal water projects have spread worldwide. An observation made decades ago about public land and water management still, for the most part, holds true in that field: "The states, as experimental bodies politic, have lagged far behind the national government agencies in pushing toward improved techniques in both management and utilization."[69] The Social Security Administration and the IRS were among the earliest in the public or private sector to make use of computers.[70] The FBI and Bureau of Prisons established early and influential models in their fields.[71] In the mid-1980s the U.S. Marshals Service created a Fugitive Investigative Strike Team which pulled off a number of celebrated "sting" operations.

Innovation depends on the ability to learn from previous mistakes. The Bureau of Reclamation was sharply criticized for errors in design that led to the 1976 failure of its Teton Dam, whose flooding killed 14 Idahoans and caused more than $400 million in damage.[72] As a result, the agency greatly strengthened its system of peer review. Indirect government is often slower to respond to its own failures, because the mistakes of one state, locality, nonprofit organization, or corporation may not be taken to heart by the others. For example, the same errors in military procurement have been repeated for decades with comparatively little improvement, and state regulators were slow to learn from the hazardous waste disasters at Love Canal and Times Beach.

In economic emergencies, when government-supported jobs need to be created, the country has often turned to projects of direct agencies like the Army Corps and Forest Service. These agencies have sometimes been criticized for keeping a backlog of plans on the shelf, ready to be unveiled when political conditions are favorable. This opportunism undoubtedly leads to some undesirable projects, but it cannot be said that the agencies suffer from insufficient initiative. In intergovernmental grant programs, the number of realistic applications received has historically been rather low.[73]

Political Feasibility

No program can survive if it lacks basic acceptance by the public, and policy analysts must consider political feasibility in their calculations.[74] Americans care how directly the federal government is involved, regarding some activities as being inappropriate for direct government.[75] Federal law makes no mention of most crimes—even murder—because of popular resistance to creating anything resembling a national police force.[76] Certain local jurisdictions resist federal aid to the poor and insist on determining amounts and conditions of cost-shared aid.[77] However, the American public also prefers to keep some activities as direct federal ones, even those that in principle could be carried out indirectly. Individual states marshalled military units in the Civil War, commercial banks printed U.S. currency until well into this century, private police services once guarded the president, and the Washington Monument was sponsored by a nonprofit organization; yet today national defense, manufacture of money, protection of the president, and operation of national memorials are seen as properly direct federal functions. Even in our present winter of discontent with government, direct federal agencies like the National Park Service, NASA, the Peace Corps, the armed services, and the FBI remain important focuses of national identity and pride for many Americans.

The administrative advantages of not relying on states, localities, nonprofit organizations, and businesses, also deprive direct government of political support of the kind that helped produce the expansion of indirect government in recent decades.[78] Still, direct government programs can have strong political support: national defense, law enforcement, the collection of revenue, the maintenance of weights and measures, and medical research have such widespread benefits that little lobbying may be needed on their behalf.[79] Other direct government programs benefit more specific groups, among them veterans, retirees, farmers, vacationers, Indians, boaters, airlines, bankers, and various manufacturers. When some of these groups were initially not as well organized as were the clients of indirect government, the agencies of direct government helped to organize them, as with the Soil Conservation Service's fostering of the nation's soil and water conservation districts (now numbering nearly 3,000) which use the agency's technical assistance and are a powerful grass roots lobby on its behalf.[80] A key means to build political acceptance is for an agency to adapt its mission to one or another set of outside demands, as in the long-time domination of the Bureau of Land Management by western livestock and mining interests.[81]

By marketing itself effectively, an agency can sometimes increase its political support without a change in policy. All agencies market themselves to some extent, but the agencies of direct government are especially good at it because of their greater resources and skills. For example, they generally employ the most public relations personnel.[82] Television series that feature the federal government have usually been about direct government. Although undoubtedly attributable in large part to the fact that viewers are more interested in direct government than in such untelegenic federal activities as regulation, grant-making, taxation, or lending, these dramatizations also have been encouraged by the agencies featured.[83]

Technical analysis is often used as a means of marketing an agency, especially to combat criticisms made by outsiders. Federal water projects have rarely lived up to claims that they "pay for themselves" (despite the addition of such rationales as flood control, navigation, irrigation, recreation, and municipal and industrial supply in an attempt to justify these claims); yet they have never lacked political support. When, despite an unpromising cost-benefit analysis by the Army Corps of Engineers, Congress and the president in the early 1970s decreed that the Tennessee–Tombigbee waterway be built, the Corps replaced the analysis with a more favorable one. Social Security Administration domination of research and expert discussion discouraged outside review of the agency's policies for several decades.[84] The massive analytical process conducted by the Forest Service under the Resources Planning Act tended to obscure key policy issues and discourage external review.[85]

Although the visibility conferred on direct government by its association with the federal "brand name" often has political advantages, at times it can be a drawback. For example, a decade of conflict and experimentation had by 1980 produced consensus on a system for sales of federally owned coal by the Bureau of Land Management. Just as the sales were beginning, however, Secretary of the Interior James G. Watt arrived on the scene. Watt's combative style antagonized many members of Congress, and even though his changes in the coal program were relatively minor, political agreement evaporated and the program faltered.[86]

Political Responsiveness

A common criticism of government bureaucracies is that they are not responsive to their clientele or to elected officials. Although it is sometimes argued that federal agencies are not subject to the competitive pressures that discipline their state, local, commercial, and nonprofit counterparts, overlap of direct government agencies is surprisingly common, spawning an active political competition by each to be the most effective, innovative, and efficient. Three agencies construct water projects, at least five have historic preservation functions, four major ones enforce civil and criminal laws, and five manage huge holdings of federal land. Others also exercise these functions on a smaller scale.[87] Even agencies with dissimilar functions compete with one another for funds, personnel ceilings, facilities, land, and new assignments.[88] Comparison of federal agencies with various nonfederal organizations is an additional competitive spur. For example, a desire to maintain the good will of the public has motivated various federal agencies in recent years to train and manage their employees for more prompt and courteous service.[89] Of course, there is much room for improvement and it is only slightly comforting that "horror stories" can be heard as well about state and local agencies and commercial and nonprofit organizations.[90]

Contrary to Max Weber's view of modern bureaucracy as being politically insulated, in the United States it is permeated with external influences.[91] The competitive pressures on agencies cause them to prospect constantly for political support. Occupational specialties inside the agencies of direct government have often become strong advocates for such popular concerns as safety and environmental quality. Agencies also respond to "regulation" by the president's Office of Management and Budget, cabinet members and their staffs, the many units of Congress, and the courts. Even agencies primarily involved in internal overhead functions must be responsive to their customers, as when the Government Printing Office receives complaints from an advisory board of agency publishers and through a governmentwide Federal Publisher's Committee of 600 members.[92]

For better and for worse, some agencies of direct government have shown a rare willingness to defy these political pressures. The New Deal land reforms instituted by the former Resettlement Administration and Farm Security Administration were successful in their assigned mission of beginning to build a rural black middle class, but this very success provoked local opposition that caused their discontinuation in the 1940s.[93] Political opponents—and nearly every program has some—may regard success in its assigned mission as a point against an agency, not for it. Nuclear wastes exist and must be put somewhere; it is difficult to imagine any location that will be welcomed by nearby inhabitants. State officials and local residents near every likely site for long-term disposal of nuclear wastes registered unhappiness with the search conducted by the Office of Civilian Radioactive Waste Management, causing Congress to intervene.[94]

When the leadership of an agency of direct government chooses to bargain with external opponents, the possibilities of political compromise can be greater than with indirect government. The managers of indirect government sometimes adopt a rigid stance for fear of losing control of a bargaining process; managers of direct government are likely to regard political bargaining as more routine because their authority is secure. For example, although state and local governments technically have no authority over federal lands, a system of "intragovernmental federalism" prevails that often represents their concerns within Congress and the executive branch.[95] Of course, an agency of direct government is also in a position, if it desires, to manipulate the process for its own purposes; the high public participation achieved by agencies like the Army Corps of Engineers and the Forest Service does not always produce equivalent changes in policy.[96] At the extreme, an agency of direct government may be able to "enact its environment."[97]

Some direct government programs are responsive to a fault, as members of Congress pressure them in a failing direction. The Agricultural Research Service lost its traditional focus on basic, nationally significant research largely in response to congressional pressure for more localized, applied work.[98] The process by which Congress authorizes and funds GSA-constructed buildings is acknowledged by many in Congress to be haphazard and wasteful.[99] Political opposition to the displacement of direct government facilities or employees sometimes blocks changes that would improve the effectiveness or efficiency of a program.[100] Efforts by several presidents to retarget the technical assistance efforts of the Soil Conservation Service more to areas with the greatest erosion problems have been largely frustrated by congressional opposition.[101] Direct agencies performed a historic mission, as mentioned earlier, in promoting the development of the South and West; but unfortunately for the East and North, these efforts continue now even after having had their intended effect of bringing the other areas up to the national average. In fact, western clients will not allow the Bureau of Reclamation to construct water projects in the East (which has most of the nation's water) and have hampered the Bureau of Land Management in its efforts to reach out more to national constituencies.[102] The geographically broader constituencies of the Army Corps of Engineers and the Forest Service have left them freer to add new missions.

At the grass-roots level, many agencies of direct government have the political advantage that their employees are located in an unusually large number of cities and towns, not concentrated just in Washington, D.C. The Postal Service is the classic example. In theory, grants or procurement contracts should be easier to shift from one region to another than federal offices or personnel; in practice, however, these policy tools are subject to similar political forces. For example, much as with Soil Conservation Service tech-

nical assistance, Congress has for the most part blocked the re-
targeting of soil conservation payments that are made by the
Agricultural Stabilization and Conservation Service. Relocation of
the huge contractor-operated laboratories that are owned by the Department of Energy would be at least as difficult politically as relocation of the government's many laboratories that are staffed by
federal employees.[103]

CONCLUSION

In contrast to the extensive research on the failures of indirect government in the United States, surprisingly little research has explored the success achieved by direct government. An earlier
tradition of research by social scientists on direct government has
weakened, and should be revived. Direct government clearly qualifies as a forgotten fundamental of public policy.

As with the other tools examined in this book, direct government
in practice is too diverse to be entirely a success or entirely a failure; a wise conclusion is that it is better suited to some tasks than
to others. Direct government's high rate of success in the United
States is in part attributable to the fact that it has not been assigned
many tasks where it would be likely to fail. Policymakers have
been very selective about authorizing new ventures of direct government. Although the general avoidance of commercial activities
by U.S. direct government has forgone some potential successes, it
has averted a greater number of potential failures. By necessarily
focusing its efforts, U.S. government perhaps does a better job at
those direct tasks that it does undertake, and these programs benefit from being able to leave some tasks to indirect government,
thereby not overloading direct government. This chapter has revealed the substantial role of direct government in providing
overhead support for federal agencies that administer indirect government programs. Clearly, a necessary condition for the success of
tools of indirect government is that direct government itself should
succeed. Here, too, direct government is a forgotten fundamental.

The performance of direct government is aided by the internali-
zation of transactions that otherwise would depend on joint action
with outside organizations, by full use of information and experts,
by reliance on organizational processes rather than legalistic ones,
and by a facility for responding to clients and the public. Direct
government has its share of failures, but many are less inherent in

the situation than those of indirect government; these failures can be remedied, moreover, and often are. Political consensus is clearly an important precondition for the success of an activity of direct government. The agencies of direct government have often achieved a responsiveness that belies the image of immovable or oppressive bureaucracy, yet playing the political market has sometimes diverted them from their intended missions.

The original dominance of direct government was overshadowed by increases in indirect government in past decades. But although Reagan-era budget cuts and deregulation reduced the scope of indirect government, direct government is becoming more significant again. In fact, contrary to the general trend of governmental cutbacks, there has been some growth in direct government. Examples in the 1980s included the expansion of the armed forces and the Immigration and Naturalization Service, the addition of museums and employees at the Smithsonian Institution, and the founding of the National Archives and Records Administration.

The success of direct government is sometimes held against it. For example, arms races and wars are largely an activity of direct government; perhaps we would all be better off if governments worldwide were less effective at such activities. In fact, the very success of the tool of direct government may be the major problem with it. Although direct government has its share of abject failures, its more characteristic drawback has been not in falling short but in carrying out its assigned goals to excess, so that the tool becomes an end in itself. Just as bureaucracies are difficult to found, they are also difficult to redirect or disband. A mission may persist far beyond the need for it, much as in the story of the Sorcerer's Apprentice, who brought a broom to life but could not reverse the spell when the broom's work was done. The indirect tools of government, too, develop their own momentum; but few can match the ability of the agencies of direct government to combat criticism by mobilizing experts, information, and political allies.

Potential excesses have given Americans an instinctive distrust of direct government, discouraging its growth. These barriers help control the excesses of direct government, an outcome much to be desired; but they also have in some cases led to a reliance on indirect government where direct government would perform better. In accepting a greater role for indirect government, we have sometimes preferred an ineffective tool to one that is more likely to succeed, leaving the impression that government cannot be made to work even when it can.

It may seem inconsistent for the public both to fear government for abuses and to ridicule government for incompetence.[104] But these views are not contradictory if the excesses are those of direct government and the failures are those of indirect government. Political and academic debates on the proper role of government need to distinguish more carefully between direct and indirect government. Some restrictions (such as shortening of federal regulations, safeguards on fraud and waste, new channels for intergovernmental review, personnel limitations, and across-the-board budget cuts) were adopted primarily to deal with the problems of indirect government, but their weight is felt also by direct government, often with perverse consequences. Remedies need to be appropriate to the problem; misapplied, they may only create new problems.

Government is a ready scapegoat for problems that originate elsewhere.[105] Much as Joseph Schumpeter argued that capitalism invites the seeds of its own destruction in the fostering of a class of unfriendly critics, the federal sector suffers attack from some whose living depends on polemics. Such attacks could become a self-fulfilling prophecy. When direct government can work but is not politically acceptable, while indirect government proves unworkable but is politically acceptable, the choice may in some cases be to dispense with the government role entirely.

Acknowledgments: The author is grateful for the assistance of personnel in many of the agencies discussed here, for the comments of Harvey Sapolsky, David Beam, Erwin Hargrove, Martin A. Levin, Paul McDaniel, the editors, and others at the conference, and for additional comments from Samuel H. Beer, Clark S. Binkley, David Campbell, Martha Derthick, John J. DiIulio, Jr., Robert J. Dilger, Charles Goodsell, Lloyd Irland, Herbert Kaufman, Robert A. Katzmann, Nancy F. Leman, Richard F. Leman, Michael G. H. McGeary, Philip Metzger, Frederick C. Mosher, Frank Popper, Alice M. Rivlin, Harold Seidman, Gilbert Steiner, Richard W. Wahl, David Leo Weimer, and Henry C. Webster, Jr.

Notes

1. Leading examples of the axiomatic critique of government include: William A. Niskanen, Jr., *Bureaucracy and Representative Government* (New York: Aldine-Ath-

erton, Inc., 1971), and his "Bureaucrats and Politicians," in *Journal of Law and Economics* 18, no. 3 (December 1975); and James M. Buchanan, Robert D. Tollison, and Gordon Tullock, eds., *Toward a Theory of the Rent-Seeking Society* (College Station, Tex.: Texas A & M University Press, 1980). A detailed exploration of this theoretical approach and its difficulties in coming to terms with the complexity of public and private institutions is Christopher K. Leman, "The Revolution of the Saints: The Ideology of Privatization and its Consequences for the Public Lands," in *Selling the Federal Forests*, Adrien Gamache, ed. (Seattle, Wash.: College of Forest Resources, University of Washington, 1984).

2. On the value of an approach that builds theory from the ground up, see Herbert Simon, *Models of Bounded Rationality*, Vol. 1, *Behavioral Economics and Business Organization* (Cambridge, Mass.: MIT Press, 1982); and Barney Glaser and Anselm Strauss, *The Discovery of Grounded Theory: Strategies for Qualitative Research* (Chicago: Aldine, 1967).

3. Many of the important books on public agencies that were published prior to the 1960s were about direct federal government. For example: Philip Selznick, *TVA and the Grass Roots: A Study in the Sociology of Formal Organization* (New York: Harper, 1966; originally published in 1949); Charles McKinley, *Uncle Sam in the Pacific Northwest: Federal Management of Natural Resources in the Columbia River Valley* (Berkeley: University of California Press, 1952); Herman M. Somers, *Presidential Agency: The Office of War Mobilization and Reconversion* (Cambridge, Mass.: Harvard University Press, 1951); Edward C. Banfield, *Government Project* (New York: Free Press, 1951); Arthur Maass, *Muddy Waters: The Army Engineers and the Nation's Rivers* (Cambridge, Mass.: Harvard University Press, 1951); Charles M. Hardin, *The Politics of Agriculture: Soil Conservation and the Struggle for Power in Rural America* (Glencoe, Ill.: Free Press, 1952); and Herbert Kaufman, *The Forest Ranger: A Study in Administrative Behavior* (Baltimore, Md.: Johns Hopkins Press for Resources for the Future, 1960). On the importance of studying successes as well as failures, see: Martin A. Levin, "Conditions Contributing to Effective Implementation and Their Limits," in *Research in Public Policy Analysis and Management*, John P. Crecine, ed. (Greenwich, Conn.: JAI Press, 1981).

4. Other agencies funded in part from their receipts include the Federal Aviation Administration, Geological Survey, Bureau of the Census, Government Printing Office, National Technical Information Service, General Services Administration, and the various land and water management agencies.

5. Other federal agencies that receive substantial funding from fellow agencies and nonfederal sources include the Bureau of the Census and the FDA's National Center for Toxicological Research.

6. Interestingly, many employees of the Department of Defense, the Veterans Administration, NASA, and other agencies are not in the federal civil service system.

7. Some offices and supplies used internally can be obtained by indirect government as, for example, if a regulated industry or grantee is required to provide them free to the federal agency.

8. Internal administrative needs can to some extent be supplied indirectly, as in the procurement of outside program evaluations and policy research.

9. These activities include Selective Service registration, assisting the Medicare program, recording vested rights in pension plans, and assisting the Internal Revenue Service in processing reports from employees. See Jack S. Futterman, "The Social Security Administration's Recent Reorganizations and Related Administrative Problems," National Commission on Social Security, *Final Report: Social Security in America's Future*, a report presenting the Commission's recommendations for changes in Social Security programs (March 1981), Appendix E.

10. The Army also managed the National Parks in the early years. The nation's first agricultural statistics were collected by the Library of Congress' Patent Office in 1839.

11. The domestic uniformed services are the Coast Guard, the Commissioned Corps of the Public Health Service, and the Commissioned Corps of the National Oceanic and Atmospheric Administration. The survey of federal laboratories is National Bureau of Standards, U.S. Department of Commerce, *Federal Laboratory Directory 1982* (February 1983), no. NBS-SP–646. The figure cited includes some nonfederal employees, especially in the Department of Energy. Libraries are also ubiquitous, with 700 belonging to a governmentwide network. The collection and analysis of statistics is also conducted throughout the federal government; see *The Federal Statistical System, 1980 to 1985*, a report prepared by Baseline Data Corporation for the Congressional Research Service of the Library of Congress, printed by the U.S. Congress House Committee on Government Operations, 98th Cong., 2d sess. (November 1984). The committee released an update on this study in May 1985.

12. A useful source on 19th century successes in direct government at the local level and the tendency to overlook them is Jon C. Teaford, *The Unheralded Triumph: City Government in America, 1870–1900* (Baltimore, Md.: Johns Hopkins University Press, 1984).

13. Employment figures are available in: U.S. Congress, Senate Committee on Governmental Affairs, *Organization of Federal Executive Departments and Agencies as of January 1, 1984*; and "The 500 Largest U.S. Industrial Corporations," *Fortune* (May 2, 1983).

14. For Weber's view of bureaucracy, see: "Bureaucracy," ch. 8 in *From Max Weber: Essays in Sociology*, H.H . Gerth and C. Wright Mills, eds. (New York: Oxford University Press, 1946). Criticisms of Weber's view are discussed in Peter M. Blau, *On the Nature of Organizations* (New York: Wiley and Sons, 1974), ch. 2 and pp. 35, 126, 246, and 406. Studies that emphasize the internal differentiation of bureaucracy and the external influences on it include Richard Cyert and James March, *A Behavorial Theory of the Firm* (Englewood Cliffs, N.J.: Prentice-Hall, 1963); Marshal W. Meyer, *Change in Public Bureaucracies* (New York: Cambridge University Press, 1979); and Donald P. Warwick, *A Theory of Public Bureaucracy: Politics, Personality, and Organization in the State Department* (Cambridge, Mass.: Harvard University Press, 1975).

15. Although one or another of these features can also be found in various indirect government activities, their combined presence is most evident with direct government.

16. This standard is similar to that applied by Regina Herzlinger and Nancy Kane, *A Managerial Analysis of Federal Income Redistribution Mechanisms: The Government as Factory, Insurance Company, and Bank* (Cambridge, Mass.: Ballinger, 1983).

17. The task of responding to an assassination attempt is much more straightforward and easier to evaluate than the task of identifying potential assailants beforehand, as can be seen by comparing Office of General Counsel, Department of the Treasury, *Management Review on the Performance of U.S. Department of the Treasury in Connection with the March 30, 1981 Assassination Attempt on President Ronald Reagan* (August 1981); with Institute of Medicine, *Research and Training for the Secret Service: Behavioral Science and Mental Health Perspectives* (Washington, D.C.: National Academy Press, 1984). In addition to protecting the president, the Secret Service has been assigned to protect an average of 25 to 30 other persons a day. It also enforces laws relating to the counterfeiting and forgery of federal documents.

18. On the changing philosophies of corrections, see Benjamin Frank, "The American Prison: The End of an Era," *Federal Probation Quarterly* (September 1979). On the changing philosophies of National Forest management, see Samuel T. Dana and Sally

K. Fairfax, *Forest and Range Policy*, 2d ed. (New York: McGraw-Hill, 1980). National security is another government mission whose meaning has shifted over the years and has frequently been a source of disagreement. See Robert E. Osgood, *Ideals and Self-Interest in America's Foreign Relations* (Chicago: University of Chicago Press, 1953).

19. Richard B. Stewart, "The Reformation of American Administrative Law," *Harvard Law Review* 88, no. 8 (June 1975): 1667–1813.

20. For example, strong endorsement of the work of the National Bureau of Standards is provided in annual reviews conducted for the National Research Council by boards whose members are drawn largely from industry. See, for example, Board on Assessment of Programs, National Research Council, *An Evaluative Report on the National Measurement Laboratory* (1984).

21. Courtenay Slater, "Opportunities for Improving Economic Statistics," Paper prepared for the Joint Economic Committee, U.S. Congress (March 1986).

22. David Packard, "The Loss of Government Scientific and Engineering Talent," *Issues in Science and Technology* 2, no. 3 (Spring 1986): 126–31.

23. On Pinchot, see the forthcoming work by Michael G. H. McGeary; on Bennett, see Hardin, *The Politics of Agriculture;* and on Hoover, see Sanford J. Ungar, FBI (Boston: Atlantic Monthly Press–Little Brown, 1976). In some cases, founding leadership can be exerted by a group of like-minded individuals. See Charles McKinley and Robert W. Frase, *Launching Social Security: 1935–1937* (Madison, Wis.: University of Wisconsin Press, 1970).

24. Recent turnover at the top of the Social Security Administration has probably reduced its effectiveness. See Jack S. Futterman, "Unburdening the Administration of the Social Security Program of Short-Term Commissioners," in Yung-Pin Chen and George F. Rohrlich, eds., *Checks and Balances on Social Security* (Lanham, Md: University Press of America, 1986).

25. This argument has been made by Philip Selznick, *Leadership in Administration: A Sociological Interpretation* (New York: Harper, 1957) and Peter Drucker, "The Deadly Sins in Public Administration," *Public Administration Review* 40, no. 2 (March/April 1980): 103–106.

26. John Crewdson, *The Tarnished Door: The New Immigrants and the Transformation of America* (New York: Times Books, 1983), 120.

27. *Report of the Presidential Commission on the Space Shuttle Challenger Accident* (Washington, D.C.) vol. 1, ch. 8 (June 6, 1986).

28. On the Interagency Fire Center, see T.R. Reid, "Wildfire Bureaucracy: Montana Blazes Spark Agency Cooperation," *Washington Post*, September 3, 1984; the Center also draws upon state, local, and other personnel where necessary. On the Federal Laboratory Consortium for Technology Transfer, see, *The FLC 1985; Special Edition* (1985).

29. There are differences. The Forest Service has long tended to contract out more work than has the National Park Service.

30. David Leo Weimer, *The Strategic Petroleum Reserve: Planning, Implementation, and Analysis* (Westport, Conn.: Greenwood Press, 1982). For a thoughtful discussion of differences in procurement of expert help, see Frank Popper, "Why I Don't Do Much Federal Consulting Anymore," *Journal of Management Consulting* 2, no. 3 (Fall, 1985): 4–9.

31. See John T. Dunlop, "The Limits of Legal Compulsion," The Conference Board Record (March 1976); Robert D. Wallick and William B. Montalto, "Symbiosis or Domination: Rights and Remedies under Grant-Type Assistance Programs," *George Wash-*

ington Law Review 46, no. 2 (January 1978): 159–99; Eugene Bardach and Robert Kagan, Going by the Book: The Problem of Regulatory Unreasonableness (Philadelphia: Temple University Press, 1982); Michael Lipsky, *Street-Level Bureaucracy: Dilemmas of the Individual in Public Services* (New York: Russell Sage, 1980); and especially Jerry L. Mashaw, *Bureaucratic Justice: Managing Social Security Disability Claims* (New Haven, Conn.: Yale University Press, 1983). Objections that have been raised as to the applicability of Mashaw's argument to regulatory agencies probably are not relevant insofar as they are applicable to the agencies of direct government. See Lance Liebman and Richard B. Stewart, "Bureaucratic Vision," *Harvard Law Review* 96, no. 8 (1983): 1952–68.

32. Personal communication, January 22, 1985.

33. Environmental Law Institute, *NEPA in Action: Environmental Offices in Nineteen Federal Agencies.* A Report to the Council on Environmental Quality (1981), 10–20; and Serge Taylor, *Making Bureaucracies Think: The Environmental Impact Statement Strategy of Administrative Reform* (Stanford, Calif.: Stanford University Press, 1984).

34. See, Jeffrey L. Pressman and Aaron Wildavsky, *Implementation*, 2d ed. (Berkeley: University of California Press, 1979); and Levin, "Conditions Contributing to Effective Implementation and Their Limits." In other countries, the most successful "megaprojects" have often been those that were managed by a single agency. See Elliot J. Feldman, "Patterns of Failure in Government Megaprojects: Economics, Politics, and Participation in Industrial Democracies," in Samuel P. Huntington and Joseph Nye, eds., *Global Dilemmas* (Washington, D.C. and Cambridge, Mass.: University Press of America and the Harvard University Center for International Affairs, 1984).

Some direct government activities depend on the voluntary cooperation of outsiders, and these activities share many of the problems of indirect government. For example, technical assistance from the Soil Conservation Service has usually been sought by the farmers who already practice conservation, and often refused by the farmers whose practices are most erosive and therefore most in need of correction.

35. For the distinction between control and influence, see Martin Landau and Russell Stout, Jr., "To Manage is Not to Control: On the Folly of Type II Errors," *Public Administration Review* 39, no. 2 (March/April 1979): 148–56.

36. Shawn P. Kelly, *The People's Printer: A Report on the Government Printing Office* (Washington, D.C.: Public Interest Research Group, 1979).

37. For an illustration of the value of decisive action in this task, see Tom Wolf, "How Lake Powell Almost Broke Free of Glen Canyon Dam: The Bureau Showed the Right Stuff," *High Country News*, December 12, 1983.

38. See Steven Lewis Yaffee, *Prohibitive Policy: Implementing the Federal Endangered Species Act* (Cambridge, Mass.: MIT Press, 1982).

39. See Dick Randall, "Survival Crisis at Meeteetse," *Defenders* 61, no. 1 (January/February 1986): 4–10, on interagency squabbles over how to protect the endangered black-footed ferret on private land.

40. This degree of cooperation is dependent on an agency's leadership. The Army Corps of Engineers has been somewhat less cooperative regarding endangered species questions.

41. Poor management is sometimes covered up within an agency. Often it has fallen to law enforcement authorities or journalists to expose serious corruption such as that found in the Immigration and Naturalization Service (Crewsdon, *The Tarnished Door*, ch. 6).

42. A consultant report commissioned by the National Park Service at the insistence of the Office of Management and Budget criticized the agency for not articulating clear

direction to its personnel or monitoring their performance. (Coopers and Lybrand, *Management Improvement Project*, report to the National Park Service, two vols., 1977–78).

43. General Accounting Office, *Tax Administration: Information on IRS' Philadelphia Service Center*, GGD–86–25FS (November 1985); Kathy Sawyer, "The Breakdown of America's Tax Factories," *Washington Post*, October 22, 1985. Not to be forgotten about the Challenger disaster is that to some extent it was a failure of indirect government, in that Morton Thiokol, NASA's contractor, ignored the advice of its own engineers in approving the fateful launch. See *Report of the Presidential Commission*, chs. 5 and 6.

44. John D. Young, "Reflections on the Root Causes of Fraud, Abuse and Waste in Federal Social Programs," *Public Administration Review* 43, no. 4 (July/August 1983), 365.

45. See Eugene Bardach, *The Implementation Game* (Cambridge, Mass.: MIT Press, 1977).

46. Internalizing transactions can also contribute to success in commercial activity. See Oliver E. Williamson, *Markets and Hierarchies: Analysis and Antitrust Implications, A Study in the Economics of Internal Organization* (New York: Free Press, 1975).

47. For unsparing accounts of abuses by members of the FBI and other federal agencies, see David Wise, *The American Police State: The Government Against the People* (New York: Random House, 1976); and Frank M. Sorrentino, *Ideological Warfare: The FBI's Path Toward Power* (Port Washington, N.Y.: Associated Faculty Press, 1985). When FBI Director Patrick Gray participated in the Watergate coverup he concealed his role from all subordinates, who continued to pursue the case. However, many FBI personnel were themselves involved in spying on Martin Luther King, Jr. through wiretaps that had the written approval of Attorney General Robert F. Kennedy. See Ungar, *FBI*. On new constraints aimed at preventing FBI abuses, see John T. Elliff, *The Reform of FBI Intelligence Operations* (Princeton, N.J.: Princeton University Press, 1979). Interestingly, the Watergate break-in could be regarded as an instance of indirect government: the burglars were contractors, not direct government employees.

48. For some alarming evidence of unchecked abuse in private debt collection, see Federal Trade Commission, "Seventh Annual Report to Congress Pursuant to Section 815 of the Fair Debt Collection Practices Act," March 27, 1985.

49. It must be conceded that segregation was also practiced for many years in the Army itself, and in Washington, D.C., the national capital. However, federal institutions were among the first to be desegregated in the 1940s and 1950s.

50. Christopher K. Leman and Robert H. Nelson, "The Rise of Managerial Federalism: An Assessment of Benefits and Costs," *Environmental Law* 12, no. 4 (Summer 1982), 988.

51. Ungar, *FBI*, 406. Again, the INS is a glaring exception, with a long history of abuses (Crewdson, *The Tarnished Door*, ch. 7).

52. The current director of the Bureau of Prisons joined the agency partly on the advice of a prisoner he had met in a state penitentiary (Pete Earley, "Chief of Prisons Bureau, a Former Guard, Stresses Training," *Washington Post*, March 15, 1984). Unfortunately, no survey data exist that would establish how widely this view is shared by today's prisoners. In the past decade federal courts have taken over the administration of prison systems of nine states, only one of which (Oklahoma) has since been returned entirely to state hands; no federal facility has been subject to such severe judicial intervention. Of course, some states have modern, closely managed systems that compare well with the federal system, and some federal prisons—especially the

maximum security facility at Marion, Illinois—have been criticized for their management. On the latter, see *The United States Penitentiary, Marion, Illinois,* Consultants'
Report submitted to U.S. Congress, House Committee on the Judiciary, 98th Cong., 2d
sess. (December 1984).

53. The distinction between cost-effectiveness and economic efficiency is widely accepted by economists. For a discussion, see Edward M. Gramlich, *Benefit-Cost Analysis of Government Programs* (Englewood Cliffs, N.J.: Prentice- Hall, Inc., 1981).

54. Thomas K. McCraw, "The Public and Private Spheres in Historical Perspective,"
in Harvey Brooks, Lance Liebman, and Corrine S. Schelling, eds., *Public-Private Partnership: New Opportunities for Meeting Social Needs* (Cambridge, Mass.: Ballinger,
1984), 32, noting that the United States is the only major country with an all-private
telecommunications network, and one of the few with no public enterprises in oil,
gas, or steel.

55. R. Joseph, M. Monsen and Kenneth D. Walters, "State-Owned Firms: A Review of
the Data and Issues," in Lee E. Preston, ed., *Research in Corporate Social Performance
and Policy* (Greenwich, Conn.: JAI Press, 1980).

56. Mathematica Policy Research, Inc., *Evaluation of the Economic Impact of the Job
Corps Program: Analysis of Program Operating Costs,* Technical Report J, prepared by
the Department of Labor, April 1980.

57. See Leman, "The Revolution of the Saints."

58. Arthur M. Okun, *Equality and Efficiency: The Big Tradeoff* (Washington, D.C.:
Brookings Institution, 1975), 62.

59. The monopoly long enjoyed by the U.S. Postal Service—technically not in most
respects an agency of direct government—undoubtedly encouraged inefficiency, but
the rise of competing services for packages, quick delivery, and electronic mail has
forced some improvements. See John T. Tierney, *Postal Reorganization: Managing the
Public's Business* (Boston: Auburn House, 1981); and Nicole Woolsey Biggart "The
Post Office as a Business: Ten Years of Postal Reorganization," *Policy Studies Journal*
11, no. 3 (March 1983): 483–91.

60. Keith B. Richburg, "Timely Bill Payments Turn a Profit for Federal Cash Management Agency," *Washington Post,* March 1, 1985.

61. Although it rarely is, indirect government can be geographically targeted, as with
grant programs like the Great Plains Conservation Program and those administered by
the Appalachian Regional Commission; loan guarantees in disaster areas; and regulatory programs like the Voting Rights Act.

62. Adding to the local impact of direct government agencies is that much of their
employment and many of their facilities are located outside Washington, D.C., and
constitute an important economic sector in themselves. Probably no government activity has shaped the country's economic development as much as has the pattern of
military bases.

63. See Christopher K. Leman, "Political Dilemmas in Evaluating and Budgeting Soil
Conservation Programs: the RCA Process," in *Soil Conservation Policy, Institutions,
and Incentives,* Harold Halcrow, Melvin Cotner, and Earl Heady, eds. (Ankeny, Iowa:
Soil Conservation Society of America, 1982).

64. Linda Cohen and Roger Noll, "The Political Economy of Government Programs to
Promote New Technology," Social Science Working Papers, California Institute of
Technology (1983), 35 and 37.

65. Classic criticisms of the economics of water projects are Gilbert White, "The Limit
of Economic Justification for Flood Protection," *The Journal of Land and Public Util-*

ity Economics (May 1936): 133–49; and John V. Krutilla and Otto Eckstein, *Multiple Purpose River Development: Studies in Applied Economic Analysis* (Baltimore, Md: Resources for the Future and Johns Hopkins University Press, 1958).

66. For a good overview, see John R. Kimberly, "Managerial Innovation," ch. 4 in *Handbook of Organizational Design*, Vol. 1, *Adapting Organizations to Their Environments*, Paul C. Nystrom and William Starbuck, eds. (New York: Oxford University Press, 1981): 84–104.

67. On the earlier history, see Alan Hogenauer, "Gone, But Not Forgotten: American's Delisted National Park Service Sites," paper presented to the annual meeting of the Travel and Tourism Research Association, Banff, Alberta, June 1983.

68. Samuel P. Hays, "Three Decades of Environmental Politics: The Historical Context," in Michael Lacey, ed., *The Evolution of American Environmental Politics* (forthcoming), 8.

69. Charles McKinley, *The Management of Land and Related Water Resources in Oregon: A Case Study in Administrative Federalism* (Washington, D.C.: Resources for the Future, 1965), 539.

70. On early advances in computers by the Social Security Administration, see Michael A. Cronin, "Fifty Years in the Social Security Administration," *Social Security Bulletin* 48.6 (June 1985): 22–24.

71. Ungar, *FBI*, 406.

72. The engineering errors that caused the disastrous failure of Teton Dam resulted in part from congressional pressure on the Bureau of Reclamation to build quickly on a geologically difficult site. Independent Panel to Review Cause of Teton Dam Failure, "Summary and Conclusion from Report to U.S. Department of the Interior and State of Idaho on Failure of Teton Dam," (Idaho Falls, Idaho, December 1976). Without excusing the error, an engineer in the Bureau states that congressional pressure to "move things out" eliminated the "sit-back-and-look time" that a project of this complexity deserves. Personal commincation, November 29, 1984.

73. Jeffrey L. Pressman, *Federal Programs and City Politics: The Dynamics of the Aid Process in Oakland* (Berkeley: University of California Press, 1975), 115.

74. For an argument on behalf of political feasibility as a criterion in policy choice, see Peter J. May, "Politics and Policy Analysis," *Political Science Quarterly* 101, no. 1 (Spring 1986): 109–25.

75. Public attitudes are explored in Seymour Martin Lipset and William Schneider, *The Confidence Gap: Business, Labor, and Government in the Public Mind* (New York: Free Press, 1983).

76. Curiously, there have not been similar objections to a national prison system.

77. See Christopher K. Leman, *The Collapse of Welfare Reform: Political Institutions, Policy, and the Poor in Canada and the United States* (Cambridge, Mass.: MIT Press, 1980).

78. For example, only one of the Smithsonian Institution's museums (the Cooper-Hewitt, in New York City) is located outside Washington, D.C. largely because of long-standing opposition from museum managements elsewhere who prefer federal aid to federal competition.

79. L.L. Wade, "Public Administration, Public Choice and the Pathos of Reform," *Review of Politics* 41 (1979): 357–9.

80. See Hardin, *The Politics of Agriculture*.

81. See Sally K. Fairfax, "Coming of Age in the Bureau of Land Management: Range Management in Search of a Gospel," in National Research Council/National Academy of Sciences, *Developing Strategies for Rangeland Management* (Boulder, Colo.: Westview, 1984).

82. Harry F. Rosenthal, "U.S. Devotes Millions to PR, Experts," *Washington Post*, May 30, 1983. Of course, recipients of government largesse, such as defense contractors, employ a large number of public relations personnel.

83. Examples have included "The Untouchables" about the Bureau of Alcohol, Tobacco, and Firearms; "Lassie" in which the dog's owner in one version was a Forest Service district ranger; "The FBI" about the FBI; and the various programs about the military services. Further reflecting the public's fascination with the direct provision of services, many television series do feature local police forces, hospitals, or schools. Although many of these institutions are on the receiving end of federal indirect government, the television series rarely acknowledge the federal role.

84. Martha Derthick, *Policymaking for Social Security* (Washington, D.C.: Brookings Institution, 1979).

85. Christopher K. Leman, "Planning Against Analysis: Forest Service Implementation of the Resources Planning Act of 1974," in *Redirecting the RPA: Proceedings of the 1987 Airlie House Conference on the Resources Planning Act*, Clark S. Binkley, Garry D. Brewer, and V. Alarik Sample, eds., Bulletin no. 95 (New Haven, Conn.: Yale University School of Forestry and Environmental Studies, 1988).

86. An interpretation of the events recounted in Robert H. Nelson, The Making of Federal Coal Policy (Durham, N.C.: Duke University Press, 1983); and Robert H. Nelson, "The Federal Coal Leasing Commission: The Story of a Minor Success," paper presented to the Association for Public Policy Analysis and Management, New Orleans, October 1984.

87. The defense and foreign policy sectors also have numerous overlaps.

88. Louis K. Bragaw, *Managing a Federal Agency: The Hidden Stimulus* (Baltimore, Md.: Johns Hopkins University Press, 1980).

89. For example, in 1977 the Forest Service initiated a "HOST" program that was patterned after those used to train commercial telephone operators, and subsequently it sponsored outside evaluations of employees' treatment of the general public.

90. For example, "horror stories" are sometimes told not only about the U.S. Postal Service, but about private carriers like United Parcel Service and Federal Express.

91. Authors who have made this point include Selznick, *TVA and the Grass Roots*; Warwick, *A Theory of Public Bureaucracy*; James Q. Wilson, *The Investigators: Managing FBI and Narcotics Agents* (New York: Basic Books, 1978); Bragaw, *Managing a Federal Agency*; Herbert Kaufman, *The Administrative Behavior of Federal Bureau Chiefs* (Washington, D.C.: Brookings Institution, 1981); and Hal G. Rainey and H. Brinton Milward, "Public Organizations: Policy Networks and Environments," in Richard H. Hall, ed., *Organizational Theory and Public Policy* (Beverly Hills, Calif.: Sage, 1982).

92. Interview with Robin Atkiss, chair of the Federal Publisher's Committee and of the GPO Advisory Board of Federal Publishers, January 9, 1986.

93. See Banfield, *Government Project*; and Lester M. Salamon, "Follow-ups, Letdowns, and Sleepers: The Time Dimension in Policy Evaluation," in Charles O. Jones and Robert D. Thomas, eds., *Public Policy Making in a Federal System* (Beverly Hills, Calif.: Sage, 1976).

94. Luther Carter, *Nuclear Imperatives and Public Trust: Dealing with Radioactive Waste* (Washington, D.C.: Resources for the Future, 1987). Many were alienated even in New Mexico, where the Department of Energy is by far the largest employer.

95. Leman and Nelson, "The Rise of Managerial Federalism," 1017.

96. One study found that in the Army Corps of Engineers some districts were considerably more responsive than others. Daniel K. Mazmanian and Jeanne M. Nienaber, *Can Organizations Change: Environmental Protection, Citizen Participation and the Corps of Engineers* (Washington, D.C.: Brookings Institution, 1979).

97. John Child and Alfred Keiser, "Development of Organizations over Time," ch. 2, in Nystrom and Starbuck, eds., *Handbook of Organizational Design*, Vol. 1.

98. James T. Bonnen, "Historical Sources of U.S. Agricultural Productivity: Implications for R and D Policy and Social Science Research," *American Journal of Agricultural Economics* 65,5 (December 1983): 958–66.

99. Congressional Budget Office, *The Federal Buildings Program: Authorization and Budgetary Alternatives* (June 1983). Among the most expensive and architecturally undistinguished federal offices are in fact the Rayburn and Hart congressional office buildings, which were designed and managed by the Architect of the Capitol under direct committee guidance. See U.S. Congress, Senate, *Rayburn House Office Building*, letter from the Comptroller-General of the United States, Doc. no. 20, 90th Cong., 1st Sess. (April 10, 1967). Even Congress has had its successes in construction, as in the restoration of the West Front of the Capitol, a project that seemingly cost less and was finished sooner than projected. See Francis X. Clines, "All Unquiet on the West Front," *New York Times*, December 8, 1985.

100. See Theodore J. Lowi, *The End of Liberalism: The Second Republic of the United States*, 2d. ed. (New York: Norton, 1979).

101. Leman, "Political Dilemmas in Evaluating and Budgeting Soil Conservation Programs."

102. Fairfax, "Coming of Age in the Bureau of Land Management."

103. Congress prohibits the Forest Service from even studying the possibility of moving or consolidating any of its nine regional offices. However, through careful political groundwork, the Forest Service over the years has been able to consolidate hundreds of lower-level offices.

104. On this contradiction, see Herbert Kaufman, "Fear of Bureaucracy: A Raging Pandemic," *Public Administration Review* (January/February 1981).

105. David G. Mathiasen, "Rethinking Public Management," *The Bureaucrat* 13,2 (Summer 1984): 9–13. Mathiasen cites a typical instance in which a tardy airline wrongly blamed the Customs Service for the delays.

FEDERAL DOMESTIC DIRECT GOVERNMENT ACTIVITIES BY FUNCTION[1]

Facilitating Commerce

Currency is manufactured by the Bureau of the Mint and the Bureau of Engraving and Printing (BEP); the latter also manufactures postage stamps.

Water and air traffic are directed, respectively, by the Coast Guard (CG), and Federal Aviation Administration (FAA).

Maps are made by the Coast and Geodetic Survey (part of NOAA, the National Oceanic and Atmospheric Administration) and the Geological Survey (GS).

Standardization of weights and measures, and the broadcast of official time, are by the National Bureau of Standards (NBS).

Property insurance in high-crime areas is provided by the Federal Emergency Management Agency (FEMA).

Labor disputes are negotiated with assistance from the Federal Mediation and Conciliation Service and the National Labor Relations Board.

Managing Public Lands

Agencies with 50 million or more acres include the Bureau of Land Management (BLM), Forest Service (FS), National Park Service (NPS), Fish and Wildlife Service (FWS), Bureau of Indian Affairs (BIA), and Minerals Management Service.[2]

Agencies with less than 50 million acres include the Army Corps of Engineers (ACE),[3] Bureau of Reclamation (BR), Tennessee Valley Authority (TVA), and many others.

Constructing Public Works and Managing Real Property

Outer space projects are operated by the National Aeronautics and Space Administration (NASA) and National Environmental Satellite, Data, and Information Service.

Storage of nuclear waste is the responsibility of the Office of Civilian Radioactive Waste Management.

Water projects are designed and/or operated by ACE, BR, and the Soil Conservation Service (SCS).[4]

Electric power is distributed by the Bonneville Power Administration (BPA), Western Area Power Administration, Southwest Power Administration, Southeast Power Administration, Alaska Power Administration, and TVA.

Other operations include fish hatcheries, cemeteries, monuments, historic sites, parkways, archives, museums, performing arts centers, and a botanical garden, an arboretum, and a zoo.

Research, Testing and Statistics

Research and testing is the dominant function of the Agricultural Research Service, Economic Research Service, National Institutes of Health (NIH, part of PHS, the Public Health Service), Bureau of Mines, and Smithsonian Institution. Other agencies involved include the Federal Bureau of Investigation (FBI), Bureau of Alcohol, Tobacco, and Firearms (BATF), Patent and Trademark Office, Environmental Protection Agency, National Transportation Safety Board, NBS, NASA, GS, NOAA, FS, FWS, BR, and ACE.

Collecting and analyzing statistics is the dominant function of the Bureau of the Census, Bureau of Economic Analysis, Bureau of Labor Statistics, and units in the departments of Health and Human Services, Education, Justice, Agriculture, and Energy. Other agencies involved include the Internal Revenue Service (IRS), and FS.

Technical Assistance and Libraries

Technical assistance is the dominant function of the National Weather Service (part of NOAA) and SCS. The National Highway Traffic Safety Administration, PHS, FBI, and IRS, among other agencies, also offer technical assistance.

Libraries include the Library of Congress, National Agricultural Library, National Library of Medicine, and hundreds of others.

Law and Justice

Law enforcement is the dominant function of the Drug Enforcement Administration, Secret Service, U.S. Marshals Service, BATF, and FBI. Other agencies involved include the Immigration and Naturalization Service (INS), Customs Service (CS), CG, ACE, BLM, NPS, FWS, and FS.

Corrections facilities are operated by the Bureau of Prisons (BP) and INS.

Health Care, Social Services, and Direct Cash Benefits

Health care is provided by the Indian Health Service, National Health Service Corps, Veterans Administration (VA), BP, and NIH, among other agencies.

Social services are provided by the Job Corps,[5] ACTION, BIA, and VA, among other agencies.

Direct cash benefits are paid to individuals by the Social Security Administration (SSA), VA, BIA, Justice Department (via the Public Safety Officer's Benefits Program), and other agencies.

Education and Training

Provided to nonfederal employees by the Merchant Marine Academy, Graduate School of the Department of Agriculture, National Institute of Corrections, Federal Law Enforcement Training Center, and by units of FBI, BP, IRS, BIA, PHS, FEMA, and FAA.

Marketing

Merchandising includes sales of publications by the Government Printing Office (GPO) and National Technical Information Service (NTIS), standard weights and measures by NBS, and federally owned natural resources such as outdoor recreation, timber, minerals, water and electricity, by such agencies as FS, BLM, ACE, TVA, BPA, and BR.

Persuasion includes efforts to encourage foreign tourism to the United States (U.S. Travel and Tourism Administration) and to discourage forest fires (FS) and tax fraud (IRS).

Supporting Internal Overhead Needs[6]

Financial services are provided by the Financial Management Service, Bureau of Public Debt, IRS, BATF, and CS.

Auditing of many domestic agencies is done by the Defense Contract Audit Agency, as well as by agencies themselves; this is in addition to auditing conducted by the General Accounting Office.

Debts are collected by IRS on behalf of VA, the Small Business Administration, and the Departments of Agriculture, Education, and Housing and Urban Development.

Personnel and labor relations matters are handled by the agencies themselves and by the Office of Personnel Management, Merit Systems Protection Board, and Federal Labor Relations Authority.

Legal advice is provided by lawyers in the Justice Department and in the agencies themselves.

Policy analysis is provided by staffs located throughout the executive branch and Congress.

Publishing (the preparation of a manuscript for printing) is done by hundreds of agencies. Printing is done by the GPO and by several agency printshops.[7]

Realty and purchasing are handled by the General Services Administration or by the agencies themselves.

Research, testing, statistics, technical assistance, and libraries that are provided by some agencies are used widely by other agencies.

Notes

1. This listing covers leading instances, and cannot be definitive. It is based on a more detailed list that is available from the author.

2. The Minerals Management Service is in charge of 3.9 billion offshore acres known as the Exclusive Economic Zone.

3. Only the civil functions of the Army Corps of Engineers are covered here. In addition, the Corps has various military functions.

4. SCS designs but does not operate water projects.

5. Some Job Corps centers are operated by the Forest Service and the National Park Service; the operation of others is contracted out.

6. The military services have large health delivery, research, fire fighting, law and justice, education, chaplaincy, transportation, manufacturing, and other systems.

7. Much of the printing by GPO is contracted out. However, most presidential, congressional, and judicial documents are printed in-house.

Chapter Four

GRANTS AS A TOOL OF PUBLIC POLICY

Donald Haider

WHAT IS A GRANT?

Federal grants are the oldest, most widely used, and probably the best-understood tool that the federal government has available to carry out public policy. Grants are the oldest government tool to the extent that land grants to the states contained in the Northwest Ordinance of 1787 predate the Constitution. The Morrill Act of 1862 shaped the modern grant economy through the conditional provision of federal land to the states to promote land grant colleges.[1]

Grants are the most widely used tool as measured by the number of authorizations and individual programs, functional scope, or federal agency participation. Grants have also been closely scrutinized as reflected in the number of grant participants or legislative committees and commissions that oversee the grant system. As a result, we know a great deal about this tool. Indeed, more has been written about federal grants than about any other form of government assistance. No form of federal assistance is as pervasive if one considers that most all governmental units are grant recipients as are many special districts and nonprofit organizations.[2] Nor has any form of governmental assistance grown so quickly— $5 billion to $112 billion between 1957 and 1987. No form of federal assistance affects as many federal departments and agencies or their state and local counterparts, as many committees and subcommittees of Congress, or as many separate interest groups and organized participants. Finally, no form of assistance generates so much conflict; one governmental branch or another regularly attempts to overhaul, reform, consolidate, simplify, or streamline grants.

Uses of Grants

At base, federal grants-in-aid are payments—in cash or in kind—mostly to lower units of government, but often to nonprofit or quasi-governmental organizations, to support congressionally determined public purposes. At an earlier point in our history, courts limited the areas where grants could function in order to prevent encroachment by the federal government into fields some thought should be reserved to the states. But these limits have since been significantly relaxed, allowing grants to be used for any purpose that served a legitimate national interest or public purpose.[3] Typically, this means an activity warranted by the presence of a problem of national scope, or significantly large regional impact, that requires for its solution some measure of national involvement: stimulation, coordination, minimum standards, experimentation, and shared involvement. Depending on the activity being supported, subnational governments, private institutions, nonprofit organizations, or private citizens can and are involved as grant agents or beneficiaries.

The compelling national interest to be served by grants can take several forms: (1) guaranteeing minimum service levels (vocational education); (2) providing income maintenance (Aid to Families with Dependent Children [AFDC] or Medicaid); (3) easing economic hardship (refugee assistance or school aid); (4) coordinating related activities (block grants); (5) stimulating economic growth (rural development); (6) promoting equal opportunity (education grants, Title I); (7) equalizing resources (hospital construction); (8) contributing to economic stabilization (job creation); (9) fostering planning (health planning); (10) promoting an activity that was nonexistent or minimal before (mental health services); (11) stimulating spending by the recipient government (matching funds above existing funding efforts); and (12) developing demonstration, research, or innovation projects (project grants).

Whether grant programs serve national interests by using state and local governments as instruments of federal policy or are designed to enable states and localities to achieve their own objectives has never been resolved in theory or in practice. Davis and Sundquist, for example, maintain that before the Great Society era of the mid–1960s, national goals in grant programs were rarely stated and, in most cases, federal assistance was aimed specifically at helping states and localities to achieve their objectives. The reverse, the authors argue, has been the case since then due to the growing amount of aid, the award of which can be used as a carrot and the threatened withdrawal of which can be used as a stick.[4]

The relative influence of parties in this partnership is secondary to the partnership's essential characteristics: a voluntary or non-mandatory relationship that is conditional in nature, in which flexibility and some degree of discretion are left to the grant recipient regarding how activities are to be carried out or the precise nature of what is produced.

Types of Grants

Broadly speaking, three different types of grants-in-aid can be distinguished: categorical grants, project grants, and block grants or general revenue sharing.

Categorical grants, the oldest form of federal financing, are used for specific, narrowly defined categories of activities and can be distributed either by legislative formula (formula grants) or by competition under agency guidelines (project grants).[5] Categorical grants typically serve some identifiable national interest and produce broadly disseminated benefits. Because some proportion of benefits accrue locally, many formula-type categoricals require matching of funds by state or local governments or both to link giver and receiver into a partnership. Such matching requirements provide a key incentive to promote participation, cooperation, and mutual stakes in a program's success on the part of recipients. To acquire federal funding, state and local officials have to buy into a program either through actual outlays of funds or through in-kind services. Matching requirements have declined as concern about the federal impact on local priorities has grown. Nonfederal matching amounted to 62 percent of all categorical grants in 1975, for example, but had decreased to about 54 percent by 1981.

The largest share of federal categorical grants is allocated through noncompetitive, open-ended matching grants that require the federal government to pay a fixed percentage of total program costs. The largest of these programs, Medicaid and AFDC, account for nearly 40 percent of all grant monies. These programs also involve grants to individuals (including in-kind transfers to beneficiaries through states) as opposed to grants to support the activities of state and local governments. Such grants to individuals have grown substantially as a share of all grants. Approximately 37 percent of all federal grant monies constituted payments to individuals in 1970, for example, a proportion that had increased to nearly 50 percent by 1987.[6]

Thus, as measured by the sheer number of grants or dollar amount, categorical grants have several distinguishing characteristics: they entail broad-based participation, exhibit narrowness of purpose, are nonmandatory, include matching requirements, and involve allocation or income transfers to individuals whose eligibility is often jointly determined by the federal and state governments, with the state acting in a fiduciary capacity.

The 200 or more *project grants* are in contrast to formula-based grants because beneficiaries compete for funds. Competition for these grants may be based on such criteria as need, competence, probability of success, previous experience, and geographic dispersion. Project grants also may carry matching requirements, in-kind contributions, and maintenance of effort or spending stimulation conditions, much like formula grants. They differ from formula grants not only because they lack well-defined measures of need, capacity, or beneficiaries, but also in the timing, duration, and administrative discretion of their allocation. Project grants also include purposes different from categorical grants to the extent that their aim is to promote innovation, demonstration, experimentation, research, technical assistance, and the like.

Block grants and *general revenue sharing* may be viewed as broader variations of categorical grants with distinctive characteristics of their own. They, too, are characterized by an outlay of government funds for national purposes, are nonmandatory, and require no matching funds; but they leave much broader discretion regarding purpose and use to the recipients, which are either states or local governments.

A Flexible Interpretation

These essential characteristics, depicted in table 4.1, provide a working definition of grants. Technically oriented officials may feel more comfortable with the Office of Management and Budget's (OMB) formal definition of grants as "budget authority and outlays by the federal government in support of state or local programs or government operations, or provisions of services to the public including direct cash grants and payments in-kind."[7] However, such a formal definition minimizes the voluntary and flexible nature of grants, their diversity and conditional nature, and the discretion left to the grant recipient to determine how activities will be carried out or how results will be achieved.

Table 4.1 SELECTED CHARACTERISTICS OF MAJOR TYPES OF FEDERAL GRANTS

Type of grant	Recipient discretion	Program scope	Funding criteria
Categorical Project	Very low	Narrow program	Federal administrative review
Formula	Low	Narrow program	Legislative formula
Block	Medium	Broad functional area	Legislative formula
General revenue sharing	High	Broad government operations	Legislative formula

Source: George E. Hale and Marian Palley, *The Politics of Federal Grants* (Washington, D.C.: Congressional Quarterly Press, 1987), 12.

Comparison to Other Tools

These distinguishing characteristics of grants are unsatisfactory to some, like members of Congress, who seek a single, clear, and consistent definition of grants. In the Federal Grant and Cooperative Agreement Act of 1977 (Public Law 94–224), Congress stated that uncertainty surrounding the definition of a grant "causes operational inconsistencies, confusion, inefficiency, and waste" for givers and recipients alike. To remedy this, Congress called for greater efforts to distinguish among such public policy tools as grants, contracts, and cooperative agreements.

An effort by OMB to achieve such clarification made little headway, however, suggesting the difficulty of making sharp distinctions among these instruments.[8] This is not to say that no differentiation is possible between grants-in-aid and other policy instruments, however. For example, on the one hand, grants are clearly different from loans and loan guarantees because they involve a direct outlay of federal funds that are not to be repaid (except where disallowance occurs). On the other hand, some grant programs permit the grant recipient to use the funds in a lending capacity. Grants are not encumbered by federal tax laws, although their agents or recipients may well be. They are not direct payments to individuals as in the case of income transfers to individuals for retirement, disability, or unemployment, but many grants deal with retired, disabled, or unemployed persons. Grants also may transfer income in conjunction with state–local participation as in AFDC, or transfer income indirectly through in-kind services such as Medicaid. Grants may contain so many encumbering regulations that rules, conditions, and requirements become as important as the grant itself; grants and regulations are separable from each other, however, in form and in substance. Grants also are an alternative to the federal government's direct provision of a service because they employ numerous public, nonprofit, and private intermediaries that carry out federally supported activities.

At least in theory, the distinctions between grants, on the one hand, and contracts, cooperative agreements, or procurements on the other,[9] depend largely on the type of relationships promoted between federal agencies and the recipient or contractor. If the work or tasks being performed require a particularly close relationship between the federal agency and the recipient and include close monitoring, supervision, and technical assistance, then a nongrant tool, such as a contract or cooperative agreement, is traditionally employed. Grants are appropriate when significant delegation or devolution of federal authority is deemed desirable. When a federal agency seeks to obtain a good or service, undertake a joint venture for a project, or become a participant in an activity, procurement contracts or cooperative agreements are the alternative tools.[10]

Grants differ further from other public policy tools to the extent that they are largely intergovernmental, involve the actual transfer of funds, are separately appropriated, tend to be allocated on a formula basis, and impose certain conditions that the grant recipient must fulfill. The recipient, in turn, is given considerable discretion in using the appropriated funds and in determining the most appropriate way relevant activities are to be implemented.

WHY GRANTS ARE CHOSEN

Broadly speaking, three sets of theories explain the heavy reliance on grants as an instrument of policy in the United States.

Political Theories

The first such set of theories is essentially political in character and emphasizes the representational and other advantages of America's federal system of government.[11] From a representational perspective, the argument is that the national government is more representative of, accessible and responsive to, various factions, interests, and minorities than many individual states and localities. Because the aggregate is seen as being greater than its discrete parts, the federal government's broader responsibility and representational basis become an underlying rationale for the use of grants. The preferred position argument follows from the national government's resource base and its ability to deal with particular problems that the states, individually or collectively, are unable to handle due to structural, legal, resource, or political constraints.[12] From a nationalization perspective, grants are seen as a highly adaptive tool, accommodating fundamental societal changes—rural to urban, manufacturing to services, younger to older. Grants function as a response to evolving problems and needs that are seen to be largely national in scope.[13]

Administrative Theories

A second set of explanations attributes the use of grants to certain administrative advantages. In the first place, the grant tool provided a vehicle to upgrade the budgeting, personnel, auditing, and related management systems of states at a time when these systems were regarded as generally weak. Stipulations that states comply with federally determined civil service, organizational, planning, auditing, and related requirements as a condition for receipt of grant funds made the grant an instrument to achieve not only programmatic but also administrative goals.[14]

Besides improving recipient effectiveness, grants were considered more efficient compared to program management from Washington, D.C. That is, grants avoid the excessive bureaucracy and inflexibility that are often associated with direct national provision of domestic services.[15] Administrative effectiveness and efficiency were also thought to be furthered through a noncentralized pooling of resources—a "collaborative" or "cooperative partnership" subject to national standards, but flexible enough to meet particular state and local needs.

Economic Theories

The third and most compelling argument for grants stems from fiscal considerations in the federal system. Federal aid supports activities that otherwise would be supported (in varying degrees, if at all) by more regressive and less elastic state–local revenue sources. At least this was the case prior to the mid-1960s when less than half the states had broad-based individual income taxes. Relying upon growing federal income tax revenues, national policymakers make use of an expanding resource base to leverage state and local resources on joint activities, and to enlist state and local policymakers and administrators in domestic program aims.[16]

Federal grants hold the prospect of redistributing federal revenues from wealthier jurisdictions or people to jurisdictions with lower fiscal capacities and to poorer people (redistribution and targeting to need), as well as stimulating states and localities to provide additional sources where a special national interest prevails. Grants also can correct problems resulting from spillovers and externalities like pollution, the effects of which go beyond a single jurisdiction. Equalization (redistribution of funds by need, by fiscal capacity, or by both) is linked to efficiency—namely, that the federal government as tax collector and resource distributor is more effective than 75,000 or so governmental units with multiple revenue sources.[17] Finally, fiscal federalism, with Washington as the dominant partner, is seen by some as a means to overcome what the late Governor Nelson A. Rockefeller called the problem mismatch: "The feds have the revenues; states and localities have the problems."[18]

HISTORICAL EVOLUTION OF GRANTS

While the basic arguments for the use of grants have remained fairly durable, the basic structure of the grant system has gone through a number of important phases. Not surprisingly, these phases are closely related to major developments in the political history of the nation.

The Pre-New Deal Era

In the pre-New Deal period, federal aid moved from land grants to monetary grants that enabled the states to meet limited objectives governed by minimal required standards. The Federal Aid Road Act of 1916, for example, provided federal aid to the states for road construction; this assistance was based on a formula and a dollar-for-dollar matching requirement. States had to establish a highway department and, in order to help the farmers "out of the mud," had to use federal funds to build roads serving communities of less than 2,500 people. One year later the federal government initiated vocational education under the Smith–Hughes Act by entering into a cooperative arrangement with state education officials. Thus the early history of federal grants may be viewed as a period during which grants were narrowly focused, categorical, specific, aimed at state government, and propelled by dominant rural interests in the Congress.[19]

Before 1932, federal grants amounted to $200 million annually, with highways accounting for nearly 70 percent of the total assistance. During the Great Depression years federal grants grew to nearly $1 billion annually, mostly for temporary, emergency-type programs that eventually were terminated in the 1940s.

The New Deal Era

President Roosevelt's New Deal of the 1930s ushered in a new era in federal grants. The principal vehicle for this was the Social Security Act of 1935, which became the basis for the nation's complex social welfare system. In addition to two national insurance components—social security and unemployment—the act authorized several categorical public assistance programs. These were Aid to Families with Dependent Children, Aid to the Blind, and Old Age Assistance—all of which were open-ended federal matching grants to the states. Under this arrangement public assistance remained largely a state function with Washington providing a helping hand.[20]

Also during this New Deal period the federal government formally bypassed state governments for the first time by dealing directly with cities and localities. The Housing Act of 1937, for example, established a federal, state, and local partnership in the public housing field.

From the early 1940s until the advent of the Great Society era in 1964, federal aid grew gradually from $1 billion annually to $2 billion in 1950, and then leaped to $7 billion in 1960. In the aggregate, federal aid as a percentage of total state–local revenues increased by less than 5 percent from 1954 to 1964. Nearly 80 percent of the grant funds to states could be accounted for in terms of public assistance and federal highway programs. Similarly, federal grant assistance to local governments was concentrated in four areas: housing, slum clearance, airport development, and modest educational assistance.[21]

The Great Society Era

The pre–1964 period was a relatively simple era of intergovernmental relationships as measured by programs, money-moving activity, scope of federal influence, and use of the grant tool in public policy. These relationships were well understood, involved relatively small-scale ventures, and were largely state-oriented and cooperative insofar as no governmental partner dominated the relation.

President Johnson's Great Society programs of 1964–66 altered this situation fundamentally and brought into public policy new constituencies, new claimants, and new instrumentalities for conducting the public's business.[22] A few indicators highlight the dramatic changes that overtook the use of grants as a policy tool from 1964 to the 1980s. In 1960, 130-odd intergovernmental fiscal transfer programs amounted to only a little over $7 billion, which represented less than 2 percent of the gross national product (GNP) and less than 15 percent of total state–local expenditures. By 1980 approximately 500 assistance programs were in existence and these amounted to $88 billion and accounted for 3.4 percent of GNP and 23.2 percent of overall state–local outlays.

Not only did the 1960s witness a growth in the scale and importance of grants-in-aid, however, it also witnessed important changes in the basic structure of the grant system. For one thing, the number of project grants mushroomed. Between 1964 and 1966 alone, Congress authorized 160 new project grants compared to only 39 new formula grants. Beyond this, the types of recipients grew in number and complexity (see table 4.2). As of 1960 the states were the prime recipients of federal assistance. By 1980 approximately 25 percent went directly to local governments, and at least 80 percent of the 80,000 subnational governments were grant recipients. The conditions attached to grants also changed in character. Prior to the late 1960s, they were program-specific with administrative and personnel requirements attached to some. By 1980 these had been augmented by at least 50 conditions that applied to nearly all federal grants.[23]

The Nixon Era

Responding in part to the complexity created by the explosion of categorical and project grant programs during the Great Society era, President Nixon promoted a variety of reforms in the grant system intended to give state and local governments greater leeway by

Table 4.2 HISTORICAL TREND OF FEDERAL GRANT-IN-AID OUTLAYS (fiscal years)

	Total grants-in-aid (billion dollars)	Federal grants as percentage of			
		Federal outlays[a]		State and local expenditures[c]	Gross national product
		Total	Domestic programs[b]		
Five-year intervals					
1950	2.3	5.3	11.6	10.4	0.8
1955	3.2	4.7	17.2	10.1	0.8
1960	7.0	7.6	20.6	14.6	1.4
1965	10.9	9.2	20.3	15.2	1.6
1970	24.1	12.3	25.3	19.2	2.4
1975	49.8	15.0	23.1	22.7	3.3
Annually					
1980	91.5	15.5	23.3	25.8	3.4
1981	94.8	14.0	21.6	24.6	3.2
1982	88.2	11.8	19.0	21.6	2.8
1983	92.5	11.4	18.6	21.3	2.8
1984	97.6	11.5	19.6	21.1	2.6
1985	105.9	11.2	19.3	21.0	2.7
1986	112.4	11.4	19.8	20.6	2.7
1987 (estimate)	109.9	10.8	18.9	n.a.	2.5

Source: Budget of the U.S. Government, 1988, Special Analysis, H-22.
Note: For additional detail, see the Historical Tables volume of the Budget of the United States Government, Fiscal Year 1988.
n.a. Not available.
a. Includes off-budget outlays; all grants are on-budget.
b. Excludes outlays for national defense, international affairs, and net interest.
c. As defined in the national income and product accounts.

merging individual categorical grant programs into broader block grants and by creating a system of general revenue sharing. The pressures for grant consolidation had already begun toward the latter part of the Johnson administration, as reflected in the passage in 1966 of the Partnership in Health Act, which consolidated nine categorical health programs. Under Nixon, additional block grants followed for other health care, manpower training, law enforcement, and community development. Then, in 1972, the Nixon administration managed to secure enactment of General Revenue Sharing, the broadest grant program in terms of eligibility, permissible uses, and recipient discretion. General Revenue Sharing essentially distributed $4.5 billion to $6 billion in federal resources each year to some 39,000 general purpose units of government on a formula basis with few restrictions on use.[24] Although proposed as a federal–state program, revenue sharing gained congressional approval once it was agreed that two-thirds of the funds would go to local governments and one-third to the states.

Reflecting these changes, the share of total grant dollars going out through broad-gauged or general purpose programs grew substantially, reaching 20 percent of the total by 1980. This was so even though the evidence to date suggests that once categorical grants are restructured into block grants, their aggregate funding grows more slowly than was the case when separate categorical programs existed.[25]

The Reagan Era

Further significant changes in the grant-in-aid system occurred during the presidency of Ronald Reagan in the 1980s. Throughout his public career as governor of California (1967–74) and as presidential candidate, Reagan asserted the need to devolve federal powers to the states and to expand the responsibilities of state government. In his inaugural address and later in his budget messages to Congress, Reagan's goals remained "to curb the size and influence of the Federal establishment," and to restore a more balanced federalism with more clearly defined roles for the various levels of government.[26]

With the passage of the Omnibus Reconciliation Act of 1981, Reagan took an important step toward achieving these goals. This act consolidated 57 separate categorical grants with a budget authority of $7.5 billion into 9 new or modified block grants. In addition, the Reconciliation Act of 1981 also made major reductions in domestic spending—$44 billion in actual expenditures in fiscal year 1982, and $45 billion in future budget authority.[27] Although federal aid to state and local governments actually peaked in constant dollars in 1978 under President Carter and a Democratically controlled Congress, that first year of the Reagan presidency constituted a turning point in grant retrenchment and devolution of power, the beginning of a fundamental shift in the balance of power and responsibilities among governmental levels.

Over the next six years, President Reagan would advocate further block grants, more federal aid reductions, and even a sweeping $47 billion "swap and turnback" initiative for decentralizing federal programs and their tax resources to redefine federalism "with a single bold stroke." Except for the passage of the Job Training Block Grant in 1982, however, subsequent initiatives fell victim to congressional battles over budget cuts and rising federal deficits. Although extensive consultations occurred between the president's staff and state and local officials on a comprehensive package of federalism legislation in 1982–83, consensus was never achieved.[28]

After 1982, federal aid to states and localities grew incrementally through 1986, but at levels less than that of total federal expenditures and less than that of state–local spending. With the termination of the $5 billion general revenue-sharing program in 1986, federal aid declined again in 1987, and averaged a growth rate of less than 3 percent for the 1981–87 period. Within that mix of federal aid, as indicated in table 4.3, further changes occurred. Grant payment for individuals (largely Medicaid) increased by nearly 7 percent annually, while grant payments for physical capital investment and other programs actually declined.

In addition to consolidating a number of grant programs and reducing grant expenditures in a number of areas, the Reagan administration also transformed many of the conditions attached to the use of federal aid. Considerable regulatory relief stemmed from the 12 block-grant programs in place in 1984, 9 of which required no state or local matching funds. A cabinet-level task force on Regulatory Relief propelled by Executive Order 12291 established central clearance for agency rulemaking and much of its attention focused upon grant deregulation. The Office of Management and Budget estimated that these regulatory changes saved between $4 billion and $6 billion in total investment costs, $2 billion in recurring costs, and reduced paperwork reporting requirements by almost 11.8 million work hours per year for states and localities. For example, under the Education Block Grant, 667 pages in the *Federal Register*

Table 4.3 COMPOSITION OF GRANT-IN-AID OUTLAYS (fiscal years)

	Composition of grants-in-aid (million dollars)				Percentage share of state and local capital expenditures financed by	
	Total	Payments to individuals[a]	Physical capital investments[b]	Other	Grants-in-aid	Own Sources revenues
Five-year intervals						
1950	2.3	1.3	0.5	0.5	8.4	91.6
1955	3.2	1.6	0.8	0.8	8.3	91.7
1960	7.0	2.5	3.3	1.2	23.9	76.1
1965	10.9	3.7	5.0	2.2	24.8	75.2
1970	24.1	8.6	7.0	8.4	24.6	75.4
1975	49.8	16.4	10.9	22.5	25.7	74.3
Annually						
1980	91.5	31.9	22.5	37.1	36.4	63.6
1981	94.8	36.9	22.1	35.7	35.9	64.1
1982	88.2	37.9	20.1	30.2	34.0	66.0
1983	92.5	41.6	20.5	30.4	33.7	66.3
1984	97.5	44.3	22.7	30.6	34.9	65.1
1985	105.9	45.1	24.8	33.0	33.7	66.3
1986	112.4	51.4	26.2	34.7	31.3	68.7
1987[c]	109.9	54.2	24.8	30.8	n.a.	n.a.
1988[c]	106.3	52.9	23.4	30.0	n.a.	n.a.

Source: *Budget of the U.S. Government, 1988, Special Analysis,* H-23.
n.a. Not available.
a. For an identification of accounts in this category, see table H-11, including its footnotes.
b. Excludes capital grants that are included as payments for individuals.
c. Estimated.

previously governing 28 categorical grants were reduced to a single set of regulations covering 20 pages and thereby reduced paperwork requirements by an estimated 90 percent.[29]

Beyond block grants, Executive Order 12372, the Intergovernmental Review of Federal Programs, required federal agencies to accommodate the recommendations of elected state and local officials where possible. The proposed bilingual education rules were rescinded. Flexibility was added to health care reimbursement levels, determination of highway maintenance standards, air quality review, and in other major intergovernmental programs. OMB Circular A–102 governing uniform requirements for grants achieved much commonality on terms and conditions of awards to grantees among federal agencies, leading to the Single Audit Act of 1984 (Public Law 98–130).

The impacts of devolution and cutbacks on recipient governments must be considered the most durable legacy of the Reagan presidency on the use of federal grants as a public policy tool. Much conventional wisdom held that social program retrenchment at the federal level coupled to devolution of responsibilities would result in state government retreat on social program responsibilities. Nathan, Doolittle, and Associates found, to the contrary, that devolution and retrenchment did not work in tandem, and that "the state and local government responses to the 1981 aid cuts— through replacement funding ... and through administrative reforms—has produced higher service levels than otherwise would have been the case due to Reagan cuts."[30] In fact, the authors' case studies suggest that states are poised to do even more in the future to protect and even extend service levels, and that social program supporters fared better in many states than they have in the nation's capital.

Unlike previous efforts during the Eisenhower years to "unwind" the federal system and President Nixon's far-reaching New Federalism initiatives, the Reagan changes have been vastly more successful because of enhanced state government capability to respond financially, administratively, and structurally to new responsibilities.[31] According to Nathan's own research and that of others, "Reagan's federalism reforms have stimulated and are continuing to stimulate state governments to increase their efforts to meet domestic needs in the functional areas in which the national government either was cutting grants-in-aid or threatening to do so."[32]

It is notable that such stimulation was a product not only of changes in the grant-in-aid tool. Changes in the use of other tools— loans, tax expenditures, and debt financing—also reduced resources available for state and local governments, increasing the pressure on these governments to sort out their respective roles and responsibilities. For example, the Tax Reform Act of 1986 ended the deductability of state and local sales taxes against federal tax liability, which had provided tax relief to itemizing taxpayers and, indirectly, incentives for higher state–local taxes and spending. The Act also limited the issuance of numerous types of previously tax-exempt securities, raising state and local government borrowing costs for private benefit or use.

In sum, as substantial as President Johnson's legacy has been in creating the modern grant-based system of federal relations, the

Reagan legacy will be equally great in fundamentally transforming it. The Reagan cutbacks and devolution of power to states did not have the disastrous consequences predicted by opponents. Nor did such changes on the federal level reduce government's role and responsibilities throughout the federal system, as some supporters had hoped. The Reagan legacy of federal aid reduction and devolved powers appears to be a durable one built on the new strengths of state and local governments and the financial constraints on federal resources.

HOW GRANTS WORK

From the discussion above, it should be clear that the grant-in-aid is, in some senses, not a single tool but a variety of tools. Not only do important differences exist among the broad types of grant programs (formula grants, project grants, block grants, and general revenue sharing), but also each separate program within each category has its own purposes, rules, and procedures. For example, varying degrees of discretion may be provided to federal agencies and grant recipients in implementing the program. Most categorical grants, except for project grants, depend on an allocation formula that itself is subject to negotiation within the Congress and, at times, between giver and receiver. Formulas often change over time, even though rarely in a radical or comprehensive way. Finally, each program differs from every other program in its arena of participants and support system.

Thus each grant has separate ingredients—purpose, program, funding and allocation, stipulations, and regulations. The perspectives and compromises contained in each ingredient may be numerous. The same variation is true in the size of the program, its intended beneficiaries or eligible recipients, and the agents responsible for implementation.

Despite these variations, however, it is possible to discern some significant operational uniformities in the various types of grant programs. These uniformities are important to review in order to understand how grants actually operate.

General Revenue Sharing

Of all the types of grant programs, general revenue sharing was the simplest. While it was in existence between 1972 and 1986, general revenue sharing distributed anywhere from $4.5 billion to $6 billion a year in federal assistance to some 39,000 general purpose state and local governments in quarterly payments according to a formula based on population, per capita income, and tax effort. Although the program included civil rights, audit, public hearing and use-reporting requirements, these were minimal; and the Treasury Department's Office of Revenue Sharing, which administered the program, was able to function with only a handful of people.[33]

Project Grants

Project grants account for two-thirds of the separate grant programs, yet less than one-quarter of all grant funds. Under most project grants federal administrators have a high degree of flexibility in developing guidelines for grant distribution and in making awards. Because project grants are awarded on a competitive basis, the key determination, which is legislatively or bureaucratically set (sometimes both), is eligibility: size of geographic inclusion; public, nonprofit, and private participation; targeted use; defined purpose or activity; previous participation or involvement in area; and the like.

The Public Health Service, for example, administers about 70 project grants ranging from drug abuse prevention programs to genetic disease testing and counseling services. The Office of Education in 1981 administered some 90 project grants from bilingual education (5 separate programs) to education for the handicapped (11 programs). Together the two agencies administered nearly half of the 316 project grants in effect in 1981. Some 50 of these were consolidated into block grants in 1982.

Generally project grants that are allocated on the basis of competition invest considerable discretion in federal agencies to determine the conditions of the grant award. These conditions often go beyond accountability for the grant (accounting, reporting, budget form, and execution) but also may involve recipients' compensation, use of time and equipment, overhead payments, ownership or use of results or product, and so forth.

Even though most project grants are not distributed by legislative formulas, as in the case of formula-based categorical grants, funds are typically distributed broadly to build geographical support for the program and to cultivate support from particularly critical oversight committees.

Numerous devices may be adopted to insulate project grant awards and their agency administrators from the political pressure of public criticism: (1) outside review and panel selection; (2) decentralized decision making; (3) guidelines that promote geographic distribution or award limits to any region, state, congressional district, or participant; (4) dollar limits on the size of any award to maximize the number of awards and to minimize the risks from a single project; (5) definitions of project merit that avoid specific details or rely on procedures, quotas, minimums or maximums; and (6) delegation of various degrees of authority to federal regional or area offices to review and approve grant applications, to commit funds, to conduct program reviews and investigations, and to provide technical assistance and financial management oversight of the grant.[34]

Formula Grants

Administrative discretion varies among formula-based grants, which constitute roughly one-third of all grant programs by number, but more than 75 percent of actual dollars. One source of this variation is the type of formula used in the program. Three broad types are in existence: strictly formula-based grants that reduce administrative discretion and review and, instead, largely guarantee funds to states and localities based on economic or demographic factors; project grants subject to formula distribution, a hybrid between formula-based allocation and project grant discretion; and open-ended reimbursements characteristic of major social welfare programs, in which discretion focuses on eligible activities, reimbursable limits, error rates, and disallowances.

Martha Derthick's classic study, *Uncontrollable Spending*, illustrates how the funding formula can affect a grant program's operation. As Derthick shows, the 1962 Public Welfare Amendments left largely open the definition of eligible state social services that were reimbursable by the federal government at 75 percent of the costs, creating a kind of "back door revenue sharing." As a result, a $350 million grant program expanded to become a $4.7 billion program in less than a decade, before funding limits were imposed by Congress.[35]

A second source of variation in the administration of formula grant programs results from the degree of latitude that such programs allow in the choice of uses for the funds. Narrowly defined categorical programs that stipulate specific uses—such as slum clearance and vocational training for temporarily unemployed autoworkers—involve much closer federal supervision and control.

Not surprisingly, they have consequently encountered more resistance from state and local officials, who typically prefer greater leeway in deciding how to use grant resources.

This resistance helps to explain the movement away from categorical grants toward block grants during the Nixon and Reagan years. Block grants have been justified on the grounds of simplicity, efficiency, decentralization, program innovation, and greater public official accountability. They also have been opposed on many of these same grounds, especially the lack of innovation and absence of targeting to need. In fact, the extensive studies that have been done on block grants have found mixed results. "They neither lived up to the high expectations of their most enthusiastic supporters," noted the Advisory Commission on Intergovernmental Relations, "nor to the devastating predictions of doom from their most ardent critics."[36]

In one of a number of analyses of the block grants created by the Omnibus Reconciliation Act of 1981, for example, the General Accounting Office found that preventive health and health services block grants led to:

□ increased flexibility to set priorities, which contributed to a greater role for governors and legislatures in some states previously dominated by federal and state program officials;
□ increased citizen involvement; and
□ interest group dissatisfaction with the block grant as being less desirable than the categorical grants.[37]

In their recent study of nine states' responses to block grants, Nathan and Associates found that replacement of cuts was greatest in programs that historically have been areas of greatest state and local activity and where organizations and politically active constituencies cared about the aid activity (day care, public health services, child abuse services). More amorphous federal aid programs (for example, community services) fared poorly under the new block grants.[38]

Grant Regulations

Although grants are often viewed as subsidies or incentives, they are accompanied by regulations, that is, by directives backed by sanctions or penalties. As a result, the distinction between grant programs and regulations has become increasingly blurred.

Table 4.4 A TYPOLOGY OF INTERGOVERNMENTAL REGULATORY PROGRAMS

Program type	Description	Major policy areas
Direct orders	Mandate state or local actions under the threat of criminal or civil penalties	Public employment, environmental protection
Crosscutting requirements	Apply to all or many federal assistance programs	Nondiscrimination, environmental protection, public employment, assistance management
Crossover sanction	Threaten the termination or reduction of aid provided under one or more specified programs unless the requirements of another program are satisfied	Highway safety and beautification, environmental protection, health planning, education for the handicapped
Partial preemption	Establish federal standards, but delegate administration to states if they adopt standards equivalent to the national ones	Environmental protection, natural resources, occupational safety and health, meat and poultry inspection

Source: Advisory Commission on Intergovernmental Relations, *Regulatory Federalism: Policy, Process, Impact, and Reform* (Washington, D.C.:ACIR, February 1984), 8.

Complaints about the regulatory provisions of grant programs are hardly new. Burdensome reporting requirements; inconsistent planning, auditing, and accounting requirements; program duplication; and confusion over eligibility and funding have long been sources of friction between the federal government and the recipients of grants. Governors, mayors, and other governmental recipients frequently railed against "red tape" and "strings" that, from their vantage point, made intergovernmental grants management unduly complex and problematic. They wanted broader based grants and less conditionality, which often brought them into conflict with categorical grant supporters in Congress and their interest group allies.[39]

In the 1970s, however, these irritants were superseded by new regulatory conditions attached to most existing grant programs. These new regulatory burdens came in several forms as indicated in table 4.4: (1) direct legal orders such as nondiscrimination in employment; (2) crosscutting requirements that affected nearly all grants relating to health, labor, housing, handicapped, and to administrative and fiscal standards; (3) crossover sanctions whereby fiscal sanctions in one area influence state and local policy in another (such as adoption of a 55 mph speed limit or loss of federal highway funds); and (4) partial preemption whereby if states do not adopt standards that are as effective as national ones (such as clean air standards), federal standards or requirements apply.[40] Between 1960 and 1980, over 1,200 new federal regulations affecting state and local governments were added, most of which were attached to new grant programs enacted in this period.[41]

Arguably, increased regulatory burdens do not change the fundamental nature of grants as a tool, but they certainly may make participation by the recipient less voluntary. In a sense, the grant relationship has allowed the federal government to enlist states and localities as enforcers of federal regulations and the state and local governments have found it hard to resist, especially after a program is well established, a supportive constituency has formed, and a degree of recipient dependency on the federal funds has developed.

CONSEQUENCES OF USING GRANTS: AN EVALUATION

How effective, then, has the grant-in-aid mechanism been in achieving the objectives of federal programs? Are some purposes better pursued through grants than others?

Clearly, the complexity of the world of federal grants makes it difficult to answer this question definitively. However, at least three tentative conclusions—or tendencies—seem to emerge from the data available.

Fiscal Equalization

In the first place, it seems clear that grants have failed in practice to provide the fiscal equalization claimed for them in theory. Income redistribution is not the major goal of most grant programs, and where per capita income or fiscal effort are distributive criteria for a program, the equalization criterion tends to be diluted by population or other factors. As Rudolph Penner, former director of the Congressional Budget Office, observed, "the grant system as a whole has never played an important role in equalizing income among states."[42] On a state-by-state basis, federal aid correlates more closely with population than any other variable.

Studies of general revenue sharing, the 1975–78 fiscal stimulation package (Comprehensive Employment and Training Act [CETA] programs, public works, and antirecession assistance) and community development block grants indicate that a similar conclusion holds with respect to redistribution among jurisdictions *within* states.[43] Even in cases where programs are intended to "target" funds or to "redistribute" revenues based on need, they lack consensus on definitions of need and hardship. Such programs experience considerable problems with eligibility and often must sprinkle funds among all jurisdictions to gain acceptance.

In an era of computer printouts of distributional benefits by locality and congressional district, and state allocations, the net result of congressional allocation practices, as one Treasury official noted in the late 1970s, is that "to get New York City one additional dollar of federal aid, we must spend 20 dollars elsewhere to gain congressional approval." Over time, federal categorical aid and block grants that contain allocation formulas have not proven to be very effective tools for targeting federal assistance. The political pressures to spread benefits in order to generate sufficient political support have simply been too great.

This reality blasts a major hole in the classical economic justification for federal aid, which focuses on benefit spillovers—fiscal equalization to finance local activities that have broader benefits than to the recipient government itself. As the Advisory Commission on Intergovernmental Relations concluded, "there is reason to doubt that existing grants-in-aid . . . can be justified or explained by reference to equity theories based on consideration of economic externalities."[44]

Physical versus Human Capital Programs

If federal grants have not been very effective in achieving equalization objectives, has this tool at least been effective in promoting more narrow programmatic objectives? The answer to this question is somewhat mixed. On the one hand, grants have been an effective vehicle for promoting capital construction and for delivering physical goods. Thus, the Hill–Burton Construction Act of 1946 promoted an enormous construction program for new hospitals and for modernization of old ones; the Federal Highway Act and its interstate program promoted the building of the 70,000-mile interstate highway system; the Special Supplemental Food Program for Women, Infants, and Children has aided low-income women by providing additional protein and other nutrients to pregnant women and newly born infants; and numerous project grants to support medical research and demonstration programs have been quite successful.

By contrast, social service programs aimed at modifying individual behavior or promoting skills acquisition have had more questionable results. Various studies of such programs as CETA, Title I of the Elementary and Secondary Education Act, the Manpower Development and Training Act, programs of the Office of Economic Opportunity, the Rural Development Act, and the Appalachian Regional Commission Act indicate that results fell short of their goals and objectives.[45]

One important reason for this may be that the legislative language identifying the goals and objectives of these programs is often either overly ambitious or overly vague and elusive. An example of the former would be the 1964 Economic Opportunity Act which launched a drive to "eliminate poverty" or the 1972 Clean Water Act Amendments whose goals were to "make all navigable rivers and lakes swimmable and drinkable by 1985." The latter may be found in social programs whose goal may be to decrease dependency or to improve the quality of life, or where the desired outcomes are couched in terms like integrated services, upgraded skills, and continuity of care. This, too, is a natural byproduct of the political process: to ensure support, program advocates have a strong incentive to overpromise results or to make goals sound like vaporous wishes. The upshot is to saddle programs with unrealistic objectives or leave them without measurable, trackable, observable criteria upon which all parties can agree.

A second reason for the difficulty in achieving complex social objectives through use of the grant tool may result from the sheer operational complexity and indirection of this form of action. This point is illustrated forcefully in Aaron Wildavsky and Jeffrey Pressman's analysis of the implementation of a federal jobs program in Oakland, California. As Pressman and Wildavsky show, the number of decision points that had to be cleared to put this program into operation made a successful outcome exceedingly unlikely.[46]

In a sense, grants vest considerable control over the successful outcome of federal programs in the hands of state and local officials over whom federal authorities have only limited influence. As a result, grant conditions and requirements are difficult to enforce, and in fact are poorly enforced, due to political and administrative limitations. One explanation is that federal officials are too few, too far away, and communication or reporting insufficient to stay on top of local performance.[47] Another is simply the reluctance to enforce rules, threaten payment suspension, or impose the ultimate sanction, the withholding of funds.[48] A third is simply with various parties unsure of the problem being addressed or the results expected from various grant program interventions, no one is really sure what does or does not work. Finally, the argument can be made that most grant programs are underfunded relative to the declared objectives.

Reflecting this, several detailed studies of individual grant programs have found a bargaining framework to be an apt characterization of how the grant tool functions.[49] Bardach, for example, uses a game metaphor to characterize the implementation process—players, stakes, strategies and tactics, resources, rules of the game, and uncertainty surrounding outcomes.[50] He goes on to identify a variety of games inherent to the implementation process, which could be matched against case studies of federal grant programs.

Players in the intergovernmental grant game have different positions, stakes, allies, and bargaining resources. Relatively equal balances of power are more characteristic of grant programs in which recipients are states or large localities because of their political resources to deal with Congress and the federal bureaucracy. A grant does not necessarily buy compliance but more likely an opportunity for negotiation between higher and lower governmental officials.[51] The broader the grant the greater is the latitude for negotiation and the greater the likelihood of elected official involvement. The narrower the grant and the more discretionary the authority over guidelines, the more likely it is that bureaucratic entrepreneurship may prevail. The greater the number of intermediaries in the grant process from giver to ultimate beneficiary, the less likely it is that federal officials will shape the resulting outcome to their satisfaction or achieve compliance with their directives.[52] The more discretionary or experimental the program the more control is open to a power struggle among competing groups.

Literature and cases also suggest that grants work better when federal and recipient governments agree on the desirability of a program's goal. The Office of Economic Opportunity's Community Action Agency program, for example, constituted a grouping of several grant programs whose purposes involved restructuring the human services delivery system by creating new administrative agencies separate from state and local agencies. The lack of agreement about "participation" and "control" created enormous tensions between the federal officials and the state and local elected officials, which was only resolved when the latter were clearly written into the program.[53] Numerous attempts have been made to bypass state government by creating a federal–local partnership (as occurred in the Community Mental Health Centers Act), and to set existing state-based, employment-oriented, institutional interests against a more dispersed set of professional interests. Efforts aimed at restructuring a human services delivery system took hold in many states largely when deinstitutionalization proved compatible with local emphasis in delivery of mental health services.[54]

Federal officials are heavily dependent upon the support, or at least the acquiescence, of local leadership to realize their aims. When federal and state–local objectives or priorities are not compatible and sanctions are not imposed, either programs become altered to meet state–local workings or lapse for lack of support. Similarly, as Martha Derthick notes, "when federal and state agencies act cooperatively, they have much protection, individually or together, against unwanted intervention from legislatures at either or both levels of the federal system."[55]

Structural, Administrative, and Fiscal Impact

One final consequence of the use of grants that is worth noting involves the impact of this tool on governmental structure, management operations, and the division of responsibilities among levels of government. As Lovell has noted, federal grants have had a growing influence on state and local functional responsibilities and on the sorting out of these functions between them.[56] This has been particularly the case under President Reagan's devolution of responsibilities and funding cutbacks, but it was true before that as well. The sheer number, organizational structure, and legal powers of subnational governments have been greatly influenced by federal grants. Grants have stimulated the creation of new, single-purpose units to receive grants (solid waste, air quality, airports); sustained small units (townships under general revenue sharing); and helped shape the metropolitan landscape (sewers and highways). In countless ways, grants have improved financial and managerial practices (personnel, accounting, planning, audits, and record keeping).[57]

Clearly a time existed in the 1960s and early 1970s when federal grants stimulated additional state spending, as evidenced by the sheer growth rate of state and local government budgets and intergovernmental programs. Such stimulation stopped not only with the slowing of state and local spending, but also reduced federal aid; the stimulation began again in the 1980s in another form— state replacement of lost federal funds.[58]

From the standpoint of the fiscal and administrative track record of grants, much conventional wisdom can be called into question. Federal and state–local fiscal fortunes have been reversed in terms of deficits and surpluses, as have the program financing needs of rising health and welfare spending at the national level versus more stabilized spending for education at the state level. Prior to the Tax Reform Act of 1986, the federal tax system on the whole had become more regressive over the years, and the state tax system less so. The federal government no longer has the market cornered on administrative competency, as indicated by cases of federal mismanagement, inefficiency, and waste. Old arguments supporting the use of federal grants have given way to new realities about the more apparent defects governing the effectiveness of this tool.

CONCLUSIONS

In the final analysis what can be said about grants as a policy tool compared to other mechanisms for achieving policy objectives? Basically, grants are a nonmandatory, immediate outlay of government funds. They are usually financed with general revenues and are given in most cases to a subnational government or to some other institution, organization, or individual acting in a public capacity other than as an ultimate beneficiary. Stipulations usually accompany the use of funds, but the grant recipient also retains some discretion regarding the implementation of the activities to be carried out or the products to be produced.

Grants can be voluntary exchanges among governmental units, although coercive elements and disincentives are readily apparent. Grants also are a malleable tool by which giver, receiver, and beneficiary presumably gain benefits without assuming full responsibility for consequences or failures. Grants have proven to be a highly flexible tool, adaptable to changes among administrations, political parties, policies, organizational structures, economic conditions, and new circumstances.

The relative success or failure of government programs is often difficult to establish. The view that little works is clearly an exaggeration as is the view that the grant system is so dysfunctional and overloaded that collapse is imminent.[59]

Even though grants are badly in need of reform, as most participants in the domestic policy arena acknowledge, they continue to function as a vital mechanism for conducting the public's business. Indeed, the recent revival of state and local government, long a goal of the grant system, seems to have occurred largely in a self-generative manner in education, economic development, environmental protection, health care cost containment, regulatory reform, and a host of other areas.[60]

From a fiscal perspective their relative importance may diminish in an era of scarce resources (as a proportion of federal expenditures and as a percentage of state and local own-source revenue), and as state governments assume more fiscal and programmatic responsibilities for their local governments. Grants have been at the forefront of "nationalizing" U.S. politics and forcing the public to decide on the appropriate roles of government and who should finance or administer what. The evolution of grants as a policy tool therefore reflects a mixture of pragmatism, politics, and theory; nothing in the immediate future suggests that this will change.

Grants receive a high rating on a scale of political acceptability as demonstrated by the number of programs, the scope of functions in which they are employed, and the durability of their use. Yet this popularity rests upon factors other than the demonstrated effectiveness of grants as a tool for achieving policy objectives.

The virtues of federal grants as a policy tool may be seen as the flip side of their deficiencies. An intrusive and burgeoning bureaucracy might correct some alleged grant deficiencies, but at enormous costs, not the least of which is the degree of autonomy exercised by state and local governments. Grants are highly compatible with shifting notions of federalism. Grants have proven effective as distributive programs, but far less so when attempts are made to redistribute or to target more effectively to need.[61] Once enacted, grant programs tend to survive even when inequities, shortcomings, and inefficiencies are fully understood to exist. Congress successfully resists efforts to subject grants to systematic appraisal, program evaluations, or full "sunset" provisions.

As with many policy tools, the theories of grants often differ from the reality. In theory, grants are a means to (1) advance major national goals; (2) equalize income among regions, states, localities, and people or equalize services; and (3) provide an effective and efficient means for administering services on a cooperative basis and a responsive mechanism to meet particular problems or to serve particular needs. But in reality research findings cast considerable doubt on whether federal grants come close to achieving any of these purposes or objectives.

Because the rhetoric and laudatory purposes of grants are typically overblown, the goals ill-defined, or funding to achieve goals inadequate, grants almost invariably fall short of performance—a victim of raised expectations and inordinate promises.[62] Furthermore, the implementation agents for most grants are subnational governments, thus frailties and shortcomings are highly visible and open to public scrutiny. Those characteristics perhaps explain why grants are so easy to criticize. How such criticism stacks up in comparison to other tools, however, remains to be seen. Once this is done, the justification for using grants, with all their discernible defects, may seem far more convincing than now appears to be the case.

Notes

1. See W. Brooke Graves, *American Intergovernmental Relations* (New York: Charles Scribner & Sons, 1964), ch. 13.

2. Advisory Commission on Intergovernmental Relations (ACIR), *An Agenda For American Federalism: Restoring Confidence and Competence*, A–86 (Washington, D.C.: ACIR, June 1981), 3.

3. ACIR, *The Condition of Contemporary Federalism: Conflicting Theories and Collapsing Constraints*, A–78 (Washington, D.C.: ACIR, August 1981), ch. 2.

4. David W. Davis and James L. Sundquist, *Making Federalism Work* (Washington, D.C.: Brookings Institution, 1969). For contrast, see David B. Walker, "Categorical Grants: Some Clarifications and Continuing Concerns," *Intergovernmental Prospective* 3 (Spring 1977), 18.

5. See ACIR, *Categorical Grants: Their Role and Design*, A–52 (Washington, D.C.: ACIR, 1977). This volume is part of a 14-part series that analyzes categorical grants, traces their history and application, describes their uses and misuses, and assesses their impact on state and local governments.

6. *The Budget of the United States Government Fiscal Year 1988, Special Analysis* (Washington, D.C.: OMB, 1987), H23.

7. ACIR, *A Catalog of Federal Grant-In-Aid Programs to State and Local Governments: FY 1981*, M–133 (Washington, D.C.: ACIR, February 1982), 9.

8. Executive Office of the President, Office of Management and Budget, Managing Federal Assistance in the 1980s (Washington, D.C., March 1980), 35.

9. See Richard B. Capalli, *Federal Grants and Cooperative Agreements: Law, Policy and Practice* (Wilmette, Ill.: Callaghan, 1982). Grants as contractual arrangements are discussed in Richard Capalli, *Rights and Remedies under Federal Grants* (Washington, D.C.: Bureau of National Affairs, 1979).

10. Nicholas L. Henry, "Bigger or Better Bureaucracy," *Assistance Mangement Journal* 2 (Fall 1980): 23–37. See also "Clarifying Grant and Procurement Relationships," *Improving Federal Grants Management*, A–53 (Washington, D.C.: ACIR, February 1977), 100–105.

11. For example, see the Commission on the Organization of the Executive Branch of the Government, *Federal–State Relations, A Report to the Congress* (March 1949): 30–36; U.S. Congress, House Commission on Intergovernmental Relations, *Message from the President of the United States*, 84th Cong., 1st sess. (June 28, 1955), 130–32; U.S. Congress, Senate, *Creative Federalism Hearing before the Subcommittee on Intergovernmental Relations*, 89th Cong., 1st sess. (1966), 2A–2B.

12. Deil S. Wright, *Federal Grants-In-Aid: Perspectives and Alternatives* (Washington, D.C.: American Enterprise Institute, 1968), ch. 4.

13. See Samuel H. Beer, "The Modernization of American Federalism," *Publius* 3 (Fall 1973): 49–95; and Michael D. Reagan, *The New Federalism* (New York: Oxford University Press, 1972).

14. See V.O. Key, *The Administration of Federal Grants to the States* (Chicago: Public Administration Service, 1937).

15. ACIR, *An Agenda For American Federalism*, 54.

16. Morton Grodzins in Daniel J. Galzar, ed., *The American Federal System* (Chicago: Rand McNally, 1966).

17. See Wallace Oates, *Fiscal Federalism* (New York: Harcourt Brace Jovanovich, 1972), ch. 3; and Wallace Oates, ed., *The Political Economy of Fiscal Federalism* (Lexington, Mass.: D.C. Heath, 1977).

18. Robert H. Connery and Gerald Benjamin, *Rockefeller of New York* (Ithaca, N.Y.: Cornell University Press, 1979), ch. 10.

19. Graves, *American Intergovernmental Relations*, ch. 15.

20. ACIR, *The Dynamics of Growth—Public Assistance: The Growth of a Federal Function*, A–79 (Washington, D.C.: ACIR, July 1980).

21. C. Martin Roscoe, *The Cities and the Federal System* (New York: Atherton, 1965), 11.

22. Donald Haider, *When Governments Come to Washington: Governors, Mayors, and Intergovernmental Lobbying* (New York: Free Press, 1974), 57; and Daniel J. Elazar, *American Federalism*, 2d ed. (New York: Crowell, 1972), 71.

23. ACIR, *An Agenda for American Federalism*, 3–5.

24. John Shannon, "Revenue Sharing for States: An Endangered Species," *Intergovernmental Perspective* 5 (Summer 1979): 14–23; and Richard E. Thompson, *Revenue Sharing: A New Era in Federalism?* (Washington, D.C.: Revenue Sharing Advisory Service, 1973).

25. See Claude E. Barfield, *Rethinking Federalism: Block Grants and Federal, State and Local Responsibilities* (Washington, D.C.: American Enterprise Institute, 1981);

Carl W. Stenberg, "Block Grants: The Middlemen of the Federal Aid System," *Intergovernmental Perspective* 3 (Spring 1977): 8–13.

26. Richard S. Williamson, "Reagan Federalism: Goals and Achievements," in Lewis Bender and James Stever, eds., *Administering New Federalism* (Boulder, Colo.: Westview Press, 1986), 41–71.

27. See John W. Ellwood, ed., *Reductions in U.S. Domestic Spending* (New Brunswick, N.J.: Transaction Books, 1982).

28. See Richard S. Williamson, "The 1982 New Federalism Negotiations"; and Stephen B. Farber, "The 1982 New Federalism Negotiations: A View From the States," *Publius* 13 (Spring 1983): 11–32; 33–38.

29. Richard S. Williamson, "A New Federalism: Proposals and Achievements of President Reagan's First Three Years," *Publius* 14 (Winter 1986): 25–26.

30. Richard P. Nathan, Fred C. Doolittle, and Associates, *Reagan and the States* (Princeton, N.J.: Princeton University Press, 1987), 8. See also, David Osborne, *Laboratories of Democracy* (Boston: Harvard Business School Press, 1988).

31. See ACIR, *The Question of State Government Capability* (Washington, D.C., January 1985).

32. Nathan, et al., *Reagan and the States*, 7.

33. Richard P. Nathan, et al., *Monitoring Revenue Sharing* (Washington, D.C.: Brookings Institution, 1975); and Richard P. Nathan and Charles F. Adams, *Revenue Sharing: The Second Round* (Washington, D.C.: Brookings Institution, 1977).

34. George E. Hale and Marion Lief Palley, *The Politics of Federal Grants* (Washington, D.C.: Congressional Quarterly Press, 1951), 77–79.

35. Martha Derthick, *Uncontrollable Spending for Social Service Grants* (Washington, D.C.: Brookings Institution, 1975), 1–6.

36. Carol Weissert, "Block Grants: The Promise and Reality," *Intergovernmental Perspective* 7 (Spring 1981), 16.

37. U.S. General Accounting Office (GAO), *State Uses Added Flexibility Offered by the Preventive Health and Health Services Block Grant*, GAO/HRD 84–4 (May 8, 1984). This is one of nine studies conducted by the GAO as mandated by Congress under the Omnibus Budget Reconciliation Act of 1981. See also GAO, *Early Observation on Block Grant Implementation*, GGD 82–79 (August 24, 1982).

38. Nathan, et al., *Reagan and the States*, 86. Amply summarized in ACIR, *Improving Federal Grants Management*, ch. 1; and Executive Office of the President, *Strengthening Public Management in the Intergovernmental System: A Report Prepared for the Office of Management and Budget*, (Washington, D.C.: 1975), ch. 2.

39. Haider, *When Governments Come To Washington*, 54–64; 123–29.

40. ACIR, *Regulatory Federalism: Policy, Process, Impact, and Reform*, A–95 (Washington, D.C.: ACIR 1984); Edward M. Koch, "The Mandate Millstone," *The Public Interest* 61 (Fall 1980), 44; and Eugene Bardach and Robert Kagan, *Going by the Book: The Problems of Regulatory Unreasonableness* (Philadelphia: Temple University Press, 1982).

41. Catherine Lovell, "Federal Regulation and State and Local Governments, in John Ellwood, ed., *Reductions in U.S. Domestic Spending*, 99–129.

42. Rudolph G. Penner, "Reforming the Grant System," in Peter Nieszkowski and William Oakland, eds., *Fiscal Federalism and Grants-in-Aid* (Washington, D.C.: Urban

Institute, 1979), 114; and U.S. Congressional Budget Office, *Troubled Local Econo-mies and the Distribution of Federal Dollars* (Washington, D.C., 1977), 34-38.

43. U.S. Congress, House Committee on Banking, Finance, and Urban Affairs, *City Need and the Responsiveness of Federal Grant Programs*, 95 Cong., 2d sess. (Washington, D.C., 1978); GAO, *Anti-Recession Assistance: An Evaluation*, PAD- 72–20 (Washington, D.C., November 1977).

44. Letter from David Beam, September 20, 1986; Lester C. Thurow, "Cash versus In-Kind Transfers," *American Economic Review* 64 (May 1974): 23–35; and ACIR *An Agenda for American Federalism*, 520–54.

45. These studies are summarized in ACIR, *An Agenda for American Federalism*, ch. 3; ACIR, *Reducing Unemployment: Intergovernmental Dimensions of a National Problem*, A–80 (Washington, D.C.: ACIR, February 1982); and James S. Larson, *Why Government Programs Fail: Improving Policy Implementation* (New York: Praeger, 1980).

46. Jeffrey L. Pressman and Aaron B. Wildavsky, *Implementation* (Berkeley: University of California Press, 1973).

47. Richard P. Nathan, "Federal Grants—How Are They Working?" in Robert W. Bur-chell and David Listokin, eds., *Cities under Stress* (Piscataway, N.J.: Rutgers, 1983), 534–35; and Jerome Murphy, "The Education Policies Implement Novel Policy: The Politics of Title I of ESEA, 1965–1972," in Allan P. Sindler, ed., *Policy and Politics in America* (Boston: Little, Brown, 1973), 184–97.

48. David B. Walker, "Federal Aid Administrators and the Federal System," *Intergov-ernmental Perspective* 3 (Fall 1977): 4–7; ACIR, *Federal Aid System as Seen By Local, State, and Federal Officials*, (Washington, D.C.: ACIR, 1977), 196–200; and David Beam, "From Law to Rule: Exploring the Maze of Intergovernmental Regulation," *In-tergovernmental Perspective* 9 (Spring 1983): 21–22.

49. Helen Ingram, "Policy Implementation through Bargaining: The Case of Federal Grants-in-Aid," *Public Policy* 25 (Fall 1977): 520–25.

50. Eugene Bardach, *The Implementation Game* (Cambridge, Mass.: MIT Press, 1977); and Theodore J. Lowi, et al., *Poliscide* (New York: Macmillan, 1973).

51. See Martha Derthick, *The Influence of Federal Grants* (Cambridge, Mass.: Harvard University Press, 1970).

52. See Steven L. Yoffe, *Prohibitive Policy: Implementing the Federal Endangered Species Act* (Cambridge, Mass.: MIT Press, 1982); and Martha Derthick, *New Towns In-Town: Why A Federal Program Failed* (Washington, D.C.: Urban Institute Press, 1972).

53. Daniel F. Moynihan, *Maximum Feasible Misunderstanding: Community Action in the War on Poverty* (New York: Free Press, 1969); and ACIR, *Improving Federal Grants Management*, 46–63.

54. See, for example, Paul E. Peterson, *City Limits* (Chicago: University of Chicago Press, 1981), 82–85; Charles M. Haar, *Between the Idea and Reality: A Study in the Origin, Fate, and Legacy of the Model Cities Program* (Boston: Little, Brown, 1975); and Joseph A. Kershaw, *Government Against Poverty* (Washington, D.C.: Brookings Institution, 1970).

55. Derthick, *The Influence of Federal Grants*, 212.

56. See Catherine Lovell, et al., *Federal and State Mandating on Local Governments: An Exploration of Issues and Impacts* (Riverside: University of California, 1979).

57. See ACIR, *Federal Influence on State and Local Roles in the Federal System*, A–89 (Washington, D.C.: ACIR, 1981), especially ch. 2.

58. See, for example, ACIR, *Federal Grants: Their Effects on State–Local Expenditures, Employment Levels, and Wage Rates*, A–61 (Washington, D.C. ACIR, 1977); and *Summary and Concluding Observations*, A–62 (Washington, D.C.: ACIR, January 1978); Edward Gramlich, "Intergovernmental Grants: A Review of the Empirical Literature," in Wallace Oates, ed., *The Political Economy of Fiscal Federalism* (Lexington, Mass.: D.C. Heath, 1977), ch. 5; and George F. Breale, "Intergovernmental Fiscal Relations," in Joseph A. Pechman, ed., *Setting National Priorities: Agenda for the 1980s* (Washington, D.C.: Brookings Institution, 1980), 248–55.

59. David R. Beam, "After New Federalism, What?" *Policy Studies Journal* 13 (March 1985), chs. 1 and 7.

60. Richard P. Nathan, et al., *Consequences of the Cuts: The Effects of the Reagan Domestic Program on State and Local Governments* (Princeton, N.J.: Princeton University Press, 1981), chs. 1 and 7.

61. Hale and Palley, *The Politics of Federal Grants*, 76–83; Albert Davis and Robert Lucke, "The Rich-State Poor-State Problems in a Federal System," *National Tax Journal* 35 (September 1982): 349–50.

62. See Eli Ginzberg and Robert M. Solow, eds., *The Great Society: Lessons for the Future* (New York: Basic Books, 1974), 211–20; see also Murray Edelman, *The Symbolic Uses of Politics* (Urbana: University of Illinois Press, 1964), chs. 1–2.

Chapter Five

BETWEEN WELFARE AND THE MARKET: LOAN GUARANTEES AS A POLICY TOOL

Michael S. Lund

Since the early 1970s federal policymakers have been trying to restrain the rapid growth of federal spending, and Washington is currently engaged in a battle over alternative ways to reduce a huge budget deficit. But during this period—when proliferating grants-in-aid, uncontrollable entitlements, wasteful defense contracts, and other spending issues have been prominent on the federal agenda—little notice has been taken of the government's growing "off-budget" programs, a wide range of public sector activities not fully accounted for in the regular appropriations process. One of the most significant and fastest growing of these off-budget tools in recent years is the loan guarantee. The loan guarantee is, in effect, an agreement by the government to cosign loans on behalf of eligible borrowers.

Rapid growth in loan guarantees over the last two decades occurred mostly in federal mortgage programs, which were the first to use the guaranteed loan device on a large scale in the 1930s. But the overall growth in the use of this technology also reflects its diffusion into new fields of federal concern. The 1980 Chrysler "bailout" through a guarantee received considerable media attention, for example, and millions of college students have benefited from guaranteed student loans. Guarantees have been used for many less conspicuous purposes as well, such as the construction of clinics by Health Maintenance Organizations (HMOs), purchase of aircraft by U.S. airlines, development of new geothermal energy projects, and purchase of U.S. goods by foreign firms. Overall, the federal government now operates well over 100 different loan guarantee programs in such diverse areas as space technology, agriculture, education, business assistance, community development, international trade, natural resource conservation, transportation and shipping, fiscal relief of local governments, foreign aid, and military defense.[1]

Despite the Reagan administration's attempt to limit loan guarantees and the enormous budget deficit which provides little encouragement for federal activism, loan guarantee programs are
likely to continue to increase in size and number and play a significant role in public policy in the coming years. Many of the largest
guarantees, such as Federal Housing Administration (FHA) and
Veterans Administration (VA) mortgages and guaranteed student
loans, are well-established programs that enjoy broad popular back-
ing. Efforts to cut back on these programs face formidable opposition. Furthermore, the loan guarantee is well equipped to survive
and flourish in a climate of fiscal austerity and governmental restraint. Because loan guarantees are largely off-budget and are
perceived as working through the private sector rather than government bureaucracy, they appear to offer an attractive way to do
something about public problems without exacerbating the deficit
or creating political conflict over enlarging the federal bureaucracy.[2]

Congress and other federal policymakers perceive them as a
simple method for producing desired public goods quickly, using
private sector resources rather than increasing public outlays and
bureaucratic involvement. Loan guarantees are, therefore, an immensely attractive policy option in a political culture that expects
government to address problems but is reluctant to give it money
or authority to achieve its goals. As the range of government's substantive responsibilities expanded and diversified beginning in the
1930s, these apparent virtues of the loan guarantee tool are likely
to continue to tempt policymakers to use it in many public policy
areas outside its original domain, housing. Finally, even if federal
use of loan guarantees declines, interest in this tool is rising on the
part of state governments. Federal program cuts have forced states
to take on more responsibility in areas such as higher education
and economic development even as they, too, are faced with severe
spending constraints. Consequently, they put a premium on policy
tools like loan guarantees that appear to require little new spending
and make use of existing resources and institutions.[3]

Clearly, loan guarantees have already played a major role in
American public policy and are likely to grow in use. Indeed, several observers cite this tool as a prime illustration of a fundamental
shift occurring over the last quarter century in the way American
government does business. Characterized by increasingly indirect,
low-profile methods of public sector involvement in the economy

and society, this trend is likely to persist in the coming years no matter which party or ideology comes to power.[4]

Loan guarantees have not received universal approval, however. Critics have long charged that guarantees have numerous shortcomings. They are attacked as not really increasing the credit supplied to a particular public purpose, but rather merely subsidizing lenders for loans they would have made anyway. They are also attacked as underwriting inefficient activities and "crowding out" other more productive borrowers, thus decreasing national productivity.

Given their rapid growth and the criticism they have received, it may seem surprising that loan guarantees have received relatively little systematic research attention. This chapter seeks to put the loan guarantee tool more clearly on the map of public policy analysis by showing what loan guarantees are, why the federal government has adopted them, how they perform in practice, and what has been done to try to improve them. The chapter argues that what we know about loan guarantees does not correspond very closely with the expectations of their advocates. Rather than a simple, self-executing mechanism, loan guarantees take a variety of specific forms, many of which are extremely complicated to design and implement properly. Many programs thus fail to achieve their intended aims. In the process, guarantees often incur higher direct and indirect costs than is generally assumed, help to reinforce social inequities, and result in undesirable side effects on the wider economy. But neither do they necessarily correspond with the charges of their harshest critics. When properly designed and fitted to appropriate problems, loan guarantees can be a workable, effective policy tool.

USE OF THE TOOL

One way government can try to promote desired activities like education, housing provision, or exports is to increase the credit available to finance these activities. Government uses many tools for this purpose. One of them is the government-guaranteed loan. Essentially, a loan guarantee is a formal pledge by government to repay some or all of the unpaid principal or interest on a loan or mortgage provided on specified terms by a commercial bank or other third-party lender to a designated borrower if the borrower defaults, or to purchase the unsatisfied portion of the loan if the borrower fails to make timely repayment.

Economic Rationale

Governments decide to guarantee loans because they believe lenders provide insufficient loans to produce a desired level of an activity, or charge interest rates that are too high. Affordable credit is unavailable because lenders perceive particular types of investments as too risky or insufficiently profitable. By shifting some of this risk to the public sector, governments hope to induce lenders to provide loans they have hitherto declined to offer or to ease the interest rates and other terms on the loans they have offered.

Two explanations are usually given for why lenders perceive particular credit investments as undesirable and therefore fail to promote an activity government wishes carried out. First, a market imperfection such as bias or lack of information may prevent normal, profitable market transactions from developing between lenders and borrowers. The lack of adequate long-term financing for exports, for example, has been attributed to the fact that many small- and medium-sized banks have limited knowledge of foreign markets and buyers and tend to exaggerate the risk entailed in financing foreign transactions.[5] A guarantee seeks to correct this misperception by substituting the credit standing of the government for that of the borrowers whom private lenders regard as financially too risky to serve. The aim is to demonstrate that profitable returns on given investments are possible and, eventually, to create normal lender–borrower transactions where they have not taken place on their own. The classic example is FHA's first mortgage guarantees. These were aimed at reviving the housing industry during the 1930s by demonstrating to lenders they could profit and would not incur high defaults from offering homebuyers long-term, high loan-to-value mortgages rather than the less favorable mortgage terms prevailing at the time.

The other circumstance in which lenders withhold credit occurs when the payoffs of such an investment are judged to be below a normal market return. The capital shortages cited as a major cause of poor economic development in rural areas may be due in part to the unwillingness of rural-area bankers to tie up their money in long-term loans. Similarly, bankers are thought to be less likely to provide loans for redevelopment in urban areas at interest rates comparable to loans in suburban areas because of above-average transaction costs incurred in urban areas.[6] In these circumstances, the objective of the government guarantee is to induce lenders to offer affordable credit by having government absorb much of the cost. Although considerable financial loss to government may result, these investments are believed to be justified because the public purpose they serve is deemed sufficiently valuable.

Political Appeal

A full explanation of why loan guarantees are adopted has to include the political benefits derived from choosing this particular tool as a method of carrying out the public's business. Though economic reasoning like that just described probably accompanies each proposal to create a guarantee program, such technical rationale is not necessarily sufficient to spur government action.

The use of loan guarantees clearly has been facilitated by certain advantages they are assumed to have over other policy tools from the point of view of the American political culture. The foremost political appeal of loan guarantees is their apparent costlessness. Since loan guarantees do not require initial monetary expenditures from government, they are not listed in the federal budget as outlays, thus avoiding the need for unpopular increases in the budget or taxes. The only immediate costs from a loan guarantee program are their modest administrative expenses. Potentially government may incur the costs of repaying defaulted loans, but these costs are in the future and in most cases will not materialize. Loan guarantees are thus relatively invisible. The observation of an early student of federal credit programs such as loan guarantees still holds:

> The single most important factor that explains the growth and proliferation of federal credit assistance is the desire to see programs funded with a minimum of scarce budget dollars. . . . [It] has undoubtedly permitted Congress and the administration to claim that wonder of wonders—something for nothing.[7]

Another attractive feature of loan guarantees is their use of existing private sector institutions rather than expanding government to do a job. Moreover, since they are justified technically only where private credit markets are inactive, loan guarantees are not perceived as displacing private resources but simply extending them through an action that will "leave intact the decision-making processes of lenders and borrowers."[8] Loan guarantee proponents can make a powerful symbolic appeal to the principles of limited government and public–private partnership.

A third advantage is that loan guarantees are not outright handouts despite the substantial subsidies often involved. Compared to nonrepayable benefits such as grants, guarantees and direct loans are less vulnerable to the charge that special interests are being indulged by government welfare; the aid is intended merely to get beneficiaries on their feet or stimulate other private action and in most cases will be repaid to the government with interest.

These selling points not only give loan guarantees broad symbolic appeal but provide concrete benefits to a number of specific governmental and nongovernmental interests, in addition to the borrowers themselves. For national administrations, loan guarantees are a way to address important national priorities without having to go to Congress with huge budget requests. For example, although the Reagan administration has cut the direct loan authority of agencies such as the Small Business Administration (SBA), Economic Development Administration (EDA), and the Export–Import Bank (EXIM), it has encouraged them to use guaranteed loans. Furthermore, since loan guarantee authority is considered separately from direct spending authority in deciding the resources an agency has to work with, loan guarantees also help particular agencies to distribute benefits to their traditional clientele without having to reduce the requests they submit to the Office of Management and Budget (OMB) and Congress for programs requiring budgeted appropriations. On the legislative side, loan guarantees allow members of Congress to provide benefits to their districts without being subject to the charge that they raised constituents' taxes.[9]

Not only do they allow various governmental actors to provide aid without pain to their constituents, but guaranteed loans also enjoy strong support from the many provider organizations involved in their distribution to the public—banks, universities, contractors, and other intermediaries. Where the programs provide sufficient return to lenders, loan guarantees make it possible to expand lending into areas formerly judged too risky or unprofitable. The funds banks use for loan guarantees do not count toward the amounts subject to federal lending ceilings and other regulations, so bankers also can take advantage of as much available loan guarantee volume as public demand is likely to absorb. Where secondary markets exist, lenders need not even reduce their liquidity by tying up assets in government loans; returns can be immediate, allowing lenders to sell their loans to investors and seek out additional borrowers. And among the prime supporters of guarantees, of course, are their ultimate beneficiaries, individual or organizational borrowers, for whom a guarantee can remove impediments to financing an enterprise from which they derive their livelihood.

In sum, loan guarantees are extremely attractive because they have strong symbolic appeal and benefit a wide array of interests without requiring these interests to impose salient costs on each other or the nation as a whole. Given these benefits, it is not surprising that guarantee programs function like traditional spending programs in binding particular federal agencies, congressional subcommittees, and interest groups together into coalitions or "iron triangles" that fight hard when the programs are threatened. The guarantees and other subsidies that go to shipbuilders, for example, have been well protected until recently by a coalition made up of the shipbuilding industry, maritime unions, the Maritime Administration (MARAD), and the members of congressional subcommittees who oversee MARAD's subsidies and receive campaign contributions from the builders and unions.[10]

Loan guarantees are not, of course, without their opponents. Although three sources of opposition can be identified, however, they have not been formidable to date. The first source includes those like Senator William Proxmire (D–Wis.) who oppose government bail-outs of particular industries or sectors on ideological grounds. A potential barrier in the way of guarantees for large corporations like Chrysler was the objection that such bail-outs convey the impression that businesses can plan on federal support even if they make poor management decisions causing them to go bankrupt.[11] Opposition also comes from interest groups that are passed over for particular subsidies or feel harmed by them. When Congress added U.S. fishermen to the list of eligible recipients of the Department of Agriculture's Commodity Credit Corporation's export credit program, for example, the U.S. soybean and rice industries protested that the program was for agriculture, not other types of business, and that the fishermen would reduce the amount of aid available for agricultural exports.[12] The most recent and potentially significant opposition to loan guarantees is composed of economists and members of the U.S. financial community who have expressed increasing concern about the seemingly uncontrollable growth of loan guarantees, the possible effect of loan guarantees and other federal credit programs in crowding out more worthy investments from private credit markets, and the high default rates and subsidy costs of some programs.

Though opposition to loan guarantees may have gained some strength over the last decade as federal commitments have appeared to explode, it is unclear how much real political clout the opposition wields. This opposition is scattered, unorganized, and episodic, whereas positive support behind guarantees within and outside government is concentrated among well-positioned bureaucrats, legislators, and organized provider and beneficiary groups.[13]

Patterns of Growth

The political benefits that loan guarantees provide go a long way toward explaining why federal guarantees have grown dramatically in recent years, as evidenced both in the amount of loans government is pledged to repay and the number of different program areas where loan guarantees now operate.

The rate of new guarantee commitments added each year remained relatively level from the early 1950s until about 1970. As the total commitments made over the years accumulated, however, the amount of guarantees outstanding—those on loans that were not yet repaid—rose at a steady pace. After 1970, however, both annual additions and outstanding guarantees began to increase much more rapidly. New commitments went from $27 billion in 1970 to $97 billion in 1983, an increase of 359 percent, and the federal government's contingent liabilities—as measured by the total amount of guaranteed loans still unpaid—rose from $125 billion in 1970 to $364 billion in 1984, or by 291 percent. Although the rate of loan guarantee growth slowed somewhat in the early Reagan years, current estimates project new guarantee commitments by 1990 to be $90 billion to $92 billion, or $3 billion to $5 billion above the highest level in pre-Reagan years.[14]

This rapid recent expansion reflects two trends. First, growing demand for cheap credit in the early mortgage guarantee and student loan programs led Congress to expand these programs by raising loan authorization limits, loan amounts, and eligible income levels. Second, executive and congressional policymakers expanded the areas where loan guarantees were used.

Significantly, as the substantive uses of the loan guarantee tool expanded and diversified, the characteristics of the policy tool itself changed in important ways. The diffusion of the loan guarantee technology from its origins in the field of mortgage insurance brought about a shift from prime reliance on the market-perfecting, less risky types of guarantee programs that are self-supporting and can return a profit, to greater use of riskier kinds of guarantees that are justified principally on social, rather than economic, grounds and are more costly to the government. It is as if, over time, the standards for what constitutes a proper loan guarantee program were gradually loosened.

The prototype loan guarantee is the FHA mortgage insurance program, created by the National Housing Act of 1934. By reducing the risks of the mortgage market, this program aimed to revive the collapsed housing industry and increase employment by inducing savings institutions to offer loans at more affordable terms to prospective homebuyers. A decade later, the VA also began to insure home mortgages and, by 1950, 97 percent of new federal loan guarantees went to housing. By and large, these early FHA and VA housing programs were actuarially sound: because they provided small loans to a large number of recipients, spread the risk in their portfolio across many borrowers, and charged default insurance premiums, the programs involved relatively little risk and were self-supporting in their financing.

Perhaps because of the perceived effectiveness and popularity of the home mortgage guarantees, subsequent decades saw the spread of the loan guarantee tool. In the 1950s loan guarantees were introduced into agriculture and rural development, domestic business assistance, and export assistance. In the 1960s they were extended to foreign military assistance, foreign investment, international aid, education, and health policy. During the 1970s loan guarantees began to be used for energy development, transportation, and the fiscal relief of local governments.

By the 1980s the federal government operated guarantees for a wide range of societal purposes and a diverse clientele. Guarantees were available to farmers to purchase or operate a farm, and to foreign companies to finance the purchase of U.S. goods. American businesses could get credit guarantees to finance new business expansion, recover from economic or natural calamities, and install environmental and safety improvements. Loan guarantees were also used to stimulate investment in geothermal and other alternative energy sources. The uses of the loan guarantee tool now range from the Defense Department's help to foreign governments in buying U.S. arms, to the Department of Health and Human Service's guarantees to HMOs for expanding health care delivery. The borrowers served include homeowners, farmers, students, small businesses, foreign exporters, public utilities, shipbuilders, railroads, and state, local, and foreign governments. Whereas the tool was once confined to FHA, VA, and the Department of Agriculture, at least 13 different federal departments or agencies now operate loan guarantee programs. Among the more recent guarantee sponsors are agencies as varied in their mandates, clientele, and size as the Agency for International Development (AID), the SBA, the Overseas Private Investment Corporation (OPIC), Environmental Protection Agency (EPA), and the Departments of Commerce, Transportation, Health and Human Services, Interior, Energy, and Education.

Many of these guarantee programs adopted since the 1960s have entailed increasingly greater risks and costs to the federal government than the original guarantee programs. Many of the newer programs provide either a large number of loans to marginal borrowers or a few large loans to a small number of financially vulnerable enterprises. Multiple-guarantee, marginal-borrower guarantees are similar to actuarially sound guarantees because they entail a large number of small loans to individuals or firms. But they also go to riskier borrowers such as low-income homeowners and students who are more likely to default or lack acceptable collateral. Total risk is pooled among the borrowers, but fees or premiums are set below the level required for fiscally sound operations. Thus these programs may require higher interest rates and the addition of other financial incentives to lenders. Examples include FHA's housing mortgage programs for declining urban areas, SBA's business loan program, and guaranteed student loans.

The third, even more recent type—the so-called discrete venture guarantee—entails much larger loans to a single borrower or small number of borrowers. Examples include the one-time New York City and Conrail guarantees and the slightly more routinized synfuels, geothermal, OPIC, and EXIM Bank guarantees. Because no sizable borrower pool exists, risk is less easily spread. Also, these guarantees go to ventures that are economically and technologically unproven, may require considerable borrower subsidies, or use for collateral assets that cannot be easily marketed in the event of default. Uncertainty regarding possible losses is high because the potential burden of any one default could impose substantial costs.

In sum, as the American welfare state grew, federal policymakers facing increasing fiscal constraints saw definite advantages in using the loan guarantee as a tool to cope with new public problems on the federal agenda. But as its usage spread, the economic and financial character of the tool changed significantly. One study shows that from 1960 to 1976 the actuarially sound programs grew in size by 240 percent, while the multiple-guarantee, marginal-borrower type grew by 1,729 percent and guarantees for discrete ventures grew by 39,240 percent.[15] While self-supporting guarantee programs still account for more than half of all federal guarantee commitments and constitute the bulk of federal financial loan guarantee commitments outstanding, this proliferation of increasingly risky guarantees into so many new fields of federal activity has led to real concern.[16]

OPERATING FEATURES OF THE TOOL

Before examining the actual effects of loan guarantees it is useful to look more closely at how such guarantees function. These operating features help clarify the differences between loan guarantees and other generic policy tools and provide much of the explanation of what happens when loan guarantees are put into effect.

Essential Tasks

Creating and operating a loan guarantee requires at least seven distinguishable steps that must be carried out by public or private organizations with differing stakes in the loan guarantee process.

STEP 1. DESIGN: FORMULATE PROGRAM RULES AND STANDARDS

This step involves the policy decisions that shape the basic components of the loan guarantee tool so they fit a particular credit need and the sponsoring agency's desired level of financial exposure. Among the more critical decisions are defining the intended uses of the guaranteed credit; stipulating the eligible clientele; and writing the rules governing the respective financial claims and obligations of the guaranteeing agency, the lender, and the borrower. Decisions are also needed regarding the financing for a program and the allocation of administrative authority over loan approval and loan account monitoring.

Some of these decisions are made by Congress and included

in the program's authorizing legislation, but many are decided through agency regulations. The choices are intertwined in complex ways, but two competing concerns are typically involved: first, the substantive aims of the program and the needs of its clientele (such as producing more low-income housing units or increasing loans to small businesses); and second, the protection of the government's financial interests. The provisions of some programs serve the interests of beneficiaries at some sacrifice of fiscal restraint; other programs are more protective of the government's financial stake.

STEP 2. MARKETING: ENLIST THE PARTICIPATION OF LENDERS AND BORROWERS

For a guarantee's substantive aims to be achieved, borrowers must apply for loans and lenders must provide them. Marketing loan guarantee programs is essential but not automatic, and requires publicizing guarantee availability and purposes, screening lenders to ensure they will be capable agents of the program, inducing certified lenders actually to offer loans, and facilitating the preparation and submission of loan applications from prospective borrowers. These tasks are carried out to some extent by sponsoring agencies, but many agencies rely on lenders to do program outreach. In the programs of SBA and the Farmer's Home Administration (FmHA), for example, the lender is usually the first to suggest a government guarantee to a credit seeker. In some programs, private consultants have emerged to assist borrowers in preparing their loan applications for submission to the bank and sponsoring agency.

STEP 3. SELECTION: EVALUATE LOAN APPLICANTS

As with other government assistance, the central task in loan guarantee implementation is selecting recipients and disbursing the award. Loan applications are scrutinized principally for whether the proposed uses are eligible and sound, the applicant is eligible and creditworthy, and the available alternatives to governmental credit have been pursued without success. Lenders often make these basic evaluations, with the guarantee agency giving final approval and reexamining borderline cases. Once approved, the loan is closed when the lender and borrower work out, within agency guidelines, terms such as loan amount, interest rate, collateral, and needed permits. The lender draws up the loan agreement and disburses funds.

STEP 4. PROJECT PERFORMANCE

Not simply a financial transaction, loan guarantees are a vehicle for assisting a borrower to undertake a desired activity. Follow-through by the borrower and project monitoring by the lender and agency are required to ensure adherence to the loan's purposes and conditions.

STEP 5. LOAN SERVICING

Servicing involves collecting fees and the payment of outstanding loans, monitoring the status of loan accounts to identify delinquencies and anticipate possible defaults, and closing out repaid loans. Once again, lenders are often the key actors in checking the progress of outstanding accounts, but agencies have varying degrees of oversight.

STEP 6. LOAN ASSET SALES

Some programs allow the agency to sell its promissory notes to private investors. This may be done by the agency or through a secondary market agency, such as the Student Loan Marketing Association or Federal Financing Bank.

STEP 7. MANAGEMENT OF "PROBLEM" LOANS AND DEFAULTS

For accounts in danger of default, agencies often rearrange repayment schedules, adjust other terms, and give management or other assistance to borrowers, in order to increase the chances of successful completion of the project and loan repayment. In some cases, the agency must declare default when borrowers are irredeemably delinquent, purchase the defaulted loan from the lender, and liquidate assets used as collateral.

Guarantee programs do not give equal attention to all seven tasks; that varies in relation to the program's objectives, administrative burden, management capacity, and shifting priorities. But with the exception of loan sales, some attention to each of the seven is necessary.

Basic Tool Components

Stepping back from those guarantee procedures, we can pick out certain generic features that distinguish the guarantee tool from other tools, and that help explain the consequences when governments put this tool to use.

THE STIMULUS

The most obvious difference between loan guarantees and other tools is the nature of the "carrot" or "stick" the sponsoring government agency uses to produce a desired policy result. As its name suggests, this tool entails two stimuli: the guarantee and the loan.

The guarantee portion is a contractual promise to fulfill a future financial obligation in the event of a contingent liability, such as a loan default. By transferring a lender's exposure to default risk to the government, the guarantee is supposed to stimulate more credit for favored activities or reduce credit costs.

Important implications follow from the guarantee stimulus. First, like all forms of nonmandatory government assistance (such as grants, tax expenditures, and income transfers)—but unlike tools such as regulation—a loan guarantee offers *inducement* rather than *coercion* to influence the decisions of lenders and borrowers. It is a conditional promise to benefit parties if they respond in specified ways, especially akin to tax expenditures, procurement contracts, government insurance programs, and price supports. Second, like tax expenditures and government insurance programs, loan guarantees involve little or no immediate physical flow of federal money, unlike grants or other cash benefits that involve immediate government outlays. If money is ever paid out it is done at some future time and only on behalf of a portion of the beneficiaries aided, that is, for those who default. Thus, only administrative costs and default payments show up in the unified federal budget. Third, although a loan guarantee may avoid the need for government to spend its own money at the outset, it can potentially incur a sizable financial obligation. By lifting the risk of loss from the shoulders of lenders, guarantees may reduce normal pressures on them to act prudently and responsibly in awarding the loan (what economists call the "moral hazard" problem), thus exposing the government to more risk than otherwise would be the case. As a result, guarantees force government to take at least some interest in the behavior of lenders since it may affect whether government's financial liability materializes due to borrowers' default. Finally, notwithstanding program restrictions, a loan guarantee by its nature does not limit the lender to apply it to specific activities.

The second stimulus—the loan—is supposed to elicit action from the borrower to achieve the desired program goal. Again, the agency guarantor is compelled, if it wants its guarantee to succeed, to take a major interest in determining whether the lender's loan terms and servicing procedures will enable the borrower to achieve the agency's societal objectives and not threaten its financial interests. Since loans, too, are potentially fungible, the agency needs to have some means of ensuring that the borrower is using the loan money for the purposes intended by the program. Unlike many assistance programs, which involve a one-time, unilateral bestowal of benefits, loans create a long-term relationship between the government and the borrower through the lender. The repayment guarantee gives the sponsoring agency a long-term stake in the lender's initial judgment and in the borrower's progress in meeting the repayment schedule.

INDIRECT DELIVERY SYSTEM

A second salient feature of loan guarantees is their highly mediated delivery system. As we have seen, guarantees are heavily dependent on two intermediaries to achieve their results: the lender, as the source of credit financing and the administrator of loan recipient selection and loan account servicing; and the borrower, as the prime agent carrying out the substantive activity desired by government. The heavy involvement of lenders in loan financing and administration, and borrowers in project execution, makes loan guarantees similar to grants to state and local governments or to other "indirect" tools that work through more than one intermediary organization. It distinguishes loan guarantees sharply from more direct tools, such as income transfer payments or government-produced services that are carried out entirely by one level of government.

MARKET-ORIENTED INTERMEDIARIES

The specific type of intermediaries involved is also important. Dominant in the implementation of loan guarantees are actors who are highly responsive to the profit motive and the vicissitudes of the economic marketplace. Most lenders are private sector, profit-seeking organizations such as commercial banks, savings and loans, cooperatives, and development organizations. Others are private nonprofits (such as colleges and universities), or governmental organizations (such as the state government agencies that supply a large portion of guaranteed student loans, or the foreign central banks that are integral to AID's housing guarantee program in developing countries). Borrowers may be private for-profit or nonprofit organizations, private individuals, or public and quasi-public bodies. Even when not actually engaged in commercial activities these actors are highly responsive to market conditions.

ADMINISTERED PROCESSES

A fourth key feature of loan guarantees is their case-by-case procedures. Loan guarantee programs require procedural tasks particular to different lenders and different borrowers. Individual lenders must be certified to participate; particular borrowers must apply and be approved; specific loan contracts must be drawn up. Loan accounts must be serviced and monitored and in some cases repaid by the sponsoring agency. This highly individualized character distinguishes guarantees from formula grants, tax expenditures, income entitlements, and economic regulation because the administration of the latter tools is simplified through application of automatic formulas or a few rules that apply to large categories. Like project grants, social regulation, and some direct services, guarantees require intensive scrutiny and involvement by the sponsoring agency in the circumstances and operations of each aided party. As a result, loan guarantees can be especially complex and burdensome to administer when the number of participants is large. But case-by-case administration also gives guarantors the opportunity—if they have the desire and sufficient enforcement powers and resources—to exert fairly close control over individual program participants.

Major Tool Variations

Although the stimuli, highly mediated character, market-oriented implementers, and administered processes of loan guarantees set them off from other generic policy tools and help to account for common problems that guarantees encounter when put into effect, all loan guarantee programs do not operate precisely the same way. As illustrated by the increasing riskiness over time of the borrowers aided by this tool, guarantee programs vary in some important ways. Three differences most worthy of brief mention are portfolio size, loan terms, and financing.

PORTFOLIO SIZE

At one extreme are federal guarantee programs involving thousands or millions of outstanding loans to individual borrowers (such as homebuyers and small businesses). At the other extreme are the single guarantees of large entities such as New York City and Lockheed. Lying in between are guarantees that involve a handful or two of accounts (such as exporting and shipbuilding). Generally speaking, the larger the number of accounts in an agency's portfolio, the smaller the dollar amounts of particular loans. Other things being equal, these differences in program scale can affect the administrative burden the sponsoring agency faces and the administrative structure it develops, its capacity to exercise detailed oversight and comprehensive assistance to recipients, and the extent of risk it is exposed to with any one loan.

Governmental sponsors of programs providing large numbers of guaranteed loans tend to be regular federal departments or bureaus, such as the Department of Education or SBA. Since these multiple-guarantee programs have a huge, widely dispersed clientele, they need to operate through a large, decentralized network of regional and local offices. To handle this volume, they delegate considerable authority over loan marketing, analysis and approval of applications, and account servicing to field offices and participating lenders. As a result, scrutiny of loans is more routinized and can become less discerning. Also, a program's loan processing and portfolio monitoring will tend to be carried out through functionally distinct organizational units within the agency, which will make them less easily coordinated with other programs or forms of assistance an agency operates. But the extent of risk in any one loan account will be small.

Programs handling fewer discrete guarantees are more centralized. This lends itself to closer, more intricate communications between the sponsor, lender, and borrower, thus increasing the opportunity for more "directive" guarantee administration as well as the high potential for loss from any one venture. Most of the big, one-shot guarantees, such as that for Lockheed, have been administered by ad hoc government boards set up solely for that purpose and composed of the Treasury secretary and other high-level officials; those providing a small number of loans often are administered by special government corporations or boards such as the Synthetic Fuels Corporation and OPIC.

LOAN TERMS

All guarantee programs are aimed at recipients perceived as potentially able to repay a loan, but some of these clients come from economic strata or localities defined as relatively more disadvantaged in the general marketplace than others. Programs thus differ considerably in the extent to which they cushion the borrower from normal market practices and conditions. Interest rates may be preset by an agency; determined by an automatic formula, such as the Treasury's current borrowing costs; or left to individual negotiations between lenders and borrowers within some maximum. Also critical to many borrowers is the maturity period allowed for loan repayment. An obstacle for some lenders in providing regular commercial loans to certain borrowers has been the recipients' inability to repay loans quickly enough. Collateral may also be significant. Banks can require collateral in home mortgage guarantees because an asset exists which the lender or government guarantor could sell upon foreclosure; but collateral is not easy to establish, for example, for a student loan.

Programs differ also in the loan covenants or other restrictions governing how the borrower can spend the loan proceeds and whether the borrower must bring about major changes in its operations or organizations in order to qualify. A critical issue in large, single-venture guarantees, for example, is what the benefiting firms must provide in return for government help, such as the portion of future earnings that Chrysler had to pledge to the government.[17]

To the extent that programs provide interest rate subsidies, lenient maturity periods, and other subsidies to borrowers, they may have to add direct monetary incentives to the guarantee stimulus itself in order to induce lenders to participate. Lenders in the Guaranteed Student Loan Program (GSLP) are paid a small participation fee by the Department of Education. Another crucial issue for lenders is whether they can sell their guaranteed loans in secondary markets such as those created by the Student Loan Marketing Association (SLMA) and the Federal National Mortgage Association (FNMA). By transferring their loan assets to some other investor, lenders can increase liquidity to make additional loans and remove a long-term servicing burden.

FINANCING

Guarantee programs finance their administrative expenses and defaults differently, which affects the legal nature of their contingent liability. Some obligations are financed entirely from premiums or fees required from borrowers, who may be charged in proportion to an actuarially determined schedule of estimated risk. Accordingly, as under FHA's 203b Home Mortgage program and the Maritime Administration's Federal Ship Financing program, the government's default liability to lenders is limited strictly to the amount of reserve funds set up to cover losses from repayment claims. Other programs may charge such fees and have reserve funds for paying out claims, while receiving congressional appropriations, interfund transfers, or payments from the Federal Financing Bank (FFB) in order to cover default losses. The FFB sells Treasury notes and bonds for over 25 federal agencies. The Farmer's Home Administration, for one, replenishes its loan funds with funds from the FFB which, in exchange, receives shares in FmHA-held loan pools. Programs with access to such outside funding can back their loans with the "full faith and credit" of the United States government.

CONSEQUENCES OF USING GUARANTEES

How well does the performance of the loan guarantee stack up to against its proponents' claims that the tool produces intended social outcomes quickly and unobtrusively, at low cost, and with minimal undesirable side effects on the economy and society. This section draws on program evaluations and other empirical research that has examined the actual impact of loan guarantee programs. Loan guarantee performance is assessed under five criteria: implementability, effectiveness, efficiency, distributional impact, and macroeconomic impact.

Implementability

Implementability refers to the ease or difficulty with which programs using a certain tool can be set up and operated according to an intended plan. Many assume that loan guarantees are relatively easy to implement. Because loan guarantee administration makes extensive use of private lenders, sponsoring governments would seem to be relieved of the need to create a new delivery system and to recruit a staff with the requisite skills. This would limit start-up time and costs, extend the program's reach, and limit government's administrative burden of monitoring.

Apparently those who attribute these virtues to loan guarantees have not come to terms with the inherent complexity that characterizes this tool as a result of the many separate tasks and implementers involved. Three implementation problems have proved especially difficult.

INSUFFICIENT LENDER PARTICIPATION

Lenders are not only the major source of project financing but often the chief vehicle for publicizing a program to potential eligible borrowers, screening applications, and servicing loans. But evidence from several programs suggests that agencies often find it difficult to induce enough lenders to offer the volume of loans that agencies are authorized to guarantee. Even if adequate levels are reached in any one year, there is no assurance that a reliable flow of loans will continue in subsequent years.

The SBA's 7(a) Business Loan program illustrates this problem. Though lenders willing and deemed qualified by SBA standards to provide loans under a federal guarantee may sign participation agreements with the agency, merely enrolling the banks does not ensure they will offer many loans to SBA's clientele. While two-thirds of the nation's banks made at least one SBA-guaranteed loan sometime during the 1970s, for example, 79 percent made less than 10 loans over that entire period, with the most active lenders averaging only about 50 per year. Of the 446 banks in one survey, 86 percent had signed participation agreements, but 21 percent made no loans at all, 55 percent made between 1 and 10 loans per year, and only 10 percent made more than 25 loans a year.[18]

Thus, though some banks may make 25 to 50 SBA loans a year, the vast majority handles very few SBA loans at all. This constrains the number of loans SBA can provide and the geographic spread it can achieve. Because of these limited channels, a large number of small businesses potentially eligible for SBA-sponsored credit must spend a great deal of time and effort finding a lender willing to participate. In fact, GAO found that 29 percent of the businesses eventually receiving an SBA loan had to contact more than one bank to find one willing to consider an SBA guarantee and almost a third of these borrowers spent over two months in their search.[19]

Lenders have stayed out or withdrawn from guarantee programs because of financial disincentives, risks in lending to a particular clientele, and the administrative complexity and costs associated with government procedures. The main financial obstacles include ceilings on interest rates and loan size, and required maturity periods. SBA loans were not popular with bankers during much of the 1960s and 1970s, for example, because of limitations on interest rates and loan size and the long maturity periods small businesses require. Banks wanted to make larger loans, which generally involve lower-risk borrowers with maturities less than 7 to 10 years— the average SBA loan—since most bankers were used to 90 day commercial loans. Even with a guarantee, some lenders have been attitudinally averse to lending to certain types of clientele. A study of the FmHA Business and Industrial (B and I) Loan program, for example, found that lenders perceived guaranteed loans by definition as riskier, and were either unaware of how these loans could increase loan volume and liquidity through loan sales, or resistant to such sales.[20]

A third obstacle is the paperwork and time required to complete guaranteed loans compared to regular commercial loans. Seventy-two percent of nonparticipating banks and 35 percent of participating banks in one study stated that the time and administrative complexity required to prepare SBA applications and disburse loans were significant deterrents to their participation.[21] Analysts have also cited red tape as the reason housing and other guarantee programs have failed to reach desired levels of lender participation. Smaller banks, especially rural ones, are often ill equipped to assimilate FHA's bureaucratic requirements. FmHA's B & I program found that banks in rural areas, because of their small staffs, have particular difficulty with federal paperwork and lengthy application procedures—several days for a guaranteed loan, for instance, compared with a half-hour for the normal commercial loan. Redundant bureaucratic reviews were found to deter participants from the Department of Energy's Geothermal Energy Loan Guarantee program. And regarding the GSLP, the Congressional Budget Office once suggested that making parents rather than students the recipients might reduce administrative burdens as well as default risks and thus increase lenders' willingness to participate.[22]

To remedy the obstacles to lender participation, agencies have added financial inducements and tried to ease lenders' administrative burden. The GSLP added special payments to lenders in 1969 to increase the program's financial appeal, for example, and a secondary market was established under the Student Loan Marketing Association in 1972 to increase loan money liquidity. FHA's Section 236 and other mortgage guarantees provide interest rate subsidies on behalf of borrowers as well as Ginnie Mae loan purchases to increase lenders' liquidity. Efforts to increase lender participation by catering more to lender financial and administrative complaints—through devices such as "early maturities" programs, anti-paperwork campaigns, raising loan and interest rate ceilings, and preferred lenders' programs—have been a recurring theme in SBA annual reports since the early 1960s. Looking back on the many changes SBA made over the years, one experienced district administrator concluded, "We've adapted to what the bankers wanted."[23] But all these remedies can add significantly to a program's direct costs and the complexity of administering it at the agency level, thus vitiating some of the original rationale for using a loan guarantee.

In sum, reliance on lenders as a financial reservoir and prefabricated delivery system has not always resulted in high-volume, widely dispersed governmental assistance. To the contrary, enticing the commercial bank delivery system to act on the government's behalf may constitute one of the major implementation problems of this policy tool.

DELAYED AND FAULTY LOAN APPROVAL

Another purported advantage of guaranteed loans is that they reduce government processing time and administrative costs by tapping lenders' expert knowledge about potential borrowers. On this argument, government needs only to spot-check lender decisions. Evidence from several programs suggests, however, that excessive delays have occurred in the processing of loan applications even by agency standards, and further, that the quality of loan evaluations has been poor. Delays affect the willingness of lenders and borrowers to participate, as we have seen. Faulty loan evaluation also gives awards to poor risks that are likely to default, or wastes credit assistance on borrowers who are able to obtain private financing without government help or use the money for the wrong purposes.

GAO reports and internal audits refer consistently to the inordinate time SBA's 7(a) program requires to approve or reject an application. One study estimated the time needed from application submission to funds disbursal at almost four months. The estimates of commercial manuals aimed at helping applicants with their application vary between one month and three years. Other studies note chronic processing delays in the HUD and VA single-family mortgage insurance programs, and similar problems in FmHA's programs.[24]

A significant factor behind these delays is the lack of sufficient staff to review the volume of applications received. Staff in charge of the 7(a) program are also responsible for SBA's other financial assistance programs, resulting in high caseloads for the average SBA loan officer. Likewise, much of HUD's and VA's delays are attributed to insufficient staff during peak workload periods.[25]

Agencies have instituted changes aimed at speeding up loan approvals, such as simplifying application forms and assigning applications from particular banks to the same loan officer. GAO once suggested that SBA and FmHA should add staff. But even if they had been able to, this would have weakened the administrative case for loan guarantees. Another remedy is to delegate more authority over loan evaluation to lenders than already exists and confine agency involvement to the bare minimum. Under SBA's pilot Certified Lender program, a good deal of analysis once conducted by both SBA and the lender was delegated solely to the lender, and SBA claimed to have reduced its applicant review time to three days. Similar efforts have been going on at HUD and VA.[26]

Although some evidence suggests that giving lenders a bigger role in loan approvals speeds up loan processing and alleviates the portion of insufficient lender participation that is due to dislike of government red tape, this can also exacerbate the critical problem of faulty loan approvals. Processing delays apparently cannot be attributed merely to excessive caution by bank or agency loan officers because many programs have not reviewed applications adequately. Lenders have misapplied program standards regarding eligibility, need, and economic soundness; and agencies have failed to enforce these standards on lenders and even on themselves.

SBA's 7(a) loans, for example, are designed to enable healthy small businesses to expand their operations, not bail them out of previous debts. GAO, to the contrary, found that too many SBA loans were being used to pay off earlier obligations to the same bank arranging the guarantee, to other creditors, or for previous SBA loans. Similarly, one of FmHA guarantees' main deficiencies has been the approval of bail-out loans that merely refinance the debt of financially unsound businesses. Such agreements serve to reduce the lender's exposure to default risk and transfer it to the sponsoring government agency.[27] GAO also found many SBA loans were provided to borrowers with access to financing without a guarantee, either through personal assets or by using personal assets as collateral in applying for a commercial loan. SBA loan officers apparently failed to examine applications thoroughly for usable alternative resources.[28]

SBA and FmHA also have been criticized for not analyzing the economic soundness of applicants.[29] Some of the faulty loan approval problem is due to the lack of sufficient staff, but one needs to look as well at the incentives and behavior of participating lenders, and the problem of "moral hazard." Agency sponsors rely heavily on lenders to gather and assess a great deal of essential information bearing on the appropriateness of the borrower's purpose, the need for the loan, and the risks of providing it. But since an agency's guarantee shields the lender from the risk of financial loss, there is less incentive than with normal commercial loans to discriminate creditworthy from risky applicants; whether the borrower repays the loan or defaults, the lender's returns may be approximately the same.

Another cause of faulty loan approvals is the failure of sponsoring agencies to enforce their own regulations on the lender or themselves. Some of this may be due to insufficient or poorly trained staff. But a more fundamental cause is lack of sufficient effort to work out clear, consistent criteria and procedures in the first place. Surveys of the management practices of federal guarantee agencies found many with vague borrower evaluation criteria, no formalized risk assessment standards and procedures, and little systematic capacity to anticipate loan problems.[30] The motivation of agencies mandated to improve the well-being of its clientele, such as SBA, may be more powerful than the competing incentive to "protect the financial interests of the United States." Though agencies may lack sufficient personnel to do thorough reviews of their awards, they also have insufficient constraints on them to worry a great deal about the proportion of their portfolios in inappropriate or unnecessarily risky awards. The chief criterion by which they judge themselves and are most often judged by Congress and incumbent administrations is whether they assist as many small businesses, students, or others as possible.

INATTENTIVE PORTFOLIO MANAGEMENT

Beyond the problems with initial awards, considerable evidence also suggests that lenders and agencies give low priority to the loan servicing tasks—collecting repayments when due, monitoring accounts for delinquencies and potential defaults, ensuring proper completion of assisted projects, assisting "problem loans" in meeting their obligations, and expediting foreclosure on defaulted accounts. Lenders have little incentive to follow through on guarantee awards in order to ensure loan repayment and project completion because their potential losses are small. If lenders often behave as if they have little at stake in the successful outcome of a project, agencies often appear primarily interested in spreading program benefits, even if this requires sacrificing federal purposes and financial interests.

If potential defaults are to be headed off by adjusting repayment schedules or providing other assistance, agencies must know which accounts are in trouble. But lenders, the agencies, and other participants have often been lax in overseeing their accounts. Much of the high default rate in the guaranteed student loan program has been attributed to the lack of strong incentives on the part of educational institutions and commercial lenders to keep track of the payment standing of the large number of students served. Debtors' addresses were lost, students were never informed of their obligations, and so on. For its part, the Department of Education failed to maintain an adequate computer information system for monitoring lenders' loan servicing and keeping on top of borrowers' progress.[31] Lenders in FmHA, SBA, MARAD, and AID programs also have failed to notify the agency of such problems, and GAO advised these agencies to establish better information management systems to keep closer tabs on their portfolios. Overall, few federal guarantee agencies have mechanisms and clear standards for defining, identifying, and dealing with delinquent loans or do not analyze default patterns.[32]

Another problem has been failure of lenders or other intermediaries to ensure that the substantive activities or projects financed by the loans have been carried out in accordance with program objectives and loan covenants. The GSLP, for example, has had difficulty enforcing meaningful standards of academic progress on aided students, so that money has continued to go out to many students who were no longer progressing toward their degrees. FmHA's programs also failed to follow up on projects to ensure that loan terms were being complied with, the project was being carried out as agreed, and the agency was providing all the management assistance it could to borrowers.[33]

Where defaults are inevitable, lenders and agencies have acted improperly or slowly in liquidating collateral to recoup the maximum from default losses. AID has paid default claims without adequate documentation, for example, and some AID host-country banks helped deplete the guarantee funds under their charge by deciding not to liquidate collateral from defaulted borrowers until economic conditions improved. The Maritime Administration suffered severe financial losses in part because bankruptcy laws put other creditors ahead of the government in the queue to receive compensation from bankrupt shipbuilders' assets. SBA also has lost money because it failed to enforce its collateral management procedures.[34]

Effectiveness

Effectiveness refers to the extent loan guarantees produce their intended results in society. Since guarantees seek, first, to induce loans, and loans are then expected to produce a social impact, effectiveness can be measured in two ways, at two points in program operation. The first looks at whether loan guarantees increase the actual amount of loan money made available for the particular activities promoted by guarantees. The second asks whether the loans supplied actually result in the social or economic benefits, primary or secondary, that are supposed to flow from them. Because of the potential fungibility of both guarantees and loans, it is critical to examine both of these performance measures.

The absolute number of loans that federal guarantees have stimulated over the years, particularly in housing and student loan programs, has been huge. But a more meaningful measure of loan production than aggregate volume is whether guarantees lead to a net increase in the credit made available in a given sector—that is, over and above what would have been provided by lenders even without a federal guarantee. Unfortunately the answer to this question is unclear.

Some studies have found guarantees to have almost no effect on net credit, whereas others have found the net effect to be significant despite some degree of substitution for private loans.[35]

The extent to which guarantee programs displace or add to net lending in a sector may depend greatly on how much lending is already occurring there. Substitution cannot occur where alternative sources of credit do not exist; thus, programs for persons or areas of low economic status or for high-risk ventures are more immune to substitution effects than others.[36] A similar argument holds that guarantees can be very successful in expanding net credit supply in areas where lenders have not operated because they have had little knowledge of likely default probabilities—the "market-perfecting" type of guarantee. Lenders may be discouraged from gathering that information through experimenting with high-risk loans because there is no financial gain from it or government regulations bar it. In these instances, guarantees are effective because of the "demonstration effect," through which government shows lenders that reasonable profits can be made in areas they have neglected, thus leading them to expand their lending into these areas.[37]

Substitution may also be minimized wherever particular program standards, such as EDA's "lender of last resort" restriction, require applicants to document that they have exhausted existing credit sources before turning to federal help. Thus bureaucratic rules may reduce guarantee fungibility. The effect of such standards depends of course on whether the staffs of guarantee programs are able to apply such "no credit elsewhere" standards rigorously and consistently.[38]

But guarantees are not aimed simply at generating loans. Ultimately they are expected to achieve the programs' objectives through the production of goods or resources the loans finance: housing units, business firm relocation decisions, jobs, expanded local tax bases, and increased income levels. The case for the ultimate effectiveness of guarantees in addressing problems is also mixed.

Studies examining primary and secondary impacts have been positive. A study of AID's housing guarantee, for example, concludes that it is likely to have a substantial impact on jobs and income both directly because of housing construction and indirectly because of housing-related spending on consumer goods such as house furnishings. Expenditures for new housing in developing countries have generated a total output double the initial outlay. Housing programs also improve long-term labor productivity through improved health.[39]

But other studies point to several ways in which guarantees are prone to ineffectiveness. One pitfall is the difficulty of determining whether a certain kind or level of guarantee is the proper incentive given prevailing economic conditions. In some cases, guarantees have been a tempting, ready-at-hand solution even where it is unclear that capital infusion is an appropriate or adequate remedy. Guarantees may fail to encourage synfuels production significantly, for example, because the problem of nonproduction is not lack of capital but competition from cheaper energy sources. What may really be needed is a purchase guarantee.[40] Guarantees for electric and hybrid vehicles have been assessed as inappropriate for stimulating that technology because the federal ceiling on the amount of the loans is too low.[41]

Ineffectiveness also arises out of the fungibility of guarantees. Stories about students using their loans to buy stereo equipment are only the better-known examples of how lenders and guaranteeing agencies have little control over the specific uses of loan proceeds. Students receiving guaranteed loans have continued to receive loans even though they were no longer moving steadily toward their degrees, and the Department of Education has had difficulty getting universities to establish and enforce specific definitions of academic progress for loan eligibility purposes.[42] Up to 30 percent of FmHA guarantees were used for debt restructuring and transfer of ownership, which do not necessarily lead to new investment.[43]

A third source of skepticism over the effectiveness of loan guarantees arises from their poor coordination with other programs. Loan guarantees, tax expenditures, and other federal and state programs for urban areas that use private intermediaries have been found to be poorly coordinated with social service programs operating through city governments. One reason may be that local business communities benefiting directly from a federal economic development programs perceive other federal programs such as employment training as "welfare." In other words, federal programs using different tools are seen as serving different groups of clients and different objectives. The small amounts of federal assistance that flow directly to local businesses may provide insufficient justification for federal officials to enforce local cooperation and coordination between them and other federal initiatives. The orientation of guarantees toward discrete projects may also contribute to lack of coordination.[44] Serious limitations on effectiveness may result when a program aimed at a complex societal or economic problem is organized around an intervention mechanism that is primarily financial and is implemented through financial intermediaries.

Efficiency

Efficiency is measured by the ratio of a program's production of desired results to its costs. A chief advantage claimed for loan guarantees is that, because they involve private financing and administration, their costs to government are extremely low, comprising mainly a few default payments; and that they operate in an efficient, businesslike manner. The available evidence suggests that this image is overdrawn. While loan guarantees generally appear to be somewhat more cost-effective compared to other tools used for similar purposes, they are less efficient than is widely assumed because of a number of subsidies and other costs that are not always recognized and have been little studied. Due to needed subsidies, moreover, cost-effectiveness of loan guarantees declines to the extent the tool is used to serve financially less-advantaged people or areas.

One way to measure efficiency is to look at the total costs to government of producing a given number of the expected outputs of a program, such as jobs or housing units. For example, CBO examined direct outlays and indirect costs over five years of serving an additional 100,000 households through several alternative housing finance mechanisms. FHA's Section 236 Mortgage Guarantee program was found to require less than half as much in budget and tax expenditures to serve the same number of households as public housing. Another cost analysis compared the total average monthly costs in 1970 of producing a two-bedroom unit in 15 sampled projects in Boston under public housing and a rent supplement program utilizing Section 236 financing. Once again the cost of public housing exceeded that of the other alternative.[45]

But cost-effectiveness depends also on the nature of the clientele served. When FHA mortgage guarantee costs are compared with public housing with respect to serving low-income people, the results are reversed. In a comparison of conventional public housing and Section 236, GAO calculated the annual discounted cost over 20 years of producing and maintaining a two-bedroom unit for a family of four with an annual income of $4,250. Despite the fact that GAO purposely overstated its cost estimate for public housing, public housing was found to cost between $100 and $435 less annually than the Section 236 loan guarantee program. The mortgage guarantee was found to be more expensive largely because it entailed higher annual debt service payments and local exemptions from property taxes. Section 236 also incurred considerable expense due to the subsidy involved in GNMA secondary market purchases. Other housing program comparisons have produced similar results.[46]

A number of factors not widely recognized add to guarantee

costs. First, the default rate on many programs is quite high. This has been true in recent years in the GSLP program, SBA's loan program, and certain AID projects. In some cases such as synfuels production, default rates may have made the program costlier than alternative subsidies. But considerable variation in default rates exists across guarantees: programs run on an actuarially sound principle that go to low-risk clientele are less prone to default than are subsidized guarantees that go to higher-risk groups. When FHA began to go into inner-city areas to serve higher-risk groups in the 1960s, for example, deficits appeared in its reserve funds for the first time.[47]

Second, many direct and indirect costs to government are built into loan guarantee programs. As we have seen, loan guarantees often involve direct outlays, tax expenditures, or other subsidies that are needed to provide lenders, project sponsors, and other intermediaries sufficient financial incentive to get involved in loan guarantee implementation. Among direct payments, for example, the GSLP pays lenders a monthly participation fee, the Section 236 mortgage guarantee pays lenders an interest rate subsidy on behalf of housing sponsors to make units affordable to lower-income tenants, and Section 236 and other mortgage programs operate in conjunction with rent supplements to enable low-income persons to reside in assisted projects.[48]

Certain hidden costs both to government and borrowers also arise because a large number of loan brokers and other parties are involved in loan guarantee implementation. Payments that drive up total costs and increase inefficiency can go to: (a) lenders in the form of excessive origination fees and favorable secondary market sales whose proceeds are not passed on to borrowers; (b) loan packagers and consultants in fees for preparing loan documents and serving as go-betweens among lenders, borrowers, and federal agencies; (c) brokers in fees for arranging secondary market sales; (d) secondary market investors who purchase guaranteed loans at premium rates; or (e) servicing agencies that manage the loans on behalf of secondary market purchasers. A study of the various fees of this sort that may be charged legally by loan consultants and lenders in FmHA's B & I program goes so far as to conclude that "lenders and purchasers have been utilizing the present regulations as a vehicle for undue profit taking."[49]

In sum, largely because of the highly mediated nature of loan guarantees, to assess their efficiency one needs to look not only at the federal government's direct outlays for administration and default payments, but also at such ancillary inducements and benefits as interest payments to lenders, rent supplements, revenue losses to federal and local governments due to tax write-offs, the cost of secondary market purchases, and loan broker fees. Taking into account all these cost sources, it is less surprising that many loan guarantees are only slightly more cost-effective than alternative mechanisms or may even be less cost-effective than other options.

Distributional Impact

Another important criterion for evaluating guarantees is how they distribute their benefits among different socioeconomic categories such as income groups, communities, and racial and ethnic groups.

The evidence suggests that beneficiaries of guarantee programs generally come from middle and lower middle economic strata; comfortably well-off groups on the one hand, and poor social groups on the other hand, are not much helped. This is not surprising since most guarantees are intended by design to serve relatively high-risk activities or groups that private sources of credit have failed to serve, but only where there is a reasonable assurance of repayment. In many guarantees, normal lender "bankability" criteria apply and actuarial principles are used to finance the program. Thus applicants perceived as low risks within the eligible category will benefit. Because lenders view low-income people or firms as high risks and possibly unable to pay loan installments, such recipients will be passed over in favor of lower-risk groups. Highly subsidized guarantees have been aimed at relatively less-advantaged groups but not the poor.

Looking first at impacts on income distribution, we find that most home buyers in the original FHA and VA mortgage programs, for example, came from moderate income brackets. In 1970, two-thirds of the homes insured under FHA's basic program ranged from $12,000 to $25,000. Similarly, student loan guarantees have gone mainly to the middle class, and increasingly so as Congress has raised the income ceiling defining eligibility in recent years. Comparing guaranteed loans to student aid grants, one study finds 94 percent of the benefits of the Pell direct grant program went to students in families with incomes below $15,000, whereas only 63 percent of guaranteed loan dollars went to this group.[50]

But not all guarantees are directed at borrowers with middle or moderate incomes; some are explicitly designed to serve primarily low-income persons or communities, although not the very poorest. Several FHA mortgage guarantee programs were started in the 1950s and 1960s in order to increase access to homeownership or apartments by low-income persons or persons living in declining urban neighborhoods. For example, the income of tenants in HUD's Section 236 mortgage guarantee and interest subsidy program for low- and moderate-income persons was $6,285 in 1977, when the median income of public housing tenants was $3,691.[51] But guarantee programs with less stringent financial risk criteria and explicit requirements to target loans to low-income recipients or areas have had to add interest rate subsidies, rent supplements, secondary market purchasing, and various tax incentives on the basic loan guarantee in order to enable these programs to reach lower-income persons.

A similar pattern is seen when looking at the distribution of guaranteed loans between richer and poorer communities as measured by urban/rural and central-city/suburb distinctions. A study of an FHA unsubsidized multifamily mortgage guarantee, for example, indicates that in 1972, 95 percent of the supported units were built within metropolitan areas (Standard Metropolitan Statistical Areas—SMSAs) while only 5 percent were outside metropolitan areas. Within the SMSAs, however, only about 27 percent were built within the central cities. While the FHA building pattern followed quite closely the urban-rural distribution of all U.S. housing units in 1970 (92 percent in SMSAs; 8.4 percent outside SMSAs), FHA favored the suburbs more than would be expected by looking at non-FHA housing distribution (only 20 percent of all units outside the central city, 72 percent inside).[52]

Among loan guarantees designed to help develop local economies, the effort to favor less well-off communities seems more evident. One study of EDA and FmHA business guarantees showed that from 1976 to 1980 72 percent of the aid provided by the former and 53 percent of the latter went to counties meeting criteria indicating economic distress such as population loss or unemployment.[53]

Data on the impact of loan guarantees on the distribution of advantages among racial groups are sketchy, but some are available for FHA mortgage guarantees. Not surprisingly, the extent to which minorities benefit varies, depending on whether the mortgage guarantees are subsidized or unsubsidized. A study of two unsubsidized guarantees indicated that around 85 percent of the housing units were occupied by white households and only 15 percent by blacks or any other minorities in 1972–73, and concluded that blacks were greatly underrepresented in proportion to their numbers in the population. But the housing occupants in two subsidized FHA mortgage programs were 66 percent to 76 percent white and 34 percent to 35 percent nonwhite.[54]

A related concern is whether FHA-insured mortgages have discriminated against blacks or other minorities by following lending institutions in their alleged discrimination against inner-city minority neighborhoods—"redlining." Considerable research has sought to determine the extent of lender redlining and FHA's possible role in it. The consensus of recent studies seems to be that although conclusive evidence on the existence of lender redlining cannot be found, if redlining does exist, FHA guarantees have not reinforced it. In fact, FHA may have had some impact in counteracting it, and in any case has played a role in encouraging movement of minorities into white neighborhoods. Specifically, FHA mortgages have been found most prevalent in low-income, minority-dominated neighborhoods with low housing prices, in areas allegedly redlined, and in "border" areas undergoing racial transition from whites to minorities. Lenders apparently substitute FHA-insured mortgages for conventional loans when lending to moderate-income households in racial-transition areas. Although some experts believe FHA may have perpetrated neighborhood segregation patterns in the past, changes in FHA lending criteria during the 1960s and the advent of more subsidized mortgage guarantees may have made it possible for many lenders to offer mortgages in inner-city areas where they ordinarily would not be active. The change in FHA's objectives in the 1960s resulted in high default rates in the mid–1970s, however, causing net losses in FHA funds.[55]

In short, guarantees by design are aimed at the broad middle of the socioeconomic strata; none seeks to aid what ordinarily would be considered the poorest income groups or communities. But where program rules encourage take-up by the upper levels within the middle band (as in student loans), guarantees exacerbate existing societal inequalities. Where lower levels within the middle band are targeted by the program design (such as in subsidized housing), guarantees can help to offset these inequalities.

Macroeconomic Impact

Another major concern about guarantee programs has been how the whole system of federal guarantees, and the interaction between it and other federal policies, may affect national economic growth, productivity, and economic stabilization.

Aggregate studies that have sought to detect whether federal credit programs (including direct loans and secondary market purchases as well as loan guarantees) have had any measurable effect in boosting the gross national product are not encouraging. According to one review, early studies found mildly positive, noninflationary impacts on national income in only some years within the several decades that were examined.[56]

While the studies of the early years revealed only occasional positive effects before the 1960s, however, they provide some grounds for expecting a growing impact since the volume of federal credit itself grew after that. But more recent simulations of the longer-term reactions of financial markets to the federal presence and the effects of a changing money supply in offsetting the federal credit impact suggest that while federal credit may have strong immediate effects on GNP, these are dissipated within a few years, so there is no long-term net impact.[57]

One way loan guarantees might have a lasting impact on economic growth is through the stimulation of financial or technological innovations that increase economic productivity. Although no comprehensive assessment has been done of the impact of loan guarantees or all federal credit on overall national economic efficiency, some analysts believe such institutional and technological innovations may be the major contribution loan guarantees and other federal credit programs make to a productive economy.[58]

GETTING A HANDLE ON THE TOOL:
LOAN GUARANTEE REFORM

The rapid rise in federal loan guarantee obligations, the sense that guarantees were spreading into too many new areas and being transformed in the process, stories about high defaults and uncollected debt in student loan and other big guarantee programs, the suspicion that guarantees may have pernicious if unknown effects in allocating resources in the national economy, and spreading uneasiness that guarantees were subject to little monitoring and fiscal discipline—all these factors combined in the late 1970s to stimulate a much greater effort within the federal government to learn more about loan guarantees and impose some control over them.

This effort was instigated mainly by analytical oversight agencies such as the Council of Economic Advisers (CEA) and OMB in the executive branch and the Congressional Research Service (CRS) and GAO on the congressional side, but included certain congressional committees as well.

The earliest reform efforts sought simply to identify the number of existing guarantee programs and to describe their programmatic variety, as a growing company of agencies were seen adapting the tool to their particular needs. This led to a tacit consensus that the administration and control of loan programs had to be reformed.

One major response to the consensus has been an effort to make the total costs of loan guarantees more visible to Congress in the course of the regular budget authorization process. Some advocated doing this by listing the total volume of off-budget, contingent liabilities from guaranteed loans within the unified budget as budget authorizations, including not only direct outlays like administrative costs and defaults but also total loan principal. A related approach was to provide a separate credit budget, which was done by the Carter administration in 1980 and has continued each year since. In 1985, the Gramm-Rudman-Hollings Act also placed the obligations being incurred by the off-budget Federal Financing Bank into the unified budget for the first time. An alternative was to indicate solely the cost of the subsidies entailed in those guarantee programs that fail to pay their own way, and these subsidy costs now also appear in the annual federal budget presented to Congress.

A second strategy for dealing with loan guarantee problems seeks more rigor and efficiency in the standards, criteria, and procedures that govern loan making and servicing by individual guarantee-sponsoring agencies. OMB had not released any circulars on credit management issues since 1965, but released two in 1985 and 1986 in order to impose more uniformity on federal agency credit practices, such as in reporting liabilities, estimating risk, servicing accounts, and writing off uncollectible debts. Changes have also been advocated to raise borrowers' fees, require agencies to hold reserves at a proportion of estimated default levels, tighten up credit needs tests, require coinsurance by lenders, employ variable interest rates across different borrowers based on the extent of risk, and require equity participation in assisted projects on the part of the borrower.

Following the passage of the Debt Collection Act of 1982, the Reagan administration also launched a major effort to ascertain and collect the large amount of debt that was owed the federal government by student borrowers and others under guaranteed and direct loan programs, and a proposal was even advanced that would have created a new, separate federal credit agency that would have centralized federal credit management and debt collection. The administration also sought to lower levels of borrowing authority for individual agencies, especially in housing, business assistance, and foreign credit assistance. As the budget deficit increased, the Reagan administration also proposed savings through selling off the loan portfolios of longstanding agencies such as SBA.

<hr>

CONCLUSION: IMAGE AND REALITY IN LOAN GUARANTEES

This effort to put loan guarantees in clearer relief has suggested that a significant gap exists between the image loan guarantees project in the public arena and the administrative realities and impacts they display in actual operation.

Part of this gap results from the fact that the operational implications of the loan guarantee instrument have not been examined closely. Although some are widely understood, the instrument's generic features often produce results contrary to conventional expectations. Against the notion that loan guarantees can quickly and unobtrusively disperse assistance due to the private lender role, for example, many programs have experienced a take-up problem. Guaranteed loans often require special handling, considerable lender patience, different rules, and time-consuming forms. Furthermore, contrary to the notion that loan guarantees impose only administrative costs on government, in practice many entail a variety of direct payments or indirect subsidies before private lenders will participate at all.

The gap between image and reality also results from lack of awareness that, beyond the basic components, loan guarantee programs have increasingly differed from one another in significant ways in programmatic content, such as loan terms and program financing. Although the early FHA guarantee was adopted as a "prototype" and applied to a large number of new and different social problems, with each new application the particular mix of incentives and regulations that made up the tool's design deviated further from the original model. These variations in the rules have corresponding effects on the guarantees' effectiveness, costs, distributional effects, and economic impacts.

The conclusion that emerges is that because of the number of steps they require, the diverse governmental and nongovernmental actors that must interact to carry them out, and the multitude of purposes and types of clientele they now serve, loan guarantees are actually one of the most complex and diversified tools in the federal repertoire. The loan guarantee is not a single tool at all or if it is, it is wobbly and flexible and can be shifted about to serve differing purposes and groups. When it comes to operational realities, we are dealing with at least three different tools or variations of guarantees, which we might call the "FHA-type guarantee," the "SBA-type guarantee," and the "Chrysler-type guarantee."

The variants within guarantees occupy a wide territory of governmental activity, ranging between market exchange processes at one end and unilateral welfare on the other. Some guarantees resemble market-responsive institutions and processes so much that they may raise the question of why government is involved at all; others involve so much government bureaucracy and costs, one might wonder why direct government provision or a grant is not a better alternative. But this variety and the flexible application of the tool have flourished under the cover of a broad mythology that is responsive to the American political culture—that guarantees are not really governmental and do not cost much, because only the capable are helped and the loans get repaid.

Given the pressures likely to continue on the federal budget for the foreseeable future, loan guarantees will retain a great deal of appeal. What is the best response to this situation? There *is* a realm of potentially beneficial activity existing between the market and welfare that government legitimately can continue to explore. Rather than uncritical championing in the public arena of the loan guarantee tool as an easy solution to new problems, at one extreme, or wholesale efforts during the budget process to curtail all guarantees, at the other, more attention needs to be paid at the microlevel of program design and administration, to matching the tool's variants to the particular objectives one wishes to achieve—with full recognition of resulting trade-offs. If maximum net credit is sought for a functional purpose, for example, the existence of private sector provision and the nature of private incentive have to be analyzed and continuously monitored, and program eligibility has to be targeted and tightly enforced, requiring bureaucracy. If efficiency is wanted, expectations of redistribution must be modest and benefit "leakage" to various intermediaries must be plugged. If greater equality is sought, eligibility has to be restricted, and government must be prepared for high subsidy costs, and so on.

This makes it all the more important to understand the actual operations of loan guarantee programs. To ensure the tool can be useful, care must still be taken to make sure it is put to use in circumstances for which it is truly suited.

Notes

1. A congressional effort to identify all federal loan guarantee programs lists 132 authorized in 1981. In the following year, a General Accounting Office (GAO) study discovered 116. See U.S. Congress Committee on Banking, Finance and Urban Affairs, *Catalog of Federal Loan Guarantee Programs* (Washington, D.C. 1982); and GAO, *Catalog of Federal Credit Programs and Their Interest Rate Provisions* (Washington, D.C.: GAO, 1982).

2. When bail-outs were proposed to Chrysler and other large, potentially bankrupt corporations and public entities in the 1970s, for example, proponents sought to win political support by arguing that guarantees do not add a dime to federal expenditures. See GAO, *Guidelines for Rescuing Failing Firms and Municipalities* (Washington, D.C.: GAO, 1984), 36; Robert B. Reich and John D. Donahue, *New Deals: The Chrysler Revival and the American System* (New York: Times Books, 1985), 120.

As concern has risen more recently over economic decline and the competitiveness of American industry, both liberals and conservatives have argued that the nation should move beyond ad hoc bail-outs to a more explicit, permanent industrial policy, and loan guarantees have been among the policy tools mentioned in such proposals. Recent proposals for loan guarantees as part of a long-term industrial strategy can be found, for example, in Ira Magaziner and Robert B. Reich, *Minding American's Business* (New York: Harcourt Brace Jovanovich, 1982); Kevin B. Phillips, *Staying on Top: The Business Case for a National Industrial Strategy* (New York: Random House, 1984); Democratic Caucus, U.S. Congress, Special Task Force on Long-Term Economic Policy, *Rebuilding the Road to Opportunity* (September 1982); and Gary Hart, *A New Democracy* (New York: Quill Press, 1983).

3. As part of their own "industrial policies," at least 19 states offered loan guarantees to promote business expansion as of 1984. See Council of State Governments, *The Book of the States, 1984–85*, vol. 25 (Lexington, Ky.: Council of State Governments, 1984), 442f. See, also, National Association of State Development Agencies (NASDA), *An Analysis of Innovative State Economic Development Financing Programs* (Washington, D.C.: NASDA, 1985), 54.

4. Salamon includes loan guarantees among the unconventional federal policy tools coming into greater use that work through administration by nonfederal actors. See "Rethinking Public Management: Third-Party Government and the Changing Forms of Government Action," *Public Policy* 29 (Spring 1981): 255–75. See also Frederick C. Mosher, "The Changing Responsibilities and Tactics of the Federal Government," *Public Administration Review* 40 (November/December 1980): 541–48; and Murray Weidenbaum, *The Modern Public Sector: New Ways of Doing the Government's Business* (New York: Basic Books, 1969). For broader analyses viewing loan guarantees as an emerging vehicle for eliminating risk for major social institutions, see Theodore Lowi, *The End of Liberalism*, 2d ed. (New York: W.W. Norton and Company, 1979): 279–92;

and Yair Aharoni, *The No-Risk Society* (Chatham, N.J.: Chatham House Publishers, 1981).

5. Harold C. Krogh, "Guarantees Against Loss to Transnational Corporations," in Annals of the American Academy of Political and Social Science, *Risk and Its Treatment: Changing Societal Consequences* 443 (May 1979), 120.

6. See John R. Kaatz and Fred A. Taysley, Jr., "The Lending Policies of Banks in Nonmetropolitan Areas and the Implications for Local Economic Development," *The Review of Regional Studies* 2, no. 2 (Winter 1972–73), 42; John A. Tuccillo, "Federal Regulations, Housing Programs, and the Flow of Urban Credit," (Washington, D.C.: Urban Institute Press, 1980), 4.

7. Bruce MacLaury, "Federal Credit Programs—The Issues They Raise," in Federal Reserve Bank of Boston, Conference Series no. 10, *Issues in Federal Debt Management* (Boston: Federal Reserve Bank of Boston, 1973), 211–14; See, also, U.S. Congressional Budget Office (CBO), *Loan Guarantees: Current Concerns and Alternatives for Control* (Washington, D.C.: CBO, 1978), 17.

8. CBO, *Loan Guarantees*, xii

9. For an illustration, see John F. Berry, "Ex-Im Financing Becoming Classic Off-Budget Case," *Washington Post*, September 14, 1980, F1.

10. Howard Kurtz, "Industry Factions Protect Their Turfs," *Washington Post*, July 18, 1985, A1 and A16.

11. Reich and Donahue, *New Deals*, 116.

12. Ward Sinclair, "Fish Industry Nets New Help," *Washington Post*, October 16, 1984, A4.

13. Loan guarantee politics thus reflect the pattern described by James Q. Wilson as "client politics," where the "benefits of a prospective policy are concentrated but the costs widely distributed." See James Q. Wilson, ed., *The Politics of Regulation* (New York: Basic Books, 1980), 369f.

14. CBO, "Federal Credit Programs: A Statistical Compilation," in *Loan Guarantees: Current Concerns and Alternatives in Capital* (Washington, D.C.: CBO, 1979), 27; CBO, *An Analysis of the President's Credit Budget in Fiscal Year 1985*, Staff Working Paper, March 1984, 5; CBO, *An Analysis of the President's Credit Budget for Fiscal Year 1986*, Spring 1985, 20–25.

15. John Mitrisin, "Federal Loan Guarantees and Their Use as a Mechanism to Correct Market Imperfections, Assist Marginal Borrowers, and Finance Discrete Ventures," Congressional Research Service, April 27, 1977.

16. See, for example, statement by Rep. William S. Moorhead (D–Pa.), in *Loan Guarantees and Off-Budget Financing*, hearing before the Subcommittee on Economic Stabilization of the Committee on Banking, Currency, and Housing (November 10, 1979), 2, quoted in CBO, *Loan Guarantees*, 16f.

17. John Brooks, "The Kicker," *New Yorker*, January 7, 1985, 44–58.

18. U.S. Comptroller General, *SBA's Pilot Programs to Improve Guaranty Loan Procedures Need Further Development* (Washington, D.C.: GAO, 1981), 18–19.

19. U.S. Comptroller General, *SBA's Pilot Programs:* 18–22. Similar problems are reported in other programs. Despite the large number of students aided by the GSLP, for example, banks in the past have not provided the total number of student loans that Congress has made it possible to offer through guarantees. CBO, *Federal Aid to Post Secondary Students: Tax Allowances and Alternative Subsidies* (Washington, D.C., January 1978), 45.

20. Coopers and Lybrand, *Assessment of Developmental and Operating Aspects of Farmers Home Administration Business and Industrial Loan Program*, Pilot Study Report submitted to U.S. Department of Agriculture, May 28, 1980, VI–19.

21. U.S. Comptroller General, *SBA's Pilot Program*, 16.

22. J.R. Kaatz and F.A. Tarpley, "The Lending Policies of Banks in Nonmetropolitan Areas," 42; Coopers and Lybrand, *Assessment*, VI–25; U.S. Comptroller General, *The Geothermal Loan Guarantee Program: Need for Improvements*, January 24, 1980, 11; CBO, *Federal Aid*, 48f.

23. Interview, Small Business Administration, October 31, 1983, Washington, D.C. District Office.

24. U.S. Comptroller General, *SBA's Pilot Program*, 12; Rich Stephan Hayes and John Cotton Howell, *How to Finance Your Small Business with Government Money: SBA Loans*, 1977, 36–38; and 1980, 26; Henry Wickmann, Jr., "Guidelines for Obtaining an SBA Business Loan," *Journal of Small Business Management* (April, 1979), 43; U.S. Comptroller General, *VA and HUD Can Improve Service and Reduce Processing Costs in Insuring Home Mortgage Loans* (Washington, D.C.: GAO, 1982), 9; U.S. Comptroller General, *Farmers Home Administration's Business and Industrial Loan Program Can Be Improved* (Washington, D.C.: GAO, 1977), 19f.

25. U.S. Comptroller General, *VA and HUD*, 9

26. U.S. Comptroller General, *SBA's Certified Lenders Program Falls Short of Expectations* (Washington, D.C.: GAO, 1983), 16f; U.S. Comptroller General, *VA and HUD*, 5–12.

27. U.S. Comptroller General, *Efforts to Improve Management of the Small Business Administration Have Been Unsatisfactory—More Aggressive Action Needed* (Washington, D.C.: GAO, 1979), 9–15; U.S. Comptroller General, *Summary of Major Deficiencies in the Farmers Home Administration's Business and Industrial Loan Program*, letter to Senator Roger N. Jepsen (R-Iowa), January 30, 1981, 5.

28. U.S. Comptroller General, *The Small Business Administration Needs to Improve Its 7(a) Loan Program* (Washington, D.C.: GAO, 1976), 21–24; U.S. Comptroller General, *Efforts to Improve Management*, 14–15.

29. U.S. Comptroller General, *The Small Business Administration Needs*, 27; U.S. Comptroller General, *Efforts to Improve Management*, 16–17. On FmHA, see U. S. Comptroller General, *Farmers Home Administration's Business*, 21–31; and U.S. Comptroller General, *Summary of Major Deficiencies*, 3–5.

30. Peat, Marwick, Mitchell, & Co., *Loan Insurance and Guarantee Programs: A Comparison of Current Practices and Procedures*, Final Report, prepared for the CBO (Washington, D.C.: Peat Marwick, Mitchell & Co., 1978), 173f and 256f, in CBO, *Loan Guarantees: Current Concerns and Alternatives for Control*, A compilation of staff working papers (Washington, D.C.: CBO, 1979); McManis and Associates, *Government-Wide Standards for Credit Allocation, Risk Analysis, and Loan Write-Off Policies and Procedures*, Report to U.S. Department of Treasury (Washington, D.C.: McManis and Associates, 1984), 23f and 39f.

31. CBO, *Federal Student Assistance: Issues and Options* (Washington, D.C.: CBO, 1981), 42; GAO, "Certain GAO Reports Concerning Federal Student Financial Aid Programs," Statement by Gregory Ahart, Director, Human Resources Division, before the House Committee on Education and Labor, February 3, 1982, 21f.

32. U.S. Comptroller General, *Summary*, 12; U.S. Comptroller General, *Improved Management of (AID) Productive Credit Guaranty Program Can Minimize U.S. Risk Exposure and Costs* (Washington, D.C.: CBO, 1983), 9f. McManis and Associates, *Government-Wide Standards*, 45 and 48f; U.S. Comptroller General, *Farmers Home Administration's Business*, iii and 42–49; U.S. Comptroller General, *Maritime Ad-*

ministration: *Efforts to Improve Data on the Federal-Ship Financing Program* (Washington, D.C.: Comptroller General, 1987), 3 and 20–24.

33. U.S. Comptroller General, *Improved Management*, 5f; U.S. Comptroller General, *Summary*, 5 and 7; U.S. Comptroller General, *Farmers' Home Administration's Business*, 49–56.

34. U.S. Comptroller General, *Improved Management*, 7 and 10; Howard Kurtz and Michael Isikott, "Shipbuilder Defaulting on Loans," *Washington Post*, November 27, 1985, A1 and A4; U.S. Comptroller General, *Better Management of Collateral Can Reduce Losses in SBA's Major Loan Program* (Washington, D.C.: GAO, 1981), i–ii and 5–19.

35. Mary Kay Plantes and David Small, "Macroeconomic Consequences of Federal Government Activity," in CBO, *Conference on the Economics of Federal Credit Activity*, Special Study, Part II Papers (Washington, D.C.: CBO, 1981), 1–65; CBO, *Local Economic Development: Current Programs and Alternative Strategies*, Staff Working Paper, June 1981, 37–40; U.S. Comptroller General, *SBA's 7(a) Loan Guarantee Program: An Assessment of U.S. Role in the Financial Market* (Washington, D.C.: GAO, 1983), 18.

36. CBO, *Local Economic Development*, 37f.

37. James Barth, Joseph Cordes, and Anthony Yezer, "Federal Government Attempts to Influence Mortgage Credit," in CBO, *Conference on the Economics of Federal Credit Activity*, 159–227.

38. CBO, *Local Economic Development*, 41.

39. Robert M. Buckley and Raymond J. Struyk, *An Economic Analysis of AID's Housing Guaranty Program* (Washington, D.C.: Urban Institute Press, 1985), 55–58.

40. U.S. Comptroller General, Letter to Senator Gary Hart, July 27, 1979, 9.

41. U.S. Comptroller General, *The Geothermal Loan Guarantee Program* (Washington, D.C.: GAO, 1980), 5f; Christopher Baum, "The Effects of Federal Loan Guarantees on Small Entrepreneurs: Focus on Commercialization of Electric and Hybrid Vehicles," in CBO, *Conference on the Economics of Federal Credit Activity*, 343f.

42. GAO, "Central GAO Reports," 1–10.

43. CBO, *Local Economic Development*, 39.

44. CBO, *Local Economic Development*, 49.

45. CBO, *Housing Assistance for Low- and Moderate-Income Families* (Washington, D.C.: CBO, 1977), 18; Arthur P. Solomon, *The Cost-Effectiveness of Subsidized Housing* (Cambridge, Mass.: Joint Center for Urban Studies of Massachusetts Institute of Technology and Harvard University, 1972), 23.

46. U.S. Comptroller General, *A Comparative Analysis of Subsidized Housing Costs* (Washington, D.C.: GAO, 1976), 20. GAO assumed the costs of constructing the units under the two methods would not differ, and it examined the Section 236 program in combination with a rent supplement so that the tenants eligible for Section 236 would also be eligible for public housing. CBO, *The Long-Term Costs of Lower-Income Housing Assistance Programs* (Washington, D.C.: CBO, 1979), 44; U.S. Comptroller General, *Evaluation of Alternatives for Financing Low and Moderate Income Rental Housing* (Washington, D.C.: GAO, 1980), 27; U.S. Congressional Research Service, *Comparative Costs and Estimated Households Eligible for Participation in Certain Federally Assisted Low Income Housing Programs* (Washington, D.C., 1976), 4.

47. U.S. Comptroller General, Letter to Senator Gary Hart, 9; Regina Herzlinger and Nancy Kane, *A Managerial Analysis of Federal Income Redistribution Mechanisms* (Lexington, Mass.: D.C. Heath, 1973), 26.

48. One study estimated, for example, that the portion of total direct benefits received by housing investors, syndicators, and government intermediaries, from two housing mortgage guarantee programs was between 17 percent and 19 percent. See Arthur P. Solomon, *Housing the Urban Poor: A Critical Evaluation of Federal Housing Policy* (Cambridge, Mass.: The MIT Press, 1974), 91.

49. James A. Flickinger and William R. Glass, "A Study of Trends in Loan Processing, Making and Servicing Fees, as Related to the Business and Industry Guaranteed Loan Program," Project Report to Institute for Applied Public Financial Management, American University, Washington, D.C., July 1979, 105.

50. Henry J. Aaron, *Shelters and Subsidies: Who Benefits from Federal Housing Subsidies?* (Washington, D.C.: Brookings Institution, 1972), 85; Herzlinger and Kane, *A Managerial Analysis*, 28; The Washington Office of the College Board, "The Guaranteed Student Loan Program: Options for Controlling Federal Costs While Preserving Needed Credit for College," Discussion Paper, May 1981, A–4; CBO, *Federal Assistance for Postsecondary Education: Options for Fiscal Year 1979* (Washington, D.C.: CBO, 1978), 24.

51. CBO, *Federal Housing Policy: Current Programs and Recurring Issues* (Washington, D.C.: CBO, 1978), 28.

52. Wilson Thompson, "Comparison of Units Financed Under FHAs Unsubsidized Multi-Family Programs and Conventionally Financed Multi-Family Units," Report, Office of Assistant Secretary for Policy Development and Research, Department of Housing and Urban Development, August 1976, 12–15.

53. CBO, *Local Economic Development*, 34.

54. Wilson Thompson, "Comparison of Units," 11–14; U.S. Department of Housing and Urban Development, *Housing in the Seventies* (Washington, D.C.: Department of Housing and Urban Development, 1974), 106 and 112.

55. John Tower, "The Mounting Evidence on Mortgage Redlining," Book Review, *Urban Affairs Quarterly*, 15, no. 4 (June 1980): 488–501; Glenn B. Canner, "Redlining: Research and Federal Legislative Response," Staff Study, (Washington, D.C.: Board of Governors of the Federal Reserve System, 1982), 4–5; David J. Fullerton and C. Duncan MacRae, "FHA, Racial Discrimination, and Urban Mortgages," *AREUEA Journal* 6, no. 4, (Winter 1978): 451–70.

56. George Aragon, "Federal Credit Programs," in U.S. Congress Joint Economic Committee, *Federal Finance: The Pursuit of American Goals*, Special Study on Economic Change 6 (Washington, D.C., 1980).

57. Ibid.

58. Ibid.

Chapter Six

TAX EXPENDITURES AS TOOLS OF GOVERNMENT ACTION

Paul R. McDaniel

The basic function of a tax system is to collect those revenues which are to be allocated to the public sector and expended for publicly determined purposes. A tax system, however, may also be used by government as a tool to implement policies of government that require the expenditure of funds. Thus, when government desires to provide a financial incentive for individuals or businesses to engage in a particular course of action or to share costs in hardship situations, it may employ either direct spending programs or special provisions in the tax system.

As noted more fully below, tax expenditures grew massively in both number of programs and dollar value up through the early 1980s. Under the Reagan administration, however, a concerted effort was made to reverse this trend as part of a broader drive to cut back the role of the federal government. This effort culminated in passage of the Tax Reform Act of 1986. Although this act eliminated a great many "tax expenditures," and reduced the value of others, it hardly did away with tax expenditures as an instrument of policy. To the contrary, such expenditures continue to play a significant role in the federal program structure.

The purpose of this chapter is to examine this role. In particular, it explores the usage, advantages and disadvantages, operating characteristics, and consequences of tax expenditures as a tool of policy. The concluding section will provide an evaluation of tax expenditures and will propose improvements if they are to continue to be used as tools for government action.

DEFINITION OF TAX EXPENDITURES

The tax expenditure concept posits that there are two components to the United States income tax system:[1] (1) the normal structural component, which contains those provisions required if there is to be an income tax at all; and (2) the tax expenditure component, which contains those provisions that are not necessary to implement the income tax but which instead provide financial incentives or assistance to particular individuals and/or corporations.[2]

Tax expenditures are provided by granting special exclusions from income, deductions, tax credits, deferrals of tax, or preferential tax rates. While these special tax provisions formerly were thought of simply as reductions in the "tax" owed by a taxpayer, it is now recognized that through such provisions government can provide financial incentives or assistance to achieve specified national policy goals.

Tax expenditures fall broadly into two categories. In one category are provisions that permanently reduce the taxpayer's tax liability and thus provide a financial benefit like that of direct governmental grants. The clearest example in this category is a tax credit, which directly reduces the amount of taxes owed, as opposed to reducing the income on which tax obligations are calculated. In the second category are tax expenditures that provide a deferral of tax liability from the current year to a later year. Tax expenditures in this category are effected by a provision that accelerates a deduction to a year earlier than the normal structural rules specify or through the deferral of an item of income to a period later than the normal rules would require. Tax deferral provisions thus provide a loan by the government to those taxpayers who benefit from them.

USAGE OF TAX EXPENDITURES

The Tax Expenditure Budget

The tax expenditure concept was developed initially by the Treasury Department and presented to Congress in 1969 in the form of a budget.[3] The budget format was selected because, upon examination of the purposes for which tax expenditures were employed, it became clear that particular tax expenditures could be assigned to the budget functions established for direct spending programs. Congress institutionalized the tax expenditure budget in the Budget Reform Act of 1974, requiring the president to submit each year with the U.S. Budget document a list and estimates of tax expenditures employed by the United States.[4] Tax expenditure lists also are compiled annually for Congress by the Staff of the Joint Committee on Taxation and by the Congressional Budget Office (CBO).[5] Tax expenditure estimates by budget function for fiscal year 1988 are set forth in the appendix to this chapter.

The use of tax expenditures to provide federal financial assistance or incentives increased substantially between 1968 and 1985. In fiscal 1968, there were fewer than 50 tax expenditure programs. In fiscal 1985, there were over 100. The more than twofold increase in the number of tax expenditure programs was accompanied by an even greater increase in the total cost of those programs. In fiscal 1968, tax expenditures totaled about $36.6 billion. In fiscal 1986, tax expenditures totaled about $424.5 billion. Even taking into account that part of the increase in the number of items and revenue costs involved was the result of more refined budget presentation techniques and inflation, there was obviously a major increase in the use of tax expenditures in the past two decades. The rate of growth in tax spending was quite rapid even though the procedures enacted in the 1974 Budget Act were intended to provide Congress with greater control over this form of federal spending. In fiscal 1976, tax expenditures totaled $98.5 billion. That number had almost tripled by fiscal 1985 and quadrupled by fiscal 1986.[6]

The growth in tax expenditures also varied between those provided to individuals and those provided to corporations. For example, in fiscal year 1978, individuals received about $93 billion through tax expenditures. That figure increased to $305 billion in fiscal 1986. Thus, tax expenditures provided to individuals during that eight-year period more than tripled in cost. By comparison, corporations received about $40 billion in tax expenditures in fiscal 1978, but that figure increased to almost $120 billion in fiscal 1986, a threefold increase in tax expenditure benefits.[7] The differential was accentuated by the 1986 Tax Reform Act: tax expenditures in fiscal 1988 fell to $62 billion for corporations and to only $259.1 billion for individuals. (See appendix.)

Tax expenditures also grew at a faster rate than direct outlays, both in relative percentages and as a percentage of gross national product (GNP). A study by the CBO revealed that tax expenditures had risen ninefold, from $36.6 billion in 1967 to $228.6 billion in 1981. In the same period, by contrast, direct outlays rose from $178.8 billion to $660.5 billion, not quite a fourfold increase. Thus, during the period of time covered by the study, the amounts involved in tax expenditures grew at more than double the rate of direct outlays. In 1967, tax expenditures represented 4.4 percent of GNP, but this figure rose to 8 percent in 1981. By contrast, federal outlays as a percentage of GNP were 21.4 percent in 1967 and 23.1

percent in 1981. Thus, while tax expenditures almost doubled as a percent of GNP between 1967 and 1981, direct outlays as a percentage of GNP rose by only 10 percent.[8]

In several budget areas, tax expenditures assumed much greater importance than direct outlays both relatively and absolutely. In the budget category "Natural Resources and Environment," for example, tax expenditures grew by more than 800 percent from 1974 to 1981 while direct outlays in that category grew by just over 140 percent. Tax expenditures in the "Commerce and Housing Credit" budget function rose by more than 800 percent between 1967 and 1981 while direct outlays actually declined in that budget category. Tax expenditures in the "Commerce and Housing Credit" budget function were nearly 25 times as great as direct outlays in 1981 ($98.2 billion in tax expenditures versus $4 billion in direct outlays).[9]

The Tax Reform Act of 1986 affected the trends discussed in the preceding paragraphs for two reasons. First, a number of tax expenditures were either eliminated (such as the investment tax credit) or sharply curtailed (such as tax shelter losses). Second, as discussed below, the amount dispensed through tax expenditures is generally a function of marginal tax rates. As a result of reductions in both individual and corporate rates in the 1986 Act, those tax expenditures that were retained will in future years cost less than they would have at pre–1987 rate levels. Nevertheless, even under the 1986 tax reform, the revenues involved will still be substantial: in fiscal 1988, tax expenditures are estimated to total $321.1 billion and will grow to $377.8 billion in fiscal 1992. The total number of tax expenditure programs will continue to exceed 100.[10]

Reasons for Using Tax Expenditures

Given the rapid expansion in the use of the tax expenditures, it is important to identify the reasons which have been advanced as to why tax expenditures represent a desirable form of offering federal financial assistance. The reasons are identified in this section; the validity of the reasons is examined in the concluding section.

TAX EXPENDITURES DO NOT INVOLVE FEDERAL SPENDING

Some favor the use of special tax provisions because they assert that no federal spending is really involved; there is only a selective "tax reduction." Correspondingly, proposals for repeal of existing tax expenditures are often opposed on the ground that repeal would "increase taxes." These views concerning tax expenditures persist despite the fact that the 1974 Budget Act delineated tax expenditures as a form of federal spending. "The President's Tax Proposals to the Congress for Fairness, Growth and Simplicity" submitted in 1985 reflected this continuing ambivalence toward the nature of tax expenditures. On the one hand, proposals to repeal or reduce certain tax expenditures were defended on the ground that the provisions were either unnecessary or undesirable. On the other hand, the overall tax reform proposal program was required to be revenue neutral because of the president's opposition to a "tax increase."

PRIVATE SECTOR CONTROL

Some favor tax expenditures because they typically employ private sector rather than governmental decision-making processes. For example, the deduction for charitable contributions is often cited as an example of the private decision making that is favored in the case of tax expenditures. The charitable contributions deduction is in effect a governmental matching grant program to encourage giving to charity, but the choice of the charities to be benefited is left to the individual donor.[11]

SIMPLICITY AND LACK OF GOVERNMENT CONTROL

Tax expenditures are asserted to have a simplicity and lack of governmental control that are not found in direct spending programs. This argument has a surface appeal and is true of some tax expenditure programs. But it does not apply to all tax expenditure programs. For example, determining the financial effects of a contribution of property to charity requires a highly sophisticated analysis for any particular donor. And the cumulative effect of over 100 tax expenditures in the Internal Revenue Code is the primary cause of the recurring calls for tax simplification.

NO NEW GOVERNMENT BUREAUCRACY

Another benefit claimed for tax expenditures is that they do not require new government bureaucracies to administer them. Every government program, however, requires some bureaucracy to administer it, and tax expenditures are no exception. It happens that the Internal Revenue Service (IRS) is the bureaucracy that will administer every tax expenditure program rather than some other agency of government. But, in order to implement a new tax expenditure, the IRS itself must train and develop personnel and expertise to carry out the program. It may be, however, that some will have a preference for using the IRS because of its reputation for honesty, efficiency, and the like, rather than another agency of government.

DIFFERENCES IN PSYCHOLOGICAL RESPONSES

It is also possible that there may be differences in the reaction of program beneficiaries to tax expenditures as compared to direct spending programs. Some assert that the tax expenditure route is preferable because program beneficiaries psychologically do not feel that they are the beneficiaries of federal subsidies. Accordingly, individuals or businesses will respond more favorably to tax than to direct subsidies, especially those of an incentive nature.

SPENDING PRIORITIES

A major advantage of tax expenditures over direct expenditures relates to spending priorities. Every tax expenditure has an automatic first priority over any direct expenditure program. All debates about direct spending priorities occur with the revenues that are left after the funding of all tax expenditures. Thus, every movie that qualified for the former investment tax credit had a higher priority than national defense or directly funded educational programs.

POLITICAL PROCESS

Another important advantage that tax spending programs enjoy is that they do not have to survive the two-step authorization and appropriations process that Congress employs for direct spending programs. Tax expenditures are written entirely in the tax writing committees. As a result, the authorization–appropriations process is collapsed into a single committee and procedure in each house of Congress. The ability to bypass the authorization–appropriations process appears to be a major reason why many in and out of Congress prefer the tax expenditure to the direct spending route.

Closely related is the nature of committee jurisdiction in Congress. All tax expenditures fall within the jurisdiction of the House Ways and Means Committee and the Senate Finance Committee. As a result, members of these tax writing committees who wish to provide financial incentives or assistance for a given objective will tend to favor the use of tax expenditures so that jurisdiction of the program will remain in the committee of which they are members.

INVISIBILITY

Finally, a program enacted in the form of a tax expenditure typically has been thought to have less political visibility than a comparable direct spending program. Beneficiaries of tax expenditure programs may see this as a significant advantage since direct spending programs tend to be subject to more regular and extensive review.

OPERATING CHARACTERISTICS OF TAX EXPENDITURES

How Tax Expenditures Work

The tax expenditure process can be thought of as the exchange of two (imaginary) checks between a taxpayer and the Treasury. First, the taxpayer remits to the Treasury a check for the amount that would be owed under the normal structure of the tax—that is, the amount that would be due if the tax were imposed on economic income (generally, the sum of the taxpayer's increase in net worth plus personal consumption expenses for the year), at the generally applicable rates, and in the proper taxable period. This check may be termed the "economic tax check" of the taxpayer. The Treasury then remits a check to the taxpayer which is an amount equal to the sum of the financial benefits from the various tax expenditure provisions for which the taxpayer qualifies. This check is the "tax subsidy" check. In practice, of course, the process of exchanging checks does not occur. Instead, the taxpayer simply computes the net of the "two-check" process when the income tax return is filled out. On April 15, the taxpayer remits to the government the difference between the tax that would be owed under the normal structure and the amount of tax expenditures for which the taxpayer qualifies. In common usage, the check sent to the government is referred to as the taxpayer's "tax liability." But tax expenditure analysis makes clear that this check is not the taxpayer's "tax liability" as such; instead it is the net of the taxpayer's economic tax liability and the tax subsidies for which the taxpayer is eligible.

The implementation of a given tax expenditure requires a number of steps. The tax expenditure must be set forth in statutory language; at this stage the Treasury and the Congress are the dominant actors. The IRS must then take that legislation and issue rulings and regulations interpreting it. In turn, the statute and the administrative interpretations must be reduced to lines, schedules, and instructions accompanying Form 1040 for individuals or Form 1120 for corporations. Taxpayers and their advisers then utilize this material in the tax return completion process. Most tax expenditure programs thus involve a self-declaration of eligibility for the program benefit by the taxpayer. The correctness of that self-declaration is the subject of possible audit when the taxpayer's tax return is examined by the IRS. Because of the self-assessment procedure employed for the income tax, of course, it is always possible that a taxpayer may improperly declare eligibility for a tax expenditure program. That error will go undetected unless the return is audited by an IRS agent and the error discovered. Finally, if the taxpayer and the IRS cannot agree on the taxpayer's eligibility for a tax expenditure program, the matter will proceed to the courts for resolution.

Institutions and Actors Involved in Tax Expenditures

The decision to utilize the tax system to deliver financial assistance brings into play a different set of institutions and attitudes than are involved when the direct spending route is adopted. Because the tax system is used, IRS personnel, taxpayers, tax advisers, and the courts bring to bear "tax attitudes" even though they are in fact dealing with spending programs. Moreover, the operational structure developed by these players in the tax system, primarily in the context of the normal tax structure, influences how the spending program will operate. Whether these attitudes and implementing mechanisms are superior or inferior to those that would be involved in direct spending programs is not an issue at this juncture; the point is that different role players and attitudes are involved if the decision is to use the tax system, and this fact may affect program outcomes.

ROLE AND ATTITUDES OF THE IRS AND TREASURY

The IRS sees its mission primarily in terms of collecting revenues. Similarly, Treasury tax policy officials see their principal task as developing a tax system which will ensure that revenues are generated as fairly and efficiently as possible. The training and experience of both sets of officials is in terms of "tax thinking"— appropriate definitions of income, which deductions are costs of producing income and which are nondeductible personal or capital expenditures, and how the accounting rules should deal with the time value of money.

But these tax attitudes and this training do not necessarily facilitate the drafting and implementation of spending programs. Treasury officials tend to be quite cool toward suggestions to use the tax system to implement spending programs. Predictably they will oppose programs or, alternatively, attempt to limit the scope of the program even if in that limitation process the inherent rationality of the statutory provision, viewed as a spending program, is undercut.[12] Similarly, IRS officials and agents are not likely to give expansive reading to tax expenditure programs because, in their view of the world, a reduction in revenues will result. Officials involved in direct spending programs, on the other hand, may be inclined to interpret their congressional mandate rather broadly in order to spread the program benefits as widely as possible. But the basic instinct of the IRS agent is precisely the opposite; that instinct is to interpret the tax expenditure program as narrowly as possible in order to maximize government revenues. The application of tax attitudes and tax analysis to spending programs may thus result in less effective and less comprehensive spending programs than would be the case if the matter were viewed entirely from a spending perspective.

The utilization of the tax system also means that the program will be developed and administered by those whose primary expertise is not in the programmatic area under consideration. Officials in the Treasury and the IRS are trained to be tax lawyers and tax collectors; they are not trained experts in environmental programs, housing, energy conservation, and all the other areas of social and economic life into which tax expenditure programs have been introduced. The results are programs designed and administered in a way that is less than optimal from a direct program perspective.

Requiring the IRS to administer spending programs complicates the process of tax collection. Each new tax expenditure program requires the IRS to promulgate regulations, prepare forms, issue rulings in response to taxpayer requests, undertake audits, and pursue litigation over disputes between the IRS and taxpayers. When the inherently complex task of administering a tax system without tax expenditures is overlaid with over 100 tax expenditure programs, the burden on the IRS may reach the point where it is not possible to administer effectively its tax collection responsibilities. This was, in fact, one of the major motivations for the reform of the tax code enacted in 1986. While some simplification was achieved by the 1986 legislation, new provisions dealing with tax expenditures actually produced further complexity.

ROLE AND ATTITUDES OF TAXPAYERS

The United States prides itself on the effective operation of its self-assessment income tax system. Under that system, various taxpayer roles and attitudes have developed about paying taxes, preparing returns, and utilizing tax advisers. The decision to use the tax expenditure route for a particular program inevitably means that taxpayers will bring "tax rules" and "tax attitudes" to the spending program. Indeed, most taxpayers appear not to differentiate in their thinking between tax expenditure programs and the normal structural features of the system.

Moreover, tax expenditures, even if rationally defensible from the standpoint of the government, may be perceived differently by taxpayers. That is, taxpayers apparently continue to view most tax expenditure programs as "loopholes" or devices for escaping one's fair share of taxes. Even though tax expenditure analysis can demonstrate as a conceptual matter that tax expenditures economically do not result in an escape from taxes, but instead representing simply one form of federal spending, that conceptual analysis has not yet been internalized by taxpayers. As a result, the existence of tax expenditures may give rise to widespread discontent with the tax system by taxpayers who do not differentiate between the tax expenditure and the tax collecting components of the system. This was clearly apparent in the push to simplify the tax system in 1986. As in prior calls for tax reform, the complaints in 1986 centered on the tax expenditure provisions despite the fact that the issue was not tax inequity but whether government should be spending money through the tax system for purposes such as medical costs, charitable contributions, and the like.

The decision to use the tax system also means that the system itself will become much more complicated. Indeed, tax expenditures are the principal cause of the present complexity of the income tax system.[13] Once again, taxpayer dissatisfaction and unhappiness with an excessively complex tax system may be triggered, as it was in 1986.

ROLE AND ATTITUDES OF THE TAX ADVISERS

Tax advisers, typically lawyers and accountants, become important players in federal spending programs run through the tax system. These lawyers and accountants, like their counterparts in the IRS and the Treasury, bring tax attitudes and methods of tax analysis to their task. They typically will have little expertise in the various areas covered by the tax expenditure programs. Most tax lawyers did not enter tax practice, for example, in order to help administer the low-income housing program of the country! As a result, tax advisers may come to see tax expenditure programs as gimmicks and loopholes by which to escape paying tax and, this, too, may have deleterious effects on the operation of the tax-collecting structure.

ROLE AND ATTITUDES OF THE COURTS

Disputes between taxpayers and the IRS over tax expenditure programs may go to the courts just as do disputes over provisions that are part of the revenue-raising structure of the system. Although courts are beginning to show greater sophistication, traditionally they have not differentiated between code sections that are tax expenditures and those that are not. Thus, constitutional issues that are imbedded in tax expenditure programs tend to be approached from a tax perspective rather than from the perspective of whether the programs would pass constitutional muster if enacted as direct programs. For example, federal aid to religion through a tax expenditure may be treated more leniently than would a similar direct aid program.[14]

Oversight of Tax Expenditures

CONGRESS

The responsibility for oversight of tax expenditures lies in the tax writing committees in Congress—the House Ways and Means Committee and the Senate Finance Committee. Of the two, the House Ways and Means Committee has exercised its responsibility for the oversight of tax expenditures more systematically than has the Senate Finance Committee.

The Oversight Subcommittee of the House Ways and Means Committee has conducted hearings on the operations of tax expenditures.[15] In addition, hearings have been held on particular tax expenditures to ascertain their impact and effectiveness.[16] The full committee, in preparation for the 1985 tax legislative program, held hearings which in part were directed at the effect on tax expenditures of various comprehensive tax reform and simplification programs that had been introduced in Congress.[17]

Tax expenditures are covered by the congressional budget process. Under the 1974 Budget Act, the CBO is required to prepare annual five-year projections of the revenue costs of existing tax expenditures.[18] Those annual reports have displayed increasing sophistication and have provided varied and informative analyses of the impact of tax expenditures on the budget and on the efforts of Congress to exert greater control over total federal spending. CBO also has prepared analyses of particular tax expenditures that have provided considerable insight into their operation, efficiency, and effectiveness.[19] In addition, the Senate Budget Committee has periodically issued a tabulation of tax expenditures, giving background information and bibliographical material with respect to each tax expenditure.[20]

Nonetheless, the budget process has not proved an effective device by which to review, control, and coordinate tax expenditures with direct spending. The review of tax expenditures has been left to ad hoc actions by tax writing committees. Tax expenditures are largely uncontrolled by the budget process because no effective limits are imposed on them. The tax writing committees are not given directions by the budget resolution as to the level of tax expenditures for a given fiscal year. Instead, the committees are given an overall revenue figure that they are to meet. But they can meet this revenue target by increasing or reducing tax expenditures or by increasing or reducing rates, personal exemptions, or the standard deduction for nonitemizers. Finally, there is virtually no coordination between tax expenditures and actions by the authorization–appropriations committees in the same budget area. The policy oversight of tax expenditure by Congress thus suffers from very serious deficiencies.[21]

Congress in some instances has exercised its oversight responsi-

bilities with respect to tax expenditures in an entirely inappropriate way. On occasion, some members of Congress have been
upset by particular actions—actual or proposed—of the IRS. The
appropriations process has been used to deny funds to the IRS to
carry out the administrative action. One particularly egregious example of this form of "oversight" technique was the denial of funds
to implement proposed IRS procedures for determining the tax exempt status of racially segregated private schools.[22] This "oversight" technique has not been confined to tax expenditures, but has
been applied to direct expenditures as well. Its potential for im-
proper intrusion of the legislative branch into the administrative
responsibilities of the executive branch is serious indeed.[23]

EXECUTIVE BRANCH

The Office of Management and Budget appears to be the one office
in the executive branch that could exercise effective oversight responsibilities with respect to tax expenditures. The Treasury Department tends to approach tax expenditures as "tax matters" for
the reasons previously discussed. The Treasury may well oppose
new tax expenditures or propose elimination of or cutbacks in tax
expenditures. It often does this on tax grounds rather than on
spending grounds. Thus, the 1984 Treasury tax reform and tax simplification proposals[24] were based largely on traditional notions of
tax equity, tax simplification, and economic efficiency. The primary
impact of the Treasury proposals, however, would have been to
reduce sharply the spending effected through the tax expenditure mechanism. Such cutbacks may be entirely appropriate, but it
strained belief that every tax expenditure program cut back or eliminated by the Treasury proposals in fact was an undesirable federal
program. What must be recognized is that the assumption underlying the Treasury proposals and ultimately adopted in the 1986 Tax
Reform Act was that all the revenue savings (tax expenditure cuts)
were to be returned to taxpayers in the form of reduced tax rates.
Other options were available with respect to the use of these funds;
for example, they could have been used to finance other spending
programs or to reduce the government deficit. It is curious that
when tax expenditures are cut, the automatic assumption tends to
be that the increased revenues should go to rate reductions rather
than to one of the other two purposes. But this is almost inevitably
the Treasury approach to the matter.

On the other hand, the Office of Management and Budget has the potential to take a broader view of tax expenditures. Thus far, it has not significantly exercised its power to do so. The annual budget documents do contain a list of tax expenditures and an association of related tax and direct expenditure programs in the budget estimates. Nonetheless, there does not appear to have been any substantial effort to institute requirements that tax and direct spending programs in the same area be coordinated, and where appropriate, one or the other type of program be cut back or eliminated because of unnecessary duplication or because the programs are in conflict. It would seem appropriate for OMB to introduce a system whereby it assigned both tax expenditure programs and direct spending programs to the appropriate department of the executive branch. It could then give a target total of combined tax and direct spending to that department. The department could meet that total by cutting back on tax expenditures or on direct expenditures, or both. Such a system would require each nontax department to take a close look at tax expenditures to ensure that priorities and program design were consistent with basic governmental policy objectives in its area of responsibility.[25]

CONSEQUENCES OF TAX EXPENDITURES

The decision to use tax expenditures as a tool of government action has produced a number of identifiable consequences. The most important of those will be discussed in this section. An evaluation of whether those consequences are desirable or necessary, or both is undertaken in the next section.

Distributional Consequences

Most tax expenditures, as presently structured, distribute benefits in an "upside-down" pattern, the financial benefits increase as the taxpayer's income increases. This result occurs because the value of any tax expenditure structured as an exclusion or an exemption from income or as a special deduction will vary according to the marginal tax bracket of the individual taxpayer. Thus, taxpayers whose income is insufficient to generate positive taxable income get no benefit from an additional exclusion or deduction, but the highest income taxpayers receive a benefit under the 1986 Act, equal to 28 percent (33 percent for some taxpayers) of the deduction or exclusion.

Table 6.1   SELECTED TAX EXPENDITURES RECEIVED BY TAXPAYERS
(percentage)

	Income	
Tax expenditure	Under $10,000[a]	Over $75,000[b]
Medical deduction	0.8	28.0
Real estate tax deduction	0.08	38.1
State and local income tax deduction	0.02	55.3
Home mortgage interest deduction	0.1	35.2
Deductibility of nonmortgage interest in excess of investment income	0.09	38.7
Charitable contributions deduction	0.02	59.5
Casualty loss deduction	0	17.4
Child care credit	0.6	4.0
Earned income credit	33.7	0

Source: Joint Committee on Taxation, *Estimates of Federal Tax Expenditures for Fiscal Years 1988–1992* (JCS-3-87), February 27, 1987.
a. 30.25 percent of total returns.
b. 3.7 percent of total returns.

Table 6.1 provides data with respect to the distribution of selected individual tax expenditures by income classes (using 1988 tax law and 1988 income levels). Those data reveal the decided upside-down effect of most tax expenditures provided to individuals. In 1988, individuals with incomes below $10,000 comprised 30.25 percent of all taxpayers. Those with incomes above $75,000 comprised only 3.7 percent of all taxpayers. But Table 6.1 shows that tax expenditures are not distributed in a similar fashion. The top 3.7 percent of taxpayers received 28 percent of the benefit of the medical expense deduction; the lowest 30 percent received only 0.8 percent of the benefit of that tax expenditure. Of the tax expenditures provided for home ownership—the deductions for home mortgage interest and property taxes—the top 3.7 percent of taxpayers received 35.8 percent; the 30 percent with incomes below $10,000 a year received only 0.1 percent. The charitable contributions deduction is the major federal program to encourage giving to charity. Almost 60 percent of this tax expenditure went to charities favored by the 3.7 percent of taxpayers with income over $75,000; by contrast, charities favored by the 30 percent of taxpayers with incomes below $10,000 received only 0.02 percent of the tax expenditure.

Thus, the decision to use special deductions or exclusions from income as the mechanism for providing tax expenditure benefits automatically produces the result that the benefits are distributed regressively to income.[26] Even when a tax credit mechanism that provides a dollar-for-dollar reduction in taxes is used, the upside-down effect remains although it is a more limited effect than in the case of special deductions or exclusions. As discussed in the following section, it is possible to avoid the regressive distribution of tax expenditures (and Congress in a few instances has done so). But, as most tax expenditures are now implemented, the upside-down effect is an inevitable consequence of the decision to use the tax expenditure tool as the mechanism to deliver federal financial assistance to individual taxpayers.

Effect on Tax Rates

Another consequence of the decision to use tax expenditures is that tax rates are required to be higher than they otherwise would be. Indeed, the rates adopted in the 1986 Tax Reform Act revealed how dramatically tax rates can be reduced if tax expenditures are reduced or eliminated.

Efficiency of the Tax Expenditure Tool

There are several different efficiency issues that the tax expenditure tool raises. The first is the so-called "windfall" effect. Tax expenditures may provide substantial windfalls to program beneficiaries: funds are provided for taking actions that the beneficiaries would have taken in the absence of the subsidy. Closely related is the inefficiency created by the fact that many tax expenditures distort free market decisions and thus misallocate economic resources by encouraging funds to be placed in investments or activities that, in the absence of the tax subsidy, would not be financially attractive. Of course, the purpose of any subsidy is to distort market decisions. Indeed, if market decisions are not distorted, then the windfall effect noted above is absolute.

The 1984 Treasury proposals and the 1986 Tax Reform Act, which responded to the second problem, were based significantly on the proposition that most tax expenditures produce economic inefficiency by distorting investment and consumption choices. To address the problem, the 1984 study advocated the total repeal of the majority of tax expenditures. The 1986 Act provisions were less sweeping, but were based on the same philosophy.

The windfall effect has been demonstrated in a number of studies that have been conducted with respect to tax exempt state and local bonds.[27] Those studies consistently showed that, where the top marginal tax rate was 50 percent, only about two-thirds of the cost of the federal tax expenditure actually flowed through to the state and local governments in the form of reduced borrowing costs. This phenomenon was produced by the interaction of the tax exemption mechanism with the tax rate structure. For example, in a perfect market in which taxable bonds bore 10 percent interest, municipal bonds had to bear only a 5 percent interest rate in order to attract a 50 percent marginal rate investor. There were not, however, a sufficient number of 50 percent bracket investors to absorb the volume of bonds issued by state and local governments. As a result, those governments were required to push their interest rates higher in order to attract the 40 percent bracket investors. When investment from that group proved insufficient, then the interest rates had to be pushed still higher in order to attract the 30 percent marginal bracket investor, the situation in which the market found itself prior to the 1986 Act. The result of this series of events was that each time the interest rate was raised to attract lower-bracket investors, all those investors above that bracket who had previously invested received a windfall. In effect those higher bracket investors received a commission for delivering the federal tax expenditure check to the state and local governments. They retained their commission out of the federal tax expenditure, and only two-thirds of that check flowed through to state and local governments to reduce their interest rates. This "middle man" effect was reduced by the Tax Reform Act of 1986 because most investors fell into a 28 percent bracket; it could be eliminated if state and local governments issued taxable bonds and the Treasury provided a direct interest subsidy to the state and local governments.[28]

The "middle man" phenomenon is also present in tax shelter operations. For example, one study[29] of a particular real estate tax shelter transaction found that about $2 million in federal tax expenditures were made available for a particular apartment project. Of this amount, approximately $1 million went to the actual builder and developer of the project. About $400,000 went to syndicators, lawyers, and accountants who developed the tax shelter project for the developer. The other $800,000 was retained by the individual investors who came into the project to purchase the tax expenditure benefits. The net result was, however, that it cost the Treasury $2 million to construct a building that could have been constructed for a $1 million direct payment to the person who actually built and developed the project. Similar kinds of waste and inefficiency have been found in other tax shelter transactions. The 1986 Act approached this problem by cutting back the tax expenditures used in tax shelters rather than by redesigning the tax expenditure to eliminate the waste—by making some tax expenditures refundable to actual participants.

There is what may be called a political efficiency issue associated with certain tax expenditure programs. As discussed above, the value of a tax expenditure provided through a special exclusion or deduction is a function of marginal tax rates. This interaction with the rate structure means that totally unrelated tax law changes can affect the amount expended for certain tax expenditure programs. Thus, for example, when the tax rates were lowered by the 1986 Act, the amount of federal funds expended for charitable contributions, medical expenses, and home mortgage interest was automatically reduced. There is no programmatic reason why the federal program to encourage home ownership should have been automatically reduced because tax rates were reduced; nonetheless, this is the effect when the tax expenditure is provided through a special exclusion or deduction. Similarly, when the personal exemptions and zero bracket amounts are increased, fewer people itemize their personal deductions, and all tax expenditure programs provided through itemized personal deductions are automatically reduced. By contrast, the rate reduction in the 1986 Act did not automatically reduce the funds available to direct programs. Of course, Congress could decide that reduced revenues from rate reductions require a reduction of direct spending programs; but that is not the automatic result as in the case of tax expenditure programs, which are affected by changes in tax rates.

Effectiveness of Tax Expenditures

Even if tax expenditures are efficient (however that standard is defined), the question remains whether they are effective in resolving the problems to which they are directed. Consider, for example, the deduction for charitable contributions. The objective is to provide an incentive to give to qualified charities. But, if the only itemized personal deduction available were that for charitable contributions, 95 percent of donors would not qualify for the tax expenditure. This is because 95 percent of donors give contributions that are smaller than the standard deduction and would, therefore, be able to deduct the same amount whether they donated to charity or not. Thus it is not the act of charitable giving that triggers the tax expenditure subsidy. Instead, the operation of the incentive depends on such diverse variables as whether the individual is a homeowner, lives in a state with high income taxes, or incurs large medical expenses. It can be questioned whether a program that introduces fundamentally extraneous actions on the part of the taxpayer or state government as a condition of obtaining the benefit of the charitable contribution deduction is rational or "effective."[30]

Similarly, tax expenditures are provided to companies that maintain operations in Puerto Rico and to corporations that set up paper "export" corporations.[31] The tax credit for Puerto Rico is intended to create jobs in Puerto Rico. But Treasury studies have shown repeatedly that the number of jobs created has been far less than anticipated from the cost of the tax expenditure program. Instead, it appears that companies arrange their affairs to maximize the tax expenditure, but very little of that tax expenditure flows through in the form of increased employment for Puerto Ricans.[32] Similarly, in the case of export corporations, Treasury studies consistently reveal that the amount of additional exports induced is far less than the revenue cost of the program would appear to justify.[33]

The lack of coordination between tax and direct spending programs within the same budget function may render one or the other ineffective. In the agricultural area, for example, a number of studies have been conducted to determine the impact of tax expenditures in light of the overall agricultural policy objectives of the country as reflected in direct expenditure programs. Those studies have revealed that the tax expenditure programs can produce diametrically opposite results from those pursued in direct programs for agriculture. For example, direct spending programs for agriculture tend to emphasize the value of the small family farm and the undesirability of absentee ownership. By contrast, the tax expenditure programs for agriculture can be effectively utilized only as the particular farm operation continues to grow larger and larger. Indeed, the farmer relying on tax expenditure agricultural programs who does not expand may well be driven into a forced sale or bankruptcy. This is because the tax expenditure agricultural program consists primarily of interest-free loans. In an inflationary economy, a farmer who relies on loans can only stay ahead of the game by continuing to take out new loans each year, larger in amount than previously borrowed. As a result, there is an inevitable drive to larger and larger farm operations which are concentrated in fewer and fewer hands. Similarly, available tax expenditure programs impose the implicit condition that the beneficiary have taxable income, a condition many farmers are unable to meet. As a result, the farm tax shelter is born, and the farm becomes the property of Wall Street bankers and investors. And this whole process defeats, the objectives both of preserving the small family farm and of discouraging absentee ownership.[34]

The ineffectiveness of a tax expenditure program may of course be due to the fact that there is really no need for the program. For example, in an era in which it is governmental policy to let oil and gas prices be governed by the market, continued provision of tax expenditures for the oil industry is both contradictory to that policy and a waste of money. Other programs appear ineffective because they are poorly designed. Thus, if it is desirable to give a benefit to homeowners to encourage them to purchase principal residences, a refundable and taxable tax credit would appear to be more effective than the home mortgage interest deduction.

Tax Policy Consequences

The decision to use tax expenditures inevitably raises what have been traditionally viewed as tax policy issues. Thus, as we have seen, because most taxpayers do not think of preferential tax provisions as spending programs, tax expenditures inevitably become entwined in tax reform efforts. As such, they tend to be analyzed as tax inequities or tax loopholes. They are seen to produce horizontal and vertical inequities and to result in low effective rates of tax paid by some taxpayers.

Reflecting this, the tax expenditure route makes programs vulnerable to tax simplification efforts. Tax expenditures are seen as a cause of tax complexity and indeed they are, viewed from the perspective of the individual taxpayer. Whenever Congress introduces a tax expenditure, every taxpayer in the country must review his or her financial affairs to see if he or she qualifies for the tax expenditure program. By and large, most taxpayers do not feel that they have to review every federal direct spending program to see if they qualify; they generally are aware of those direct programs that may be applicable to them. Thus, while individuals on welfare may be puzzled as to the extent of their qualification for welfare programs, they do not have to concern themselves with whether they also qualify for subsidies for political contributions, energy conservation equipment, and the like. But if the tax system tool is used, taxpayers must run the whole gamut of tax expenditures to determine if they qualify. Thus, a side effect of tax expenditures is that they will be subject to attack on the grounds that they create tax complexity; likewise, they may be eliminated on the ground of tax simplification.

Another consequence of using the tax system in the business and investment context has been the rise of the tax shelter industry. Tax shelter transactions at bottom are based on the sale of tax expenditure benefits by taxpayers who cannot use them (because their tax liability has already been reduced to zero) to taxpayers who can use them. The purchase and sale of tax expenditure benefits may give rise to congressional concerns about tax equity and thus invite the introduction of legislative and administrative weapons and penalties to curb what is seen to be an abuse of the tax expenditure provision. The 1986 Act provisions with respect to "passive activity losses" and the alternative minimum tax were examples of legislative responses reflecting these concerns.[35]

Tax Administration Consequences

As we have seen, the decision to utilize a tax expenditure program places on the IRS the responsibility for auditing its results. The IRS must insure that the individual program beneficiaries in fact qualify for the program and, if so, determine the extent to which they were entitled to the financial benefits. This decision in turn automatically invokes the audit practices and coverage of the IRS. At present, less than 1.5 percent of individual tax returns are audited each year. This means that tax expenditure programs are given a similar audit coverage. Conversely, the income tax returns of large corporations are audited annually. As a result, their use of tax expenditure programs is given much more sustained and systematic audit scrutiny. It is doubtful that this same pattern of audit coverage exists in direct spending programs.

Moreover, as noted above, IRS auditors are not likely to be experts in every one of the more than 100 different tax expenditure programs now in effect. As a result, program expertise that might be brought to bear were the audit conducted by an agency or department responsible for comparable direct programs will not be available.

Significant compliance problems are experienced in the tax system.[36] When tax expenditures are involved, problems of tax noncompliance are in fact problems of spending program noncompliance. Existing data do not permit an informed judgment of the extent to which tax noncompliance problems are spending noncompliance. But it may well be that there is greater noncompliance when a spending program is run through the tax system because the taxpayer is willing to play the "audit lottery." Moreover, since the audit coverage is so minimal in the case of individual taxpayers, it is not surprising that the data indicate that in certain areas compliance with direct spending programs is much greater than is the case with comparable tax expenditure programs. It is also possible that taxpayers, who tend to view tax expenditure programs as loopholes for those who benefit from them, may be tempted to create tax expenditures on their own by claiming deductions to which they are not entitled or by failing to report income which properly should be subject to tax. Again, existing data do not permit an informed judgment as to whether the mere existence of tax expenditures causes noncompliance with the normative provisions, but there is considerable anecdotal evidence among tax advisers that this phenomenon occurs.[37]

Budget Policy Consequences

Tax expenditure programs, once introduced, cannot easily be controlled because individuals or businesses become eligible for the benefits by meeting the qualification criteria. They are, in this respect, like direct entitlement programs. Congress establishes criteria which, if met, entitle the taxpayer to the benefits provided. Given this fact, the control of the amount of funds dispensed through tax expenditures is difficult.[38]

EVALUATION OF TAX EXPENDITURES

Tax expenditures thus have a variety of disadvantages. However, many of these turn out to result not from the inherent characteristics of the tool but from the way it has been structured. In view of this, what recommendations can be offered about the use of this tool? It is to this question that I now turn.

Negative Aspects of Tax Expenditures that Can Be Corrected

One negative aspect of most tax expenditures is that they provide no financial benefit or incentive to those whose taxable income is insufficient to enable them to use the tax expenditure provision. Thus, granting a special tax deduction to an individual whose taxable income is not high enough to reach the first positive tax rate will have no effect on that individual; similarly, a tax credit made available to an individual who has no tax liability will provide no financial benefit. Tax expenditures can, however, be designed to remedy this defect. The technique is to make the tax expenditure refundable—the individual receives a check from the Treasury to the extent his or her tax expenditure benefit exceeds tax liability. This technique has been adopted in the case of the earned income credit for low-income workers.

As discussed earlier, most tax expenditures provide benefits that increase with income, a feature that many would find objectionable from a programmatic standpoint. This objection too can be overcome, for example, by requiring that tax expenditures in the form of tax credits be included in income. The result of such a provision—which has been adopted for several of the business tax credits[39]—is that the tax expenditure is no longer provided in an upside-down fashion but instead is made available on a basis that is progressive to income. For example, if a tax credit of $100 is provided which must be included in income, a 28 percent bracket taxpayer would pay $28 in tax on the subsidy and derive a $72 after-tax benefit from the tax subsidy. A 15 percent bracket taxpayer, on the other hand, would pay only $15 in tax on the subsidy and receive an $85 after-tax benefit. The tax subsidy has thus become progressive to income.

In the case of tax expenditures that provide for a deferral of tax—in effect, an interest-free loan—the upside down problem can be solved by imposing an interest charge on the amount of the tax expenditure. Congress has also adopted this technique in the case of several tax expenditure provisions in the tax code.[40]

If the above steps were taken with respect to tax expenditures, then the upside-down objection to the structure of tax expenditures would be eliminated and tax policy concerns would be met since the tax expenditure benefits would be subject to income taxation in full.

Budgetary Issues

Also potentially remediable is the inadequate handling of tax expenditures in the budget process. In the executive branch, as we have seen, there is little coordination between tax expenditures and direct expenditure programs in the same budget area. Closely allied with this problem is the fact that, while great efforts have been made to exert budgetary controls over direct spending programs, little effort has been made to impose similar controls or limitations on the growth of tax expenditures. The solution to this problem would appear to be within the reach of the Office of Management and Budget. It should assign to the individual agencies and departments that have responsibility for administering direct expenditure programs the tax expenditures that fall within the same program jurisdictions. A total amount of spending, both tax and direct, should then be imposed on the agency. Each agency would be required to reach its budget target by considering both tax and direct spending programs. Where the total of the two exceeded the amount allocated to the department by OMB, it would be the responsibility of the agency to cut tax expenditures or direct expenditures in order to meet the budget target.

Similar problems exist in the congressional budget process. There is little coordination between the committees that control direct expenditure programs and the tax writing committees that control tax expenditure programs. Likewise, the Budget Act itself imposes no meaningful limits on the growth of tax expenditure provisions. Either of two actions could address these problems. One approach would require that the appropriate nontax legislative committees authorize tax expenditures, with the tax writing committees then serving in effect as appropriations committees to vote the funds. This procedure would insure that the committees charged with program responsibility consider both direct spending and tax expenditure approaches to their particular program areas. An alternative approach, similar to the one recommended for use by the executive branch, would require the budget committees to allocate both tax and direct spending by functional categories to the appropriations committees. A total that included both tax and direct expenditures would be assigned to each budget function. The appropriations committees would then be required in each budget category to stay within the expenditure total by considering both tax and direct expenditures. If tax expenditures were to be increased in a particular category and the budget total was thereby exceeded, direct outlays would have to be correspondingly reduced. If the tax writing committees wished to initiate tax expenditure legislation, the appropriations committees would have to consider and approve that legislation before it could proceed to a floor vote.

Negative Aspects of Tax Expenditures that Cannot Be Corrected

One negative aspect noted with respect to the use of tax expenditures is the administrative burden which it imposes on the IRS, an agency that would have more than enough work to do if there were no tax expenditures in effect at all. Moreover, the general lack of sufficient IRS personnel to audit returns means either that the tax expenditure programs are going to be inadequately overseen by the IRS or that the tax collecting responsibility of the IRS will suffer.

A second objection to tax expenditures that cannot be cured is the tax complexity created for taxpayers and the government by the decision to use the tax expenditure tool. Every tax expenditure requires at least one additional line on the income tax form, many require entirely separate schedules, and all require regulations, rulings, and instructions to implement them.

It is also unlikely that taxpayers' perceptions that tax expenditures are the cause of inequity and unfairness in the tax system can be overcome, even if steps are taken to make sure either that the tax expenditures are included in income or that an interest charge is imposed for those that represent tax deferrals. It would take a massive educational effort to convince the average taxpayer that a tax expenditure is in fact not a loophole for those who benefit from it. Given this fact, the use of tax expenditures as a tool for government action means that they will continually be under attack as sources of tax unfairness and, hence, as objects for tax reform efforts.

THE CHOICE OF THE TAX EXPENDITURE TOOL AS OPPOSED TO OTHER TOOLS OF GOVERNMENTAL ACTION

Very little work has addressed why governments choose to use tax expenditures in lieu of other tools of government action. Nor has much work been done on the related question of why tax expenditures are used in a particular area as opposed to one of the other governmental tools. As this chapter has noted, there are a number of observable differences in the effects of using tax expenditures from those that would be applicable, for example, under direct spending programs, and many persons perceive advantages in the use of tax expenditures.

Many of the perceived advantages of tax expenditures over other forms of governmental action are neither inevitable nor actual. Thus, an examination of tax expenditure provisions reveals that many are not simple at all and that in the aggregate they cause great complexity for the tax system; government bureaucracy is involved in the administration of the tax expenditure provisions—it is only a question of which bureaucracy; government funds are expended through the tax system and the questions of proper control and coordination of that form of spending with other forms of spending exist; windfall effects in tax expenditures are no different from those experienced in direct expenditure programs; the misallocation of resources that occurs as a result of tax expenditures is no different from the resource misallocation that occurs when direct subsidies are provided; tax expenditure programs are often poorly designed with resulting inefficiencies and ineffectiveness. These are characteristics that hardly serve to distinguish them from other forms of government action. It must be recognized that many differences experienced between tax and direct expenditures in their operation really result from different program designs rather than from inherent differences in the tools themselves. Any proposed governmental expenditure program to address a particular policy goal can be drafted either as a tax expenditure or as a direct expenditure, with identical effects in terms of impact on beneficiaries, allocation of resources, distributional effects, and the like.

Most important in the deciding whether to use tax expenditures as a tool of government action is to determine whether the consequences that follow the decision are preferable to those that would follow from using an alternative tool of government action. Thus the decision to use tax expenditures will involve the actors and agencies identified in the preceding discussion. Whether those attitudes and actors are preferable from the standpoint of the implementation and administration of a particular program compared to the attitudes and actors brought into play by an alternative form of governmental action is a question that must be addressed as each tax expenditure is considered.

On balance, the problems of administering the tax system and the perception of taxpayers that tax expenditures involve tax inequities and tax loopholes create a presumption against the use of tax expenditures as a tool for government action. Moreover, once this tool has begun to be used, present procedures within Congress and the executive branch provide no real opportunity to limit the growth and controllability of tax expenditures. Although it is arguable that the use of the tax expenditure tool might be preferable to alternative forms of government action tools in selected areas, past experience does not indicate any optimism that the use of the tool can be kept within bounds that will permit efficient administration of the revenue collecting responsibilities of tax administration and that will alleviate concerns of taxpayers over issues of tax fairness.

Notes

1. This chapter examines tax expenditures in the context of an income tax. The analysis, however, is equally applicable to any tax of global reach as, for example, wealth transfer taxes, net wealth taxes, national sales taxes (including value-added taxes), and national property taxes. For a comparative application of the tax expenditure concept to the major type of taxes employed by six OECD countries, see Paul R. McDaniel and Stanley S. Surrey, eds., *International Aspects of Tax Expenditures: A Comparative Study* (Deventer, Netherlands: Kluwer, N.V., 1985).

Closely associated with the tax expenditure component is the tax penalty component of the income tax system—much smaller than the tax expenditure component—which contains special provisions that have effects similar to direct governmental fines or penalties. Because the focus of this chapter is on methods of providing governmental assistance, tax penalties will not be discussed.

2. It is beyond the scope of this chapter to explore the conceptual subtleties involved in the classification of provisions of the Internal Revenue Code (IRC) as tax expenditures or as part of the normal structure. Those issues are explored in detail in Stanley S. Surrey and Paul R. McDaniel, *Tax Expenditures* (Cambridge, Mass.: Harvard University Press, 1985), 184–230 (hereafter cited as "Tax Expenditures").

The term "tax expenditure" was coined by the late Stanley S. Surrey during his tenure as assistant secretary of the Treasury for Tax Policy. The first comprehensive exposition of the concept appeared in Stanley S. Surrey, *Pathways to Tax Reform* (Cambridge, Mass.: Harvard University Press, 1973).

3. Ibid.

4. Budget Act of 1974, P.L. 93–344, Section 3(a)(3) (1974). Since 1975 the executive branch tax expenditure list has been set forth in Special Analysis G of the Budget.

For analyses of the impact of the 1974 Budget Act on tax expenditures, see Stanley S. Surrey and Paul R. McDaniel, *The Tax Expenditure Concept and The Budget Reform Act of 1974*, 17 Boston College Industrial and Commercial Law Review 679 (1976); Stanley S. Surrey and Paul R. McDaniel, *The Tax Expenditure Concept: Current Developments and Emerging Issues*, 20 Boston College Law Review 225 (1979).

5. See, for example, Joint Committee on Taxation, *Estimates of Federal Tax Expenditures for Fiscal Years 1982–1998* (JSC–3–87), February 27, 1987; Congressional Budget Office, *Tax Expenditures: Current Issues and Five-Year Budget Projections for Fiscal Years 1984–1988* (Washington, D.C., October 1983).

6. The data in the text are derived from CBO, *Tax Expenditures: Budget Control Options and Five-Year Budget Projections for Fiscal Years 1983–1987* (Washington, D.C., November 1982), 11–16, and the references cited in supra note 5.

7. Ibid.

8. Ibid.

9. Ibid.

10. Ibid.

11. See Paul R. McDaniel, "Study of Federal Matching Grants for Charitable Contributions," in Department of the Treasury, *Research Papers Sponsored by the Commission on Private Philanthropy and Public Needs*, Vol. 4, *Taxes* (1977), 2417.

12. For example, the former 10 percent investment credit was generally limited to some percentage of tax liability, ranging from 80 percent to 90 percent. This limitation was understandable from a "tax" viewpoint since it prevented businesses from reducing tax liability to zero, a result that would be perceived as "tax inequity." But if the

investment credit were a direct government grant, no one would even think of limiting the amount of a business's grant to some percentage of its income tax liability.

Other examples of the process described in the text are discussed in Paul R. McDaniel, *Federal Income Tax Simplification: The Political Process*, 34 Tax Law Review 27 (1978).

13. Ibid., at 32–36.

14. See *Tax Expenditures*, supra note 2, 118–55.

15. See, for example, Subcommittee on Oversight, House Ways and Means Committee, *Hearings on Tax Expenditures*, 96th Cong., 1st sess. (1979).

16. See, for example, House Ways and Means Committee, *Hearings on Targeted Jobs Credit*, 98th Cong., 2d sess. (1984).

17. House Ways and Means Committee, *Hearings on Tax Reform and Deficit Reduction*, 98th Cong., 2d sess. (1984).

18. See supra note 4.

19. See, for example, CBO, *Containing Medical Care Costs Through Market Forces* (Washington, D.C., May 1982); CBO, *Tax Subsidies for Medical Care: Current Policies and Possible Alternative* (January 1980), CBO, *Tax-Exempt Bonds for Single-Family Housing*, A study prepared for the Subcommittee on the City of the House Committee on Banking, Finance and Urban Affairs, 96th Cong., 1st sess. Comm. Print, 96–2, (Washington, D.C., April 1979); CBO, *Federal Aid to Post-Secondary Students: Tax Allowances and Alternative Subsidies* (Washington, D.C., January 1978); CBO, *Real Estate Tax Shelter Subsidies and Direct Subsidy Alternatives* (Washington, D.C., May 1977).

20. Senate Budget Committee, *Tax Expenditures: Relationships to Spending Programs and Background Material on Individual Provisions*, 97th Cong., 2d sess. (Washington, D.C., 1982).

21. For an expanded discussion of these issues, see *Tax Expenditures*, supra note 2, 31–98.

22. See Treasury, Postal Service and General Government Appropriations Act, 1980, P.L. 96–74, sec. 614 (1979).

23. See Archie Parnell, *Congressional Interference in Agency Enforcement: The IRS Experience*, 89 Yale Law Journal 1360 (1980).

24. U.S. Treasury Department, *Tax Reform for Fairness, Simplicity and Economic Growth* (Washington, D.C., November 27, 1984).

25. A system such as that outlined in the text has been used in Canada. See Canadian Department of Finance, *The New Expenditure Management System* (December 1979); Richard Bird, *Tax Expenditures: The Canadian Experience*, 14 Tax Notes 423 (1982).

26. Of course, Congress could structure a direct spending program in such a way that the benefits would rise with income. Congress apparently has not taken this step with respect to any direct expenditure programs.

27. See, for example, the CBO study cited in supra note 19.

28. See, for example, Emil Sunley, Jr., "State and Local Governments," in Henry Owen and Charles L. Schultze, eds., *Setting National Priorities: The Next Ten Years* (Washington, D.C.: Brookings Institution, 1976), 395–400.

29. Paul R. McDaniel, *Tax Shelter and Tax Policy*, 26 National Tax Journal 353 (1973): 367–73.

30. For a more extended analysis, see the references cited in supra note 11.

31. The subsidy for Puerto Rican operations is contained in IRC sec. 936, which provides a tax credit for taxes imposed by Puerto Rico even though the taxpayer does not in fact, pay any such taxes. The export subsidy was formerly contained in the Domestic International Sales Corporation provisions; it is now found in the Foreign Sales Corporation provisions.

32. See the annual reports of the U.S. Department of Treasury, *The Operation and Effect of the Possession's Corporation System of Taxation.*

33. See the annual reports of the U.S. Department of Treasury, *The Operation and Effect of the Domestic International Sales Corporation Legislation.*

34. Charles Davenport, et al., *The Effects of Tax Policy on American Agriculture,* U.S. Department of Agriculture, Agricultural Economic Report no. 480 (Washington, D.C., 1982); Paul R. McDaniel, *Tax Expenditures in the Second Stage: Federal Tax Subsidies for Farm Operations,* 49 Southern California Law Review 1277 (1976).

35. "Passive activity losses" are losses resulting from investments in tax shelters where the investor does not play an active management role. The "alternative minimum tax" is a provision designed to insure that despite any loopholes, every taxpayer pays tax of at least 21 percent of his true economic income.

36. In general, see the studies in *Income Tax Compliance. A Report of the ABA Section of Taxation Invitational Conference on Income Tax Compliance* (Washington, D.C.: American Bar Association, 1983) (hereafter cited as *"Income Tax Compliance"*).

37. See Paul R. McDaniel, "The Effect of Tax Preferences on Income Tax Compliance," in *Income Tax Compliance, supra* note 35, 259–74.

38. See Paul R. McDaniel, *Tax Expenditures and Federal Spending Limitations,* 10 Tax Notes 475 (1980); Paul R. McDaniel, *Institutional Procedures for Congressional Review of Tax Expenditures,* 8 Tax Notes 659 (1979).

39. The alcohol fuels tax credit provided in IRC sec. 40 is required under IRC sec. 87 to be included in the income of the taxpayer. In some instances, the mathematical equivalent of taxability is reached by denying a deduction for the costs which generated a tax credit. Thus, in the case of the targeted jobs credit, the amount of the taxpayer's wage deduction is reduced by the amount of the credit. IRC sec. 280C.
The result of reducing the wage deduction is exactly the same as requiring the amount of the credit to be included in income. In other instances, the amount of the credit is required to be included in the income of the taxpayer by requiring the taxpayer to reduce the basis of an asset; the effect of the reduction in basis is the same as requiring the amount of the credit to be taken into income over the depreciable life of the asset. This technique is followed with respect to the general business credit provided in IRC sec. 38.

40. For example, an interest charge is imposed on the tax deferral accorded certain Domestic International Sales Corporations. IRC sec. 995(f).

TAX EXPENDITURE ESTIMATES BY BUDGET FUNCTION, FISCAL YEAR 1988
(billion dollars)

	Corporations	Individual	Total
National defense	0.0	1.9	1.9
International affairs	1.5	1.4	2.9
General science, space, and technology	4.0	0.2	4.2
Energy	−0.6	1.2	0.6
Natural resources and environment	1.0	3.0	4.0
Agriculture	0.6	0.1	0.7
Commerce and housing	49.9	80.3	130.2
Financial institutions	4.8	5.0	9.8
Housing	0.9	49.7	50.6
Other business and commerce	44.2	25.0	69.8
Transportation	0.0	0.1	0.1
Community and regional development	0.1	1.1	1.2
Education, training, employment and social services	2.2	20.6	22.8
Education and training	0.6	2.7	3.3
Employment	1.2	5.5	6.7
Social Services	0.4	12.4	12.8
Health	0.3	30.1	30.4
Medicare	0.0	5.7	5.7
Income security	0.0	80.7	80.7
Social Security	0.0	18.5	18.5
Veterans benefits and services	0.2	2.1	2.3
General purpose fiscal assistance	3.5	26.4	29.9
Interest	0.0	0.8	0.8
TOTAL	62.0	259.1	424.6

Source: Joint Committee on Taxation, Estimates of Federal Tax Expenditures for Fiscal Years 1988–1992 (JCS-3-87), February 27, 1987.

Chapter Seven

SOCIAL REGULATION AS A
GENERIC POLICY INSTRUMENT

Eugene Bardach

In its ideal form, social regulation aims to enforce "responsible" conduct on business enterprises, nonprofit organizations, and even agencies of government that might otherwise act less than "responsibly." Programmatically, social regulation is recognizable by the conjunction of three characteristic elements: (1) a body of governmentally adopted rules or standards prescribing "responsible" behavior; (2) a cadre of enforcement agents and auditors to monitor, and thereby to deter, deviations from these rules or standards; and (3) a schedule of sanctions to be applied to persons or organizations who deviate from the rules and standards to an unacceptable degree. A representative specimen of social regulation is enforcement of restaurant sanitation standards by the local or state health department. Other examples from the local level would include: construction standards enforced by the building department; the accuracy of weights and measures enforced by a county consumer affairs office; housing habitability standards enforced by the city housing department; and various fire safety standards enforced by the local fire marshall. At the federal level one of the most commonly adduced examples is the inspection of workplaces by the Occupational Safety and Health Administration (OSHA) in order to promote compliance with standards aimed at preventing occupational disease and workplace accidents. Other examples include the screening of new drugs by the Food and Drug Administration (FDA) and the policing of fraud and other deceptions in the stock market by the Securities and Exchange Commission (SEC).

State and federal regulation often overlap and cover such areas as exposure standards for workers in sites where toxic chemicals are produced or used; design standards for safeguarding machines used in manufacturing; false and deceptive advertising; quality of care of patients in nursing homes; quality of care of residents in community halfway houses for the mentally ill; honest labeling of fur and textiles; sanitation in food processing plants; the health of livestock; the transportation of hazardous materials by road; non-discrimination in tenant selection by landlords; automobile emission standards; election laws concerning campaign expenditure limits; and the storage and disposal of hazardous wastes. These are of course but a tiny sample of the objects of federal and state regulation.

Social versus Economic Regulation

Social regulation is sometimes known as "protective regulation," inasmuch as it often deals with the vulnerability of individual citizens to various hazards and injustices, against which it is hoped to protect them. It shares certain features with "economic regulation," which typically deals with pricing patterns, entry and exit, and economic output in an industry or economic sector, such as rail freight transportation or broadcasting. Both forms of regulation act through the legal instrumentality of formal regulations, and both affect, even if indirectly, prices, market entry and exit, firm profitability, and firm market share.

However, the differences between the two forms of regulation are, for most analytic purposes, much more important than their similarities. They differ, for example, in their intentions, their methods of implementation, and their political dynamics. They also differ in the rationale underlying each: whereas economic regulation may be conceived as addressing suspected imperfections in the structure and workings of markets (such as monopoly, cartel restrictions, chronic capacity excesses), protective regulation may be conceived as addressing imperfections in the liability law and other institutions for litigation.[1] The regulation of air and water pollution is a peculiar hybrid of social and economic regulation, mingling the objectives and some of the methods of social regulation with the political dynamics and economic effects often observed in economic regulation.[2]

Government as Object of Regulation

I have indicated above examples of social regulation as diverse as the enforcement of restaurant sanitation standards and the control of fur and textile labeling. Yet all these examples referred to programs in which private firms and private nonprofit organizations are the main objects of regulation. My definition of social regulation, however, also fits the many programs that apply to state and local governments (including school districts) and appear in conjunction with grant-in-aid, loan, or other sorts of subsidy programs. The regulatory aspect of these programs is simply that compliance with certain rules becomes a condition of eligibility for receiving the grant, loan, or subsidy. For instance, as state governments have assumed the role, in recent years, of major financier of local school districts, they have also tended to impose more and more regulations. In many cases, the state's withdrawal is unthinkable; and as a consequence what began as a subsidy program has now literally turned into a regulatory program, though its form retains the elements of each and it is conventionally still considered a subsidy program. In the education area, the regulatory implement has been used by the federal government as an adjunct to grant programs to promote racial integration of students and of teachers, to introduce "mainstreaming" for handicapped students, and to promote the spread of bilingual education. In the area of transportation, the federal government succeeded in imposing a national 55-mile-per-hour speed limit by threatening to withhold highway aid funds from states that refused to adopt this limit as their own.

Similarly, the reach of regulation has been extended by attaching regulatory conditions to eligibility to receive governmental contracts. In this case, the threat to withdraw access to contract funds is the relevant sanction. The federal government has used this sort of regulation to promote "affirmative action" hiring in private businesses and in institutions of higher education, for example. Regulations that make use of the sanction of denying eligibility for a broad spectrum of governmental grants and contracts for reasons basically unrelated to the programmatic ends for which the grants and contracts are awarded are generally known as "cross-cutting regulations."[3]

In practice, it is often difficult to withhold grant and contract funds from governmental units. Political pressures plus a lingering respect for the ideology of federalism and decentralization bar the way. Thus, one important element of regulatory strategy, the threat to apply sanctions for non-compliance, is defective. However, regulators *can* harass administrators in other levels of government in a way that might not be so available in the case of private business. In any event, so little is known about how regulation actually works in the case of governmental agencies as objects of regulation that such regulation will not be a principal focus here.[4]

THE GROWTH OF SOCIAL REGULATION

Social regulation is by no means a recent invention. The standard-ization of weights and measures and of coinage was attempted in biblical times and in classical antiquity. Colonial Massachusetts required each town to appoint a "gager or packer" to prevent short-weighting of packaged beef and pork. The penalty for sale without the gager's approval was forfeiture of the goods (with "one halfe to the Informer and the other halfe to the countey"). In the early 19th century New York had an "inspector general of provisions" with authority to confiscate unwholesome food.[5] In 1906 the United States adopted the federal Pure Food and Drug Act and the Meat Inspection Act, both products of the "muckraking era" and, partic-ularly, of the exposures in novels by Upton Sinclair.

The great growth of federal interest in social regulation, however, began only in the mid–1960s. The National Highway Traffic and Motor Vehicle Safety Act was passed in 1966 (on the heels of Ralph Nader's allegations of safety problems with General Motors' Cor-vair). The Coal Mine Health and Safety Act was passed in 1969, the Occupational Safety and Health Act in 1970. The Clean Air Act amendments were passed in 1970, the Water Pollution Control Act in 1972. Strip mining was regulated by the Surface Mining Control and Reclamation Act, passed in 1977. In addition, new enforce-ment powers were added to existing regulatory agencies, some-times by statute, sometimes administratively, and sometimes, indirectly, by the courts. During the late 1960s and early 1970s the Civil Rights Division of the Department of Justice became more ag-gressive in its enforcement of the Civil Rights Act of 1964; and the Office of Federal Contract Compliance extended its antidiscrimina-tion powers throughout the 1970s. In 1975 Congress passed the Magnuson-Moss Federal Trade Commission (FTC) Improvement Act, which codified hitherto informal powers of the FTC to pursue its consumer protection programs through means of industrywide "trade regulation rules" as opposed to case-by-case regulation. And these are but some of the most prominent instances of the new so-cial regulation adopted in the last two decades. Reflecting this, the overall number of federal regulatory agencies grew from 28 in 1960 to 56 in 1980.[6]

Another quantitative indicator of regulatory growth is the in-crease in the number of pages in the *Federal Register*: in 1940, about 8,000 pages were published, and in 1964, 20,000; but only one decade later the figure was roughly 60,000, and in 1980 it hit 88,000—a peak from which it subsequently declined in the Reagan years.[7] The budgets of federal regulatory agencies grew threefold (in constant dollars) between 1970 and 1980.[8] An indication of the substantial scope achieved by federal regulation in this period is the dollar cost of compliance. Economists Robert E. Litan and William D. Nordhaus compiled estimates of compliance costs for 1977 from a number of sources. In that year, environmental regulation cost between $13.4 billion and $37.9 billion; health and safety regulation cost between $7.4 billion and $17.1 billion. These costs represented between 1.1 percent and 2.9 percent of gross national product (GNP).[9] What accounts for the remarkable growth of social regulation during this period? There are many explanations, all of them mutually compatible, that together go some—though probably not the whole—distance toward explaining this phenomenon.

First, there has been an increased public demand for protection from the various risks of a complex and rapidly changing technological society. In the last 20 years we have become more aware of the toxic properties of various chemicals in everyday use, the potentially dangerous defects in household products, the carcinogenic properties of certain pesticides, and so on. While it is likely that many of these risks are, objectively, overestimated by the public at large, and even by specialists with technical knowledge about them,[10] public perceptions drive the political process. Moreover, many people's tolerance for risk has declined. In the late 1960s a growing counterculture, environmental and consumer protection organizations, and public interest advocacy groups stressed the undesirable side effects of technological change and the allocation of goods via markets. Growing affluence, coupled with a belief that an abstract entity called "business" was technically and financially capable of preventing the harms in question, sustained the illusion that "what could be should be." Furthermore, the "should" increasingly acquired a moral dimension: the reformist activism of a generation that had created a civil rights revolution and was effectively protesting the country's involvement in the Vietnam War aimed to define as "rights" what had hitherto been seen as individually earned rewards—decent housing, a job in a safe workplace—or else simply as "blessings"—good health, clean air, and water.

Changes in the political elite also played a role in the growth of protective regulation. Individual senators and congressmen cultivated a more entrepreneurial legislative style and sought out issues with media appeal and hence the possibility of attracting national attention. Budgetary politics also played a role; a crucial political advantage that regulation enjoys over various other forms of subsidies (such as grants-in-aid and loans) as a generic policy tool is that the costs of achieving the stipulated goals show up principally in the ledgers of private business rather than government. This was particularly important in the earliest phase of the new wave of protective regulation, when President Lyndon B. Johnson sought ways to launch new and politically popular governmental initiatives without draining funds from the increasingly expensive Vietnam War effort.[11] In addition, as Irving Kristol and others have argued, an expanding "new class" of college-educated professionals working in the postindustrial "knowledge industries" sought psychologically satisfying jobs in the public sector.[12] Finally, it is in the nature of regulation to feed on itself; once a program is launched, a certain deductive logic forces its expansion to neighboring domains (racial equality generalizing to gender equality and "equal access" for the handicapped, for example). This same logic then promotes the augmentation of enforcement efforts, and increases the level of sanctions available to regulators.[13]

Attempts by the Reagan administration to "relieve" business of "the burden of federal regulation" have generally not resulted in much reduction in the scope or impact of federal regulation. The regulatory history of this period seems, by and large, to confirm the "ratchet" theory of social regulation advanced by Robert A. Kagan and myself in 1982, to wit, that regulation can be held down to some current level but not significantly rolled back.[14] The Reagan presidency was most successful in introducing a less stringent enforcement style in several agencies (notably the Office of Surface Mining, the Consumer Product Safety Commission [CPSC], the Equal Employment Opportunities Commission, the National Labor Relations Board, the FDA, OSHA, the EPA, and the FTC), although in the important cases of OSHA and the EPA the administrators who took over in the closing years of the Reagan administration appear to have reinstated the tougher style that was disdained in the early Reagan years.[15] The administration also devolved a number of regulatory responsibilities to state governments, although the announced intention—and perhaps, in some cases, the result—of these shifts was not so much to "reduce" regulation as to "improve" it.[16] The first Reagan budget slashed social regulatory agencies severely in terms of both dollars and manpower but these cuts were in some—though not all—cases partially restored in later years.[17] Although the Reagan administration drastically slowed down the promulgation of new regulations, mainly by means of subjecting proposed regulations to merciless review by the Office of Management and Budget (OMB), it did not succeed in removing many existing regulations from the books. In particular, it did not reform or reduce the vast and costly structure of environmental regulation.[18]

TECHNICAL ISSUES IN REGULATORY DESIGN

I remarked at the outset that social regulatory programs enforce standards of "responsible" conduct on various enterprises and agencies, and that they do this by means of the threat to apply sanctions in the event that violations of standards are detected by inspection and audit officials. In this section I explore some of the technical design issues that a legislator or a top-level program manager might encounter in establishing and running a program of social regulation.

The Choice of Regulatory Rules and Standards

Regulatory standards typically specify some minimum level of acceptable performance. In the product safety area, the CPSC standard for baby cribs stipulates that crib slats must be spaced no less than 2⅜ inches apart. Regulations under the Clean Air Act amendments of 1977 specify ambient air standards of no more than 12 parts per million of ozone in any given hour. As in these examples, most standards are expressed in quantitative terms. However, regulatory standards may also be expressed qualitatively, as in the statutes requiring new drugs to be proven "safe and effective" before they may be marketed.

A distinction is often drawn between "design" (or "specification") and "performance" standards, the latter specifying results to be achieved and the former specifying the means that regulators believe will produce the desired results. The crib slat standards are of the design type; the new drug standards are performance standards. Although performance standards give regulated parties the flexibility to adopt more cost-effective measures than design standards might permit, and in principle are widely endorsed for this reason, they are far less prevalent than design standards. The reason is that they often present enforcement problems. Consider, for example, the results one desires from a design standard requiring that community residential facilities for the mentally ill house no more than two residents per room. These results have to do with the dignity and comfort of the resident, which may in some cases be better achieved by having three or even four residents in a room, but which in other cases may depend on having the resident live alone. In these cases the design standard is ineffective or downright harmful, and an enforceable performance standard would surely be superior. Yet, how is one to write such a standard, employing highly subjective terms like resident "dignity" and "comfort"? The task is extremely difficult, even impossible; hence regulators settle for the design standard. Moreover, regulated parties frequently like the clarity and specificity of design standards, even when they complain about their rigidity and lack of realism for the situation at hand.

A common difficulty in writing design standards (and sometimes performance standards as well) is the lack of consensually acknowledged causal relationships between certain design "inputs" and desired policy "outputs." In setting its crib slat standard, the CPSC relied on extensive technical research which reached a relatively unambiguous conclusion (depending, as it did, merely on the body measurements of a large number of infants). But it is a lot harder to know the degree to which space per halfway house resident is causally related to resident dignity and comfort. Probably the most politically vexed issue of technical uncertainty occurs in the field of toxic chemicals (in the workplace, in the ambient environment, and as food additives), where tests for carcinogenicity and other harmful properties are typically carried out on mice and rats rather than humans, making the results of such tests a quite unstable scientific foundation for setting regulatory standards aimed at protecting people.

The writing of standards also forces a trade-off between simplicity and "congruence," that is, the fitting of regulatory language to the exact objects intended, being neither "overinclusive" nor "underinclusive." The variety and complexity of the real world of people, things, and institutions is not easily captured in regulatory language. More precisely, they may be captured only through the elaboration of manifold categories, conditions, and contingencies. Yet such elaboration can make regulations too dense and too voluminous to be mastered either by the regulated parties or by the regulatory officials. On the other hand, simplicity is purchased only at the price of ignoring some of the real complexity and variety in the world, thereby justifying complaints of regulatory overkill, insensitivity, and inadequacy.

Enforcement Strategies

The first major design question with regard to enforcement strategies concerns whether or not to screen individuals or firms *before* they begin to carry out some regulated activity or to restrict regulatory efforts to surveillance of their activities once they have begun. Prior screening is often accomplished through "licensing," though this is not the only function of licensing as a regulatory instrument.[19] Prior screening potentially offers greater protection to the public than ongoing surveillance by itself, and it also permits the regulatory agency to obtain a better "map" of the regulated activities under its jurisdiction. It has the substantial disadvantages, however, of delaying legitimate activities pending the sometimes lengthy processes of bureaucratic review, discouraging innovation, and concealing both these faults from public scrutiny because they entail sins of omission rather than commission.[20]

Perhaps the second most important design question in the enforcement area concerns the choice between sending agency inspectors into the field and requiring self-reports from the regulated parties, which reports are then audited (usually on a sampling basis) and verified (systematically, if infrequently) in the agency offices. Self-reporting can be more comprehensive and more informative than direct surveillance, since the reports are prepared by insiders who know their own local situation better than inspectors do. It is certainly a less costly form of monitoring to the regulatory agency, since the regulated parties bear most of the costs. On the other hand, direct inspections may produce more trustworthy information, at least with respect to the matters that inspectors are able to attend to, and may permit inspectors to gain information not easily conveyed in written reports.[21]

Another strategic choice concerns the use of complainants and other third parties (including "informers") as auxiliary enforcement resources. Workers may complain to OSHA, for instance, about suspected hazardous conditions and, under some conditions, can thereby trigger an inspection. In some states nursing home regulators receive complaints from nursing home residents and target at least a portion of their investigations accordingly. Many state and local consumer protection agencies rely almost exclusively on complainants to generate their caseload. Despite the evident desirability of mobilizing unpaid third parties to assist the regulatory agency, however, there are drawbacks to this strategy as well. Complainants may be motivated by spite, or they may use the threat to complain as a form of blackmail against an employer or a seller. Complainants often are ignorant of the law and of what truly constitutes a breach of regulations. Complaints also tend to come from the most articulate sectors of the population, not necessarily from the sectors exposed to the most problems or in need of the most help. Furthermore, an agency relying on complaints usually must find a way to balance the right of an accused to know his accuser against the complainant's desire or need for anonymity; and in cases where anonymity must be, or is likely to be, breached the agency must typically find a way to offer the complainant protection from reprisal. Reliance on complainants, therefore, may amount to an inefficient and troublesome strategy.

The targeting of scarce field-enforcement resources also poses a strategic choice for agency managers. A certain number of random (and unannounced) inspections may be thought useful for their supposed deterrence effect. On the other hand, they may miss sites with the most serious problems. Concentrating on the problem sites is a good strategy for the nonrandom inspections an agency conducts—but only if there is a substantial probability that agency intervention in these sites will actually lead to improved compliance. This latter condition is not necessarily easy to meet, inasmuch as the same conditions underlying the original problems might also underlie a commitment not to comply with enforcement orders— lack of social conscience, risk of insolvency, cash-flow problems, a principled belief that the agency's standards are wrong-headed or inapplicable in the circumstances at hand, and so on.

The recruitment, training, supervision, and motivation of field-level enforcement officials present numerous problems. Frequently government regulatory agencies compete directly with private industry for the technically qualified personnel that can best perform the agencies' inspectorial (and standards-writing) functions. Safety engineers, industrial hygienists, food chemists, building trades specialists, conservation biologists, automotive engineers, accountants, lawyers, architects—these and other professionals may find a niche equally well in the regulated firms as in the regulatory agencies. Indeed, salaries and working conditions in the regulated sector are often superior to those in government. Agency recruitment efforts must often rely, therefore, on agency claims to be serving some broader, higher, and perhaps nobler purpose than private sector entities. Sometimes such claims may be persuasive (and perhaps justifiable), but frequently the regulatory employer loses the competition for the highest-quality or the best-trained professionals to the private sector.[22] In-house training may be able to overcome some deficiencies in the background of agency recruits, but agencies appear to vary greatly in how much energy and resources they devote to this function.

Because regulatory agencies deploy inspectors whose work takes them to off-site locations and brings them into direct contact with regulated parties, the opportunities for corruption are abundant. Corruption can take the form of underenforcing the law in exchange for bribes, or threatening to enforce the law punitively or with excessive stringency in order to extort "protection money." Supervisory strategies to deter corruption of both sorts include: rotating inspectors periodically to new "beats," pairing inspectors in the field, requiring that inspectors "go by the book" in enforcing all relevant regulations, requiring inspectors to document thoroughly the reasons for deviating from what "the book" calls for, forbidding inspectors to accept even token gestures of hospitality from regulated parties, and reinspecting certain sites to evaluate the quality of the initial inspection. All such strategies entail costs, of course. Rotation of personnel implies that the site-specific knowledge or expertise that an inspector manages to acquire through experience is soon dissipated. "Going by the book" implies rigidity and eliminates discretionary underenforcement as a method of compensating for overinclusive rules. Documenting the reasons for discretionary actions is time-consuming and might require subtlety of expression and analysis. Forbidding hospitable interactions can create unnecessarily hard feelings in those being regulated or can, in any event, shrink regulators' opportunities for motivating compliance through informal or nonlegalistic means. Both double-teaming and periodic reinspections consume budgetary resources.

Many strategies can be used to motivate performance, but the one most worth mentioning here involves the use of quantitative measures of enforcement activity, which include the number of sites visited, the number of violations cited, and the amount of fines assessed. The design problem here concerns the possible distorting effect of such measures. On the assumption that field-enforcement officials will actually be motivated to produce more of what is measured by these indices, the results will not be desirable unless there is a good correspondence between the measured output and the desired output—such as a reduction in otherwise expectable injuries or injustices. Yet this correspondence is necessarily attenuated by the fact that measures of actual enforcement activity never can capture the deterrent effect of regulatory efforts—the violations that never occurred because the program was in place.[23] Furthermore, quantity is not the same as quality: "nitpicking" violations might be numerous and easily detectable, but even in large numbers may not add up to a genuinely serious condition deserving of remedy and, hence, enforcement attention.

Finally, the emphasis on finding and recording violations might displace energies better directed at developing a consultative and cooperative relationship between the enforcement officials and the representative of the regulated enterprise. The "good inspector," like the "good cop," is not a zealot for tough, stringent, legalistic enforcement of the laws. Rather, the good inspector relies on a mixture of persuasion, bargaining, charm, and threat to induce compliance. Quantitative measures of enforcement activity cannot capture the beneficial results attributable to these more psychological tactics, many of which are, in any case, only indirectly connected with "enforcement."[24]

Regulatory Sanctions

The sanctions imposed in social regulatory programs typically include money fines, withholding or revocation of permits to operate or to market goods, enforced restitution of damages by the offending business to the injured party, and the seizure and destruction of noncomplying goods or other items of property. Some regulatory agencies have the authority to enjoin "imminently dangerous" activity on an emergency basis, for example, closing down hazardous work sites or banning the marketing of contaminated products. A related power is that of ordering manufacturers to recall defective products (such as automobiles) for the purposes of making repairs. In cases of willful noncompliance, fraud, or other such purposive offenses, criminal sanctions might also be invoked.

The design and application of sanctions is the most fragmented area of social regulation. The legislative branch characteristically specifies the schedule of sanctions associated with general classes of violations. The field-level enforcement official gathers the evidence required to persuade administrative superiors and/or a court to apply the sanction. Within the regulatory agency sanctions must normally be approved by one or more hierarchical levels above the field agent. Often there is a semi-autonomous "appeals board" within the agency to review line supervisors' decisions to proceed with sanctions. Agencies that lack the legislative authority to impose sanctions on their own must turn to the courts; this step in turn requires that the agency persuade the district attorney's office to take up the matter—not always a simple step, as these offices normally are overworked and burdened with "more serious offenses." Even when the agency does have the authority to impose sanctions without court orders, the accused party always has the right to appeal to the courts against the agency's decision.

Official sanctions are often accompanied by unofficial sanctions, which may or may not be intended by the agency, and which sometimes can be quite potent. The adverse publicity associated with a product ban or recall, for instance, can be extremely damaging to a company's overall sales. More than one food processor, bakery, or restaurant has been shut down following reports of sanitation violations or suspected product contamination. Furthermore, many firms, especially large and nationally visible corporations, dislike the scofflaw or "bad citizen" image associated with regulatory noncompliance. In the worker safety case, publicizing safety and health violations can lead to increased pressure from local unions. And in some cases, the threat of repeat inspections and intensive future surveillance by the regulatory agency also amounts to a considerable sanction ("the hassle factor"). Since the legislated schedule of money fines is often low, these informal sanctions may often be more important in inducing compliance than the formal sanctions.

Among formal sanctions the control over a firm's products or marketing opportunities constitutes a much more powerful sanction than fines. The threat of an automobile recall, for example, is a much more powerful weapon in the hands of the National Highway Traffic Safety Administration than its schedule of fines for noncompliance. Building inspectors are powerful because they can prevent the occupancy of a building. (Conversely, housing inspectors are not powerful because they cannot normally threaten to vacate an occupied unit.) Any agency that relies on screening, like the FDA with respect to new drugs, or a state agency that licenses child day care facilities or residential care, like halfway houses for the mentally ill, is in a powerful position before the license is granted. On the other hand, since license revocation requires substantial proof and therefore is very costly to the regulatory agency, once a license has been granted its value as a potential sanction is much diminished.

So far we have discussed the choices of standards, enforcement measures, and sanctions independently, but in fact they are interdependent in important ways. Overinclusive standards and rules, or excessively potent sanctions, can be corrected by discretionary underenforcement (as the police commonly do with regard to the criminal law). Inadequate formal sanctions can be supplemented by informal sanctions or the threat of such sanctions. Technical uncertainty that inheres in particular standards may be offset by more careful enforcement judgments and by hearings or appeals connected with the application of sanctions. Inadequate budgets for enforcement personnel can lead agencies to adopt standards that permit self-reporting plus auditing (specification standards that are easy to monitor) and to eschew the enforcement of standards that involve sanctions likely to provoke legal contestation.

PHILOSOPHICAL ISSUES IN REGULATORY DESIGN

This sketch of the technical issues involved in regulation suggests certain value choices that are inherent in regulation. Social regulation is one of the most politically and ideologically controversial of all the policy tools examined in this volume. Citizens, political elites, and scholarly observers are quite divided on whether we have too much or too little social regulation; how cost-beneficial or cost-effective it is; how much it honors or violates norms of fairness and administrative due process; and whether superior alternatives may be found in private institutions like the unregulated market, the liability law, and professional ethical codes. Even when there is agreement on the desirability of a particular regulatory intervention, consensus may easily fail with respect to the many technical issues that attend regulatory design, since these usually have philosophical or ideological as well as merely technical implications.

Political liberals have often supported social regulatory programs as a means of aiding interests deemed to be "weak" or "vulnerable" in the face of excessively powerful or "predatory" forces. Liberal ideology has posited an "imbalance of power," originating in unjustly operating markets or legal institutions (particularly the law of torts and contracts), which government should redress. Conservatives, on the other hand, have objected to the supposed intrusiveness of regulation; its interference with enterprise, personal freedom, and privacy; and to the financial costs seemingly borne by business.[25] (Although both conservatives and liberals often assume that the economic costs of regulation are borne by "business," it is usually hard to determine in what fashion costs are distributed among shareholders, employees, and product consumers.)

Concern over the procedural aspects of regulation cuts across political ideology—almost everyone believes in fairness, due process, and elimination of unnecessary coercion. Ordinary citizens who become the objects of regulatory attention also demand "reasonable," rather than "inflexible" or "rigid," application of the rules to their own particular cases.

Academic economists have introduced into the debate criteria concerning some proportionality between social benefits and economic costs. Unlike the conservatives, however, their conception of "costs" is much broader than simply the financial costs imposed (in the first instance) on business firms. The economic conception covers all the "resources" that go into compliance with regulatory standards, including those spent by government in administering the standards; and it also covers the benefits lost to society (if any) by restricting productive activities to those allowed by the particular standards adopted. An auto safety standard, for instance, that prevented consumers who preferred the risks of possible crash injuries to the costs of bigger, heavier bumpers from satisfying their preferences would be counted as imposing social costs. The economist also counts on the cost side of the ledger the inefficiencies of any cartel-like strategies that an industry may be able to carry out when it can indirectly control firms' product qualities and prices.

The economic perspective elevates two criteria to positions of pre-eminence: net-benefit-maximization and cost-effectiveness. The first holds that neither gross costs nor gross benefits are important by themselves; what counts is net benefits (benefits minus costs), which are to be maximized. This criterion is not inherently more favorable to either the liberal or the conservative perspective as described above, although in practice it has been used so often as an argument against specific regulatory standards and even programs that liberal advocates of regulation have come to regard it with suspicion. The cost-effectiveness criterion holds that once some budget (cost) is adopted or, alternatively, some target benefit level selected, the ratio of benefits to costs should be made as high as possible. In principle, therefore, cost-effectiveness analysis should be acceptable to liberal partisans of regulation who, in the name of protecting the weak, implicitly set some target level of protection and let the costs take care of themselves. So long as the target level is achieved, these liberal partisans should be pleased if costs are held to the minimum efficient level. Thus reason the economists, at least. In the real world of policy making, however, it is often hard to distinguish cost reductions that are designed to hold benefits constant while economizing on resources from cost reductions that are simply indifferent to benefits or to "justice." Hence, liberal partisans of regulation are often suspicious of both of the criteria that seem to make such good sense to the academic economist.[26]

The evolution of any particular regulatory program reflects to some extent the conflicting ideological forces that are present at its birth and that impinge on it during its subsequent implementation. This means that certain policy values move into ascendancy for certain periods and may sink into decline during others—though not necessarily permanently. Just as we spoke of technical trade-offs above, then, we may speak of value trade-offs, the most important of which we examine in the rest of this section.

Regulatory "Capture" versus Rigidity and Legalism

Because so many of the important decisions in regulatory programs are technical and take place within regulatory agencies far from public view, the ideological constituency that dominated the legislative struggle over policy design may be beaten by other constituencies in administrative arenas. To the original partisans, especially to liberal advocates of new regulatory initiatives, this process has earned the epithet "capture": agency officials become "coopted" by the businesses with whom they were supposed to have an adversarial, or at least an "arms-length," relationship.[27] In the last two decades, the capture motif has entered the conventional wisdom of political discussion as well, largely due to the rhetorical efforts of Ralph Nader and his "Raiders," whose critiques of various federal regulatory agencies from the FTC to the FDA have all leaned heavily on "capture" as an explanation for agency "failure" or "weakness."

The reasoning as to why capture occurs ranges from the subtle corruption of regulators by the implicit and explicit offers of lucrative jobs in the regulated industry to the regulators' inevitable dependence on information supplied by the regulated industry as a partial basis for regulatory decisions. Aggravating conditions include vague statutory mandates, a low level of prescribed penalties for violations, lack of judicial scrutiny, difficulty of access on the part of "the public" to regulatory decision arenas, and the atmosphere of privacy if not secrecy that surrounds regulatory decision making. The design solution is thought, therefore, to be

□ explicit statutes and statutorily prescribed penalties
□ avoidance of statutory language that would permit legalistic defenses by business or excessive latitude on the part of regulators
□ the supplanting, to the extent possible, of state and local regulation by federal regulators, presumably less accessible to localized business pressures, and
□ facilitating "public access" to the regulatory decision process by such means as granting legal standing to citizens with policy grievances to sue the agency and making funds available to citizen "intervenors."

The reformers' agenda, which can be summed up as "centralization" and "legalization," was implemented to some extent, by a cooperative judiciary and journalism profession.[28]

Through such remedies capture can indeed be avoided, or at least mitigated, but these remedies carry a price. The internal structure of the agency is made hierarchical, rule-bound, and centralized; the external environment of the agency is kept in flux; and the boundary between the two is weakened so as to permit easy scrutiny and political pressure from a multiplicity of interested parties, including the courts, the press, legislators, and the chief executive. These design features, unfortunately, are as inhospitable to policy stability and rationality as they are to would-be captors. The congressional design of OSHA serves as a useful example. Its rigidity and inflexibility have angered many regulated firms. Its emphasis on safety at the expense of worker health issues initially satisfied political demands for agency visibility, but to the detriment of workers' most serious real needs. The initial reluctance to have OSHA inspectors play the role of "friendly consultant," and a presumption instead, in favor of the "tough cop" role, was a strategy to prevent cooptation at the field level; this strategy worked but also made businesses unwilling to consult OSHA experts about safety and health matters on which they might indeed have been helpful. Worse yet, OSHA inspectors did not in fact develop the expertise that would have proved helpful, since it was not to be their role to furnish it. Of course, it is possible that a design for OSHA which built in more flexibility and rationality would have led to agency capture and even less effective policy than what emerged.

Costs versus Benefits

The original capture theory held forth the possibility that regulated businesses would manage to win enough regulatory power to dilute agency effectiveness. It did not contemplate the possibility that (1) regulatory "zealots" committed to effectiveness (that is, the attainment of public health, consumer protection, gender equality, etc.) at any cost might capture programmatic control, or (2) one segment of the regulated industry might manipulate regulatory authority to impose high compliance costs on its competitors—and indirectly on the public—in order to secure a competitive advantage: a process known as "rent-seeking." Yet these are always lively possibilities, and sometimes actualities.

It was alleged during the Carter administration, for example, that regulatory zealots had seized control of the regulatory agencies. The "iron triangle" linking legislative subcommittees, regulatory agency managers, and business interests was not abolished, only reoriented so that liberal and environmental interest groups substituted for business interests at the third apex.[29] The most visible evidence for this development was the presence of several individuals who had risen to prominence with Nader's Raiders in top regulatory positions in the administration, such as, Joan Claybrook, who headed the National Highway Traffic Safety Administration.

One of the most notorious examples of how economic rivals use regulation to secure a competitive advantage comes from the 1977 amendments to the Clean Air Act. Eastern coal producers and the United Mine Workers joined forces with environmentalists to require, in effect, the installation of very expensive sulfur scrubbers on all new coal-burning power plants, independently of the sulfur content of the coal being burned. This requirement eliminated the cost advantage of low-sulfur western coal relative to high-sulfur eastern coal and protected unionized mineworkers' jobs in the east from their nonunion rivals in the west.[30]

Effectiveness Constrained by Fairness and Budgets

If directed at the truly "bad apples" in the regulated population, harassment, intimidation, and outright bullying might be both effective and morally appropriate. However, norms of fairness, especially as embodied in respect for legal due process, bar such tactics. They may even inhibit the sort of informal bargaining that would be appropriate in dealing with regulated parties more generally. This sort of bargaining often takes the form of the inspector trading noncompliance for lesser matters, or (with purely technical or procedural standards) for substantive improvements that would be hard to embody effectively within the strict framework of the law. Such informal bargaining, however, opens the door to shake-downs, bribes, corruption in general, and ultimately to a reduction in effectiveness. Knowing how much informality to tolerate in the face of such risks and costs poses a significant design dilemma.

Another related question concerns the trade-off between regulatory effectiveness and restricting the scope and intrusiveness of government. This generally takes the form of decisions over the enforcement budget and the number of inspectors to deploy. The Internal Revenue Service, for instance, is constantly denied resources to expand its audit staff significantly, even though it is acknowledged by OMB and the Congress that the revenue yield would probably justify the dollar investment by a factor of eight or more. It is felt that "the public just would not stand for it."

Cost-Effectiveness and Other Values

All other things equal, because the world is so complex and variegated, customizing the regulatory rules and enforcement techniques to individual cases would be socially efficient (that is, cost-effective). The particular costs and benefits of particular actions by particular parties in particular situations would be taken into account by the regulatory agency. But this conclusion holds only if we ignore the various costs of detailed, case-by-case decision making. Some of the costs of customized treatment are easily translated into dollars, but others are expressed as potential threats to less tangible values like equality, fairness, simplicity, and honest government. Once these are taken into account, a degree of standardization is desirable. A high degree of standardization seems to ensure that people will be treated fairly and, in a certain sense, "equally." While standardization does not make corruption impossible, it does make corruption harder to conceal and therefore works to discourage it. And, by ignoring differences, standardization makes rules and procedures simpler, easier to master, both for the regulated parties and for the regulators themselves. Probably, fewer lawyers and accountants would be needed on either side of the table.

Yet there are also costs to standardization. Whatever the standard, there will be cases that deviate from it. Some parties will bear compliance costs that, in their particular situations, yield little or no benefits. A factory may be obliged to install guards on machines soon to be replaced and presently used only by highly experienced and careful workers. Or a village public library may, if it wishes to continue to receive federal or state subsidies, be obliged to undertake expensive renovations to improve wheelchair accessibility when it could more cheaply serve its two wheelchair-bound patrons by continuing to deliver books to their homes. In some cases, the costs of regulatory compliance may be so high that firms or governmental agencies opt altogether out of the otherwise beneficial activity that had drawn regulatory attention. For example, the library in question may to forgo federal subsidy altogether because it is simply too expensive to comply with the conditions under which it was offered. In addition, imposition of "unreasonably" high costs on regulated parties contributes to alienation from government and undermines respect for governmental requirements or activities more generally—including the more reasonable requirements of the regulatory agency in question.

The alternative way of handling the possible costs of standardization is to set the general level of regulatory requirements *too low* or their scope *too narrow*, relative to what policymakers ideally desire. Doing so would mean that some potential beneficiaries of the regulatory program would not be aided.[31]

Presumably, the promulgation of cost-effective rules requires some degree of thought, time, and perhaps research. The rationality of the rule-making process, however, may be at odds with other values that are supposed to be enshrined in the administrative process. When the factual issues involved in rule-making are complex—perhaps scientific information concerning risks is lacking, or economic information concerning abatement costs is thought to be unreliable or distorted—the most expeditious method for reaching an honest approximation to their solution is often that of discussion, persuasion, bargaining, and compromise. This method typically requires *ex parte* proceedings, the convocation of informal workshops or other such forums, and the aggressive canvassing of opinions that might not turn up in formal hearings or comments. The adversarial type of process so central to administrative rule-making in the United States, which discourages such *ex parte* and informal activities, may be reasonably good at settling certain kinds of relatively well-focused disputes, but it is not well adapted to the analytical elucidation of complex and ambiguous technical issues.

In addition, deliberative time spent on promulgating some standards is time not spent on others. The regulation of various kinds of toxic chemicals (in pesticides and industrial solvents, for instance) is beset by the problem of excessive attention to a few substances driving out time for modest consideration of a greater numbers of substances.[32]

Competing Equities

A great deal of social regulation is directed at conduct or products or environmental conditions that pose some hard-to-assess risk or threat. In addition to the problem of determining accurately the facts of the case (and thus determining the extent to which variable x is a cause of outcome y), the agency also faces the task of estimating how much people would value a reduction of a particular magnitude of this particular outcome. These conditions ensure that when the regulatory agency carries out its own assessment it will make a certain number of errors. In general the agency makes errors of (1) underestimating or (2) overestimating the real value of reducing the danger or risk in the object of its assessment. Typically, the procedures and approaches that tend to reduce errors of one type tend to increase errors of the other type. The distributive implication of this fact is that either too few potential beneficiaries are actually helped by regulatory efforts, or too many costs (without corresponding social benefits) are imposed on regulated parties.

As noted above, the regulatory agency usually has a choice between having its inspectors play the role of "tough cop" or that of "friendly consultant," or some blend of these two. But however desirable it might be for the agency to synthesize the right blend of the two approaches for any given person or situation, in practice it is quite difficult to customize the correct approach for each occasion. For one thing, it is often hard to know in advance which approach would really work for each case; for another, the costs of training and supervising field enforcement personnel could easily be prohibitive. Hence, an agency must usually decide to err in one direction or another, acting "on average" either a little too tough or a little too friendly.

This fact too has distributional implications. In general, the tough cop approach is most appropriate to the "bad apples," who normally constitute merely one tail of a distribution of attitudes among regulated parties. But if it is applied across the board, the "good apples" find themselves "treated like criminals" and subjected to a variety of overly stringent reporting requirements and the like. On the other hand, a generalized friendly consultant strategy risks failing to deter misconduct by the bad apples. If, indeed, as we have assumed, the bad apples are a minority, then the regulatory dilemma is to choose between protecting a relatively small population of potential beneficiaries (or at least making the effort, whether or not it is successful) and treating too harshly the majority (good apples) of regulated parties.[33]

The political environment of the agency and the degree of the agency's insulation against, or permeability to, that environment is likely to powerfully affect this choice. An environment densely populated by the regulated parties themselves, and by legislators or politically powerful executives who represent the interests of these parties, will very likely produce a bias in favor of accommodating the good apples. Sanctions will be low, the regulatory impediments to applying them will be high, field enforcement officials will tend to be "flexible" and act more as friendly consultants than as tough cops. On the other hand, a political environment dominated by beneficiary groups or their representatives, or by liberal sympathizers with the regulatory mission of the agency, will push the agency in the opposite direction. The push in this latter direction has another source as well. The fact that injustices, accidents, injuries, fatalities, and catastrophes are always bound to occur, even under the most scrupulous regulatory regime, guarantees a permanent vulnerability of the agency to criticism for being insufficiently vigorous, vigilant, and "tough." To deflect or neutralize such criticism when it does come, agencies are more inclined than they otherwise might be to treat regulated parties as though they were bad apples or likely to become so.[34]

APPRAISING SOCIAL REGULATION

As we proceed to evaluate past experience with social regulation and to speculate on its prospective potential, it is worthwhile keeping in mind the variety of philosophical and ideological perspectives that observers can and do legitimately bring to bear on the phenomenon. It is also useful to recognize that reliable and systematic evaluative data do not exist with respect to several important performance criteria, and that with respect to other criteria the available evidence may provide a somewhat distorted picture.

Consider first the criterion of "reasonableness" in particular situations, so important to the ordinary citizen. The subjective experience of the ordinary citizen who becomes the object of some sort of regulatory control is characteristically annoyance or frustration. This is so no matter how beneficial, intelligently conceived, and well-executed the regulatory program. Even the most virtuous and compliant citizens must periodically demonstrate to regulatory officials their actual rectitude. They must complete the relevant paperwork and host visits by the inquiring field-enforcement officials. Unfortunately, there are no systematic data on the level of citizen dissatisfaction with being the object of surveillance. In many cases it could be small, especially if the citizenry generally understands and appreciates the reasons for the regulatory program. But the sheer number of citizens subject to compliance reporting probably multiplies individually small annoyances into a rather substantial social cost.

In addition, it is virtually certain that some regulated parties will be the object of genuinely intrusive and unreasonable regulatory structures. There is always a rule that does not make sense in at least one case but is enforced nonetheless. The essentially ambiguous and uncertain tasks that are at the foundation of many or most programs of protective regulation—tasks which are nonetheless carried out in the context of legal norms that require the pretensions of rationality, due process, and consistency—virtually guarantee that these problems will occur. Moreover, in this large and imperfect world there is always an inspector who exceeds his authority or who harasses "innocent" businessmen or who attempts a shakedown. Unfortunately, we have no systematic data on how extensive these virtually inescapable problems of legalism (overinclusive rules) and petty tyranny may be. In the case of legalism, we may speculate that the problem is aggravated to the extent that (1) regulatory rules are written primarily to deal with the social problems created by a particularly troublesome subset of regulated entities, and (2) this subset is a relatively small and unrepresentative tail of the entire distribution (the bad apples).

Let us turn now to certain areas in which more systematic data are available: effectiveness, economic costs, and social benefits. In general, the available literature paints a very discouraging picture indeed of the value of protective regulation. Regulation appears in many cases to be ineffective, costly, and—when effective at all—of only modest value to the parties supposed to benefit from it. This, at any rate, is the conclusion of most academic students of the subject, though optimism is somewhat higher in the analyses produced by advocacy groups.[35] It should be emphasized, however, that one should generalize only with great caution from the existing academic literature to the whole domain of protective regulation. Academic analysts have probably tended to focus on those programs that they suspected, on theoretical grounds, were poorly conceived.[36] Secondly, most of the published studies concern proposed or actual regulatory *standards* rather than programs in their entirety. The selective bias toward studying inefficient and ineffective standards can have an even more severe distorting effect than studying poor programs, as even programs that are "good" or "desirable" overall are bound to incorporate at least some costly standards of dubious benefit. Furthermore, studies focused on standards alone do not usually attempt to assess the degree to which poor standards are in fact underenforced by field personnel and by administrators or judges involved in the application of sanctions for noncompliance.

However, it is also true that programs which look good in principle—that is, intervene in markets where the conditions for consumer sovereignty appear to be notably absent, such as nursing homes—may be imperfectly implemented. Whereas the academic literature may perhaps overemphasize overregulation, underregulation is also likely to be a significant problem in certain areas, such as the management of toxic substances and hazardous wastes. Hence, the documentation of the poor performance of protective regulation may tend to understate, rather than overstate, the case.

Given the limitations of the literature, then, I merely sketch here the types of appraisals one finds in this field. There would be no point in providing a definitive survey of the literature, since the conclusions reached in the literature do not permit us to appraise the past performance of "protective regulation" considered as a generic tool.

One probable success may be found in the area of coal mine safety. Mining fatalities per man hour declined after the passage of tough safety laws in 1941 and again in 1969, though not after the passage of a merely "symbolic" law in 1952.[37] In the worker safety area, regulation by OSHA appears to have had either no impact or a very small positive impact on workplace accident rates.[38] In the area of worker health, it is likely OSHA has done relatively little to ameliorate the problem of exposure to dangerous chemicals. It has adopted very few exposure limit standards relative to the number of probable dangerous substances to which exposure is common.

But some of these have been extremely costly and the exposure reductions they sought could have been achieved at much lower cost through the use of personal-protection devices (such as masks and protective clothing) rather than through engineering controls.

In the realm of product safety, Viscusi's careful review of the work of the federal Consumer Product Safety Commission is able to find no measurable effect on product-related injuries in the aggregate and little or no effect for any of nearly a dozen specific products regulated by the commission. In the case of child-resistant medicine bottle caps mandated by the commission, there may have been a perverse effect: parents may have relied too much on these caps and reduced their vigilance against their children's access to medicine bottles; furthermore, due to the difficulty of removing the caps, more bottles may have been left around without being capped at all.[39]

Environmental protection is probably the area in which the total costs of regulation are the highest. In 1979, the Council on Environmental Quality projected the annual costs of water pollution control regulations through 1985 at $18 billion to $19 billion. It estimated the benefits, however, to fall into some range around $12 billion.[40] With regard to air pollution control, there is a substantial consensus that there have been large benefits, although the estimates of the magnitude of these benefits vary between $5 billion and $60 billion. In pure physical terms, the number of "unhealthful, very unhealthful, and hazardous" days per year in 23 major metropolitan areas declined 18 percent in the period 1974–78.[41] There is also no consensus on whether total benefits exceed total costs, although it seems quite likely that air pollution abatement targets at the margin are too ambitious and costly given the relatively small probable benefits for health.[42]

The FDA screens all new drugs for safety and efficacy. The screening process does effectively hold dangerous drugs off the market but it also delays or inhibits the introduction of valuable new drugs. A number of studies have concluded that the excessive caution of the FDA (instilled in part by congressional sentiment as well) has been extremely costly in terms of delaying the marketing of new and beneficial drugs in the United States.[43]

Since 1970, recipients of federal contracts (and grants) have been obliged, pursuant to an executive order of the president and subsequent judicial and bureaucratic adjustments, to carry out "affirmative action" hiring of minorities and women. The Office of Federal Contract Compliance Programs (OFCCP) in the Labor Department has borne chief for responsibility enforcement. Only one recent statistical study of this program is available, but it is quite sophisticated. It shows that OFCCP pressures have indeed been effective in producing more employment of persons in the "protected" categories. It also shows that the effects have been concentrated in white-collar jobs, and that regulatory pressure has been directed disproportionately at firms that were performing better than average, and not at all effectively at firms with extremely poor hiring records. It appears that the aim of the enforcement effort has been less that of eliminating discrimination than of redistributing jobs from white males to women and to blacks.[44]

Though hardly a systematic sampling from the universe of regulatory studies, this brief review gives the general tenor of the academic evaluation in this field. Two generalizations drawn from the literature are:

☐ Many regulatory interventions prove to be ineffective and excessively costly because they aim at situations reasonably well managed by the forces of the marketplace and the liability law.
☐ Those interventions that in principle *could* usefully supplement market forces and the threat of litigation do indeed do so, up to a point; but they also tend to be pushed to a point beyond the optimum, where the marginal costs exceed the marginal benefits.

PROGNOSIS AND PRESCRIPTION

It is unlikely that there will be a new wave of regulation in the foreseeable future of anything like the magnitude of the wave that moved across the country from about 1965 to 1980. First, that historical wave probably covered most of the remaining domains that had previously been unregulated or relatively lightly regulated. New domains will appear in time, of course, but probably slowly and erratically. Secondly, the various costs of regulation, economic and otherwise, have become more salient in recent years, and their saliency has energized an antiregulatory backlash that will persist for a long time. Nevertheless, enough new opportunities to extend or adopt protective regulation will appear in the future, as well as demands to modify existing regulatory programs, so that a final cautionary word is in order about the intrinsic limits and potentialities of regulation as a generic policy tool.

First, I cannot overemphasize the inescapability of the various trade-offs, both technical and philosophical (or ideological), delineated above. Perhaps the fundamental dilemma can be summarized as an "essential mismatch between the formalism of government—which we impose because we demand equal treatment before the law, due process, and the trappings of rationality—and thriving diversity of everyday life in the great wide world."[45] This mismatch ensures that protective regulation will always appear, and actually be, clumsy. It will be unprepared to deal with the new, the subtle, the ambiguous, and the unusual—and it will also be oppressively constricting and costly when it does make the attempt.

Second, the effectiveness of government regulation is limited in many cases by the same technical problems that limit the effectiveness of nongovernmental institutions like the marketplace, collective bargaining, the liability law, and professional ethical commitments. That is, the sources of risk, hazard, and injustice are often hidden or, more precisely, extremely costly for citizens themselves to detect and guard against. Workers cannot tell whether the fumes to which they are exposed to will ultimately make them ill or at what level of control they will become safe. The woman denied a promotion cannot tell whether the supervisor's decision was based on legitimate job-related factors or on sexist prejudice. Yet regulators may not be able to resolve such uncertainties either.

Third, government regulation is likely to impose inefficient costs on the society when it is overlaid on an already more or less efficient marketplace. "More or less" is the operative phrase in this case. No marketplace is perfect, and one can always find lamentable instances of "hidden" risks, hazards, and injustices that one might hope to prevent by regulation. Yet it is essential to estimate realistically the prevalence of such problems. The horror stories and catastrophes that reveal the existence of some problems may be very imperfect indicators of their true prevalence. In some cases a realistic assessment may lead to a conclusion that regulation is uncalled for. In others, it may lead to better-focused regulation: less sweeping rules, more targeted enforcement, and sanctions more tailored to the motivations and capacities of the subpopulation whose conduct is to be altered.

Fourth, it is important for the society to explore ways to design regulatory programs that will, over the long run, be more susceptible to modification—especially modification that entails streamlining and paring down regulatory control—through trial-and-error learning. Overly broad and diffusely targeted regulatory sallies would not be so troublesome if subsequent evaluation and redesign could focus and narrow the program's thrust or improve its armament of weapons. At present, however, our ability to make such adjustments is quite limited. It is as though protective regulation were governed by a ratchet mechanism that allows it to move upward but never, or at least infrequently and only by small degrees, downward.[46] Constituencies concerned about the protective mission of the regulatory program will fear that even the smallest "slippage" in regulatory control will eventually bring down the whole programmatic edifice; they protest the incipient "retreat" or "sellout." Business firms that have already undertaken the costs of compliance may object to any change that allows competitors who have not yet complied to escape these costs. Regulatory bureaucrats are typically more interested in programmatic expansion than in contraction. And the broad public that indirectly bears the costs of excessive regulation through higher product costs and taxes, while perhaps desiring to reduce "regulation" in general, has little interest in the details of trimming down particular programs.[47]

Fifth, it will sometimes be profitable to search for "alternatives to regulation." The literature on this subject commonly explores ways to improve what are in effect private systems of regulation, such as, provision of better information to workers and consumers concerning safety and health hazards, revising the liability law and associated institutions of litigation, and strengthening the loss prevention arm of the liability insurance industry.[48] Unfortunately, the modifications needed to make some of these alternatives work may also depend, to some degree, on governmental regulation and could therefore be subject to many of the difficulties described above.

Sixth, because regulatory programs address real or alleged failures of social "responsibility," one way to reduce reliance on regulation is to reduce the need to rely on people to behave "responsibly" in the first place. As I pointed out above, regulation often deals with "hidden" or hard-to-assess risks or motivations, such as product defects or racial discrimination in hiring. However, at least some such elusive qualitative characteristics ultimately may be made more visible and therefore more manageable by virtue of technological change or change in industrial structure. For many people the problem of how to find a "good, clean, reasonably priced" hotel in a strange city has been solved by the rise of nationally known motel and hotel chains. The incidence of milk-borne disease has been radically reduced by the consolidation of small dairies and milk processors into larger and more vertically integrated firms, as well as by the development of cheaper and more reliable methods to test product quality. Imagine how much less we would need to depend on nursing home regulators if potential residents (or their families) could check a facility's record for "tender loving care" and "competent medical practice" before moving in! What, if anything, government might do to promote the technological and organizational changes needed to displace the need for regulation would, of course, need to be evaluated case by case.

Finally, the social systems underlying the problems addressed by regulation are typically multifaceted. The curing of "irresponsible" action might be only one of several possible points of intervention. In the case of nursing homes, for example, higher Medicaid payments or more subsidies for the training of nursing home personnel could be partial substitutes for (as well as partial complements to) regulation.

In short, while regulation may have its place in any system of government action, it is important to keep it in that place and not count on it to achieve results for which it is unsuited.

Notes

1. Because market imperfections and legal imperfections are often somewhat interdependent, this distinction sometimes becomes blurred. Scholars searching for a general explanatory theory of regulation have not been too successful, though, precisely because the two types of imperfections are generally more independent than interdependent. Hence the two types of "regulation" are relatively independent of each other. The most important things they have in common are the designation "regulation" and the fact that the adoption of administrative regulations in both cases conforms to the same sorts of due process requirements. Otherwise, thinking of "protective" regulation and "economic" regulation as mere variants of the same underlying phenomenon is a category error.

2. See Donald F. Kettl, *The Regulation of American Federalism* (Baltimore, Md.: Johns Hopkins University, 1987), 35–36 and note 41.

3. Ibid., see esp. 43 and 132–33. See also ch. 4 in this volume.

4. James Q. Wilson and Patricia Rachal, "Can Government Regulate Itself," *Public Interest* 46 (Winter 1977): 3–14.

5. Eugene Bardach and Robert A. Kagan, *Going by the Book: The Problem of Regulatory Unreasonableness* (Philadelphia: Temple University Press, 1982), 8 and references cited therein.

6. Ronald J. Penoyer, *Directory of Federal Regulatory Agencies* (St. Louis, Mo.: Center for the Study of American Business, Washington University, 1981), cited in Kenneth J. Meier, *Regulation: Politics, Bureaucracy, and Economics* (New York: St. Martin's Press, 1985), 2.

7. Office of the Federal Register, Regulatory Information Service Center; processed, n.d. These figures include both social and economic regulation. Before 1964 the bulk of regulation was economic; it is safe to assume that most regulations added in the 1964–80 period were in the social sphere.

8. Penoyer, cited in Kenneth J. Meier, *Regulation*, 1985, 3.

9. Robert E. Litan and William D. Nordhaus, *Reforming Federal Regulation* (New Haven, Conn.: Yale University Press, 1983), tables 2.4, 2.6, and 2.7.

10. Yair Aharoni, *The No-Risk Society* (Chatham, N.J.: Chatham House, 1981).

11. Mark Nadel, *The Politics of Consumer Protection* (Indianapolis, Ind.: Bobbs Merrill, 1971), 66–70.

12. Irving Kristol, *Two Cheers for Capitalism* (New York: Basic Books, 1978), 26. See also Paul H. Weaver, "Regulation, Social Policy, and Class Conflict," *Public Interest* 50 (Winter 1978): 58–59.

13. Bardach and Kagan, *Going by the Book*, 19–22.

14. Ibid., 184–213.

15. See, for instance, the agency write-ups in *Congressional Quarterly, Federal Regulatory Directory*, 5th ed., 1986; also, Claudia Deutsch, "The Pollution Hounds Get Ready to Pounce," *New York Times*, September 6, 1987, F–6; Cathy Trost, "Job-Safety Agency Is Firing Buckshot Again, and Industry Runs for Cover as Penalties Fly," *Wall Street Journal*, April 22, 1987, 70; William Glaberson, "Is OSHA Falling Down on the Job?" *New York Times*, August 2, 1987, 3–1.

16. See Michael Fix, "Transferring Regulatory Authority to the States," in George C. Eads and Michael Fix, eds., *The Reagan Regulatory Strategy* (Washington, D.C.: Urban Institute Press, 1984), 153–79.

17. Paul N. Tamontozzi with Kenneth W. Chilton, "U.S. Regulatory Agencies under Reagan 1980–1988," Center for the Study of American Business, Washington University, St. Louis, Mo., May 1987. To take one example where resources did not bounce back up, the Food Safety and Inspection Service of the Agriculture Department received $407 million in 1981, $351 million in 1982, and $398 million in 1986. Comparable staffing figures for the same years were 12,411; 10,151; and 9,700.

18. An important exception was the formal adoption of the "bubble" policy as a method of implementing air pollution abatement. This policy was developed during the Carter years, however, and would likely have been adopted during the 1980s no matter who the president would have been. See Michael H. Levin, "Getting There: Implementing the 'Bubble' Policy," in Eugene Bardach and Robert A. Kagan, eds., *Social Regulation: Strategies for Reform* (San Francisco: Institute for Contemporary Studies, 1982), 59–92.

19. In some areas, notably professional licensing, very little post-licensing surveillance takes place once the practitioner has received the license.

20. Peter Huber, "Exorcists vs. Gatekeepers in Risk Regulation," *Regulation* (November/December, 1983): 23–32.

21. Eugene Bardach, "Self-Regulation and Regulatory Paperwork," in Bardach and Kagan, eds., *Social Regulation*, 315–40.

22. One likely implication of this self-selection process is that the high-quality employees the agency does manage to find are likely to be particularly dedicated to the agency mission, sometimes to the point of zealotry.

23. Thus, high levels of observed enforcement activity could suggest either that the agency and its inspectors are performing poorly or that they are performing well.

24. Enforcement that is both flexible and effective is not easy to produce. It depends on training and the budgetary resources that support training. It also helps to have the technical means of verifying inspector decisions at low cost so that supervisors and others may have confidence that inspectors are not being corrupted.

25. See Mark Nadel, *Politics of Consumer Protection*; also, Michael Pertschuk, *The Revolt Against Regulation* (Berkeley and Los Angeles: University of California, California Press, 1982); Susan J. Tolchin and Martin Tolchin, *Dismantling America: The Rush to Deregulate* (Boston: Houghton Mifflin, 1983).

26. The cost-effectiveness criterion is often misidentified with the net-benefit-maximization criterion, even though it is quite separate. The paradigmatic cost-effectiveness slogan is: get the biggest bang for the buck. It assumes that the buck will be spent, and simply asks that the most efficient way of spending it be chosen. If no conceivable way of spending it produces at least a buck's worth of benefits, net-benefit-maximization comes down against the expenditure; but cost-effectiveness is unconcerned.

27. Bardach and Kagan, *Going by the Book*, 331. In the last 15 years, economists have joined the "capture" theorists of political science with their own theory of "rent-seeking" on the part of interests seeking to restructure their competitive environment to greater, and sometimes mutual, advantage.

28. On the role of the judiciary, see especially R. Shep Melnick, *Regulation and the Courts: The Case of the Clean Air Act* (Washington, D.C.: Brookings Institution, 1983); and Jeremy Rabkin, "Office for Civil Rights," in James Q. Wilson, ed., *The Politics of Regulation* (New York: Basic Books, 1980), 304–53.

29. Weaver, "Regulation, Social Policy, and Class Conflict," 1978.

30. Bruce A. Ackerman and William T. Hassler, *Clean Coal/Dirty Air* (New Haven, Conn.: Yale University Press, 1981).

31. It should be emphasized that the norm of "equal treatment" is not necessarily served by greater standardization. A proper understanding of quality means that irrelevant distinctions are ignored; but ignoring relevant distinctions may actually work against equality. Suppose, for example, that a law required all firms to reduce particulate emissions by 10 percent. To excuse certain firms from complying on the grounds that they were owned by local business leaders rather than multinational corporations would violate equality norms. But these norms would not be violated were the exemption to be granted on the grounds that a company had already, and at great cost, cut its past emissions by a large margin. Indeed, it would be imposing a competitive burden—and represent a loss for equality—to insist on further reductions.

32. For a related argument, see John Mendeloff, "Does Overregulation Cause Underregulation? The Case of Toxic Substances," *Regulation* (September/October 1981): 47–52.

33. The terms "good apples" and "bad apples" should not be taken literally. All "apples" fall on a continuum; moreover, some good apples can fall into bad-appledom if not discouraged by regulators from doing so. However, the relative minority status of bad apples in the total population of regulated parties is attested to by many veteran regulators. See Bardach and Kagan, *Going by the Book*, 64–66.

34. In the argot of regulators, this tendency is known as "CYA" ("cover your ass") behavior.

35. Among the latter, see, for instance, Mark Green and Norman Waitzman, *Business War on the Law: An Analysis of the Benefits of Federal Health/Safety Enforcement* (Washington, D.C.: Corporate Accountability Research Group, 1979); for a more favorable view, see also Martin Tolchin and Susan Tolchin, *Dismantling America;* and Nicholas A. Ashford, *A Crisis in the Workplace: Occupational Injury and Disease* (Cambridge, Mass.: MIT Press, 1976).

36. Most high-quality academic studies of protective regulation have been carried out by economists, who have worked from the premise that government was disrupting the relatively efficient operation of the unregulated marketplace.

37. John Braithwaite, *To Punish or Persuade: Enforcement of Coal Mine Safety* (Albany: State University of New York Press, 1985), 79. Unfortunately, the author does not indicate the costs associated with these desirable effects.

38. W. Kip Viscusi, *Risk by Choice: Regulating Health and Safety in the Workplace* (Cambridge, Mass.: Harvard University Press, 1983); Albert L. Nichols and Richard Zeckhauser, "Government Comes to the Workplace: An Assessment of OSHA," *Public Interest* 49 (Fall 1977): 36–39; and John Mendeloff, *Regulating Safety: An Economic and Political Analysis of Occupational Safety and Health Policy* (Cambridge, Mass.: MIT Press, 1979). Needless to say, the estimation of benefits and costs is a complex, uncertain, and controversial matter. For a brief and lucid discussion of many of the important issues, see Viscusi, Ibid., esp. ch. 6. The greatest difficulty comes in evaluating the benefits of fatalities or injuries prevented. Conceptually, the currently accepted approach is to use the aggregate "willingness to pay" of the program's beneficiaries for whatever decrement in risk they enjoy. Hence, if 100,000 persons are, on average, willing to pay $50 apiece for an annual reduction of .01 percent in the likelihood of dying from a particular kind of accident to which they are exposed, the annual benefit of a program that produces this reduction is $5,000,000. This translates, for some purposes, into a value of $500,000 of one life saved—speaking, of course, in a statistical sense only.

39. W. Kip Viscusi, *Regulating Consumer Product Safety* (Washington, D.C.: American Enterprise Institute, 1984).

40. Council on Environmental Quality, *Tenth Annual Report* (Washington, D.C., December 1979), 655–66.

41. Litan and Nordhaus, *Reforming Federal Regulation*, 15–16.

42. Philip E. Graves and Ronald J. Drumm, *Health and Air Quality: Evaluating the Effects of Policy* (Washington, D.C.: American Enterprise Institute, 1981). Protective regulation is particularly unsuited as a generic policy implement to the solution of problems posed by air and water pollution. The interdependency among the various dischargers of pollutants—the dumping of pollutants into common watersheds or airsheds to produce undesirable ambient levels—makes the firm-by-firm and site-by-site approach inherent in protective regulation wholly irrational. The only known social mechanism capable of adjusting these interdependencies relatively efficiently is a market. Hence, it is not surprising that policy analysts interested in this area have turned to inventing policy instruments utilizing pseudo-markets and pseudo-prices to replace or at least complement the existing programs. See, for instance, Michael H. Levin, "Getting There: Implementing the 'Bubble' Policy," in Bardach and Kagan, eds., *Social Regulation: Strategies for Reform*, 59–92.

43. Henry G. Grabowski and John M. Vernon, *The Regulation of Pharmaceuticals* (Washington, D.C.: American Enterprise Institute, 1983).

44. Jonathan S. Leonard, "Affirmative Action as Earnings Redistribution: The Targeting of Compliance Reviews," Working Paper No. 1328, National Bureau of Economic Research, Cambridge, Mass., April 1984; and Jonathan S. Leonard, "What Promises are Worth: The Impact of Affirmative Action Goals," Working Paper No. 1346, National Bureau of Economic Research, Cambridge, Mass., May 1984.

45. Bardach and Kagan, eds., *Social Regulation*, 18.

46. Bardach and Kagan, *Going by the Book*, 184–213.

47. A certain amount of deregulation occurred during the first term of the Reagan administration, though not nearly as much as the administration rhetoric promised or claimed. These effects were achieved mainly through cuts in enforcement budgets and devolving certain regulatory responsibilities to the states. It does not appear that nearly so much attention was given to the objective of *improving* regulation through streamlining or program redesign as to the objective simply of reducing the visible costs and presence of regulation. See George C. Eads and Michael Fix, *Relief or Reform: Reagan's Regulatory Dilemma* (Washington, D.C.: Urban Institute Press, 1984).

48. See, for instance, David Leo Weimer, "Safe—and Available—Drugs," in Robert W. Poole, ed., *Instead of Regulation: An Alternative to Federal Regulatory Agencies* (Lexington, Mass.: Lexington Books, 1982), 239–84; Bardach and Kagan, eds., *Social Regulation*; and Bardach and Kagan, *Going by the Book*, chs. 8–10.

Chapter Eight

THE GOVERNMENT-CORPORATION TOOL: PERMUTATIONS AND POSSIBILITIES

Lloyd D. Musolf

Government corporations are separately constituted agencies established by government to pursue particular public purposes. Government corporations are typically characterized by a greater degree of autonomy and freedom from administrative controls (such as budget controls, personnel regulations, procurement regulations) than is normally available to regular government agencies. Such freedom tends to be justified in terms of the missions of the corporations, which often involve commercial-type activities and close interaction with private businesses.

To conceive of federal government corporations as a single instrument or tool of government action admittedly requires some imagination, however. There is, for example, disagreement even on the number of such corporations. In 1983 the General Accounting Office (GAO) counted 47, while in the same year the Library of Congress found only 31.[1] There are other complications. Corporate purposes differ widely, as do the corporations' authorized powers and organizational features. Perhaps more significant is a psychological barrier. In Western Europe and the Third World government business ventures—usually organized as corporations—commonly have been thought of as a tool of government action under the rubric of "public enterprise." Americans, because of their traditional regard for the concepts of "free enterprise," tend to be hesitant to view government business ventures a collectivity, least of all one with the legitimizing name of public enterprise. Partly for this reason, but also because various federal government corporations have been used for operations remote from business purposes, it is appropriate to employ the more neutral term, government corporations.

THE INSTRUMENT

In elaborating the notion of government corporations as an alternative tool of government, it will be helpful to outline its shape or silhouette, its uses, and operating methods associated with its use.

Silhouette

This description of the shape of the tool begins with some definitions and classifications, compares them with actual examples, and notes some organizational arrangements. A useful starting point are the definitions developed in 1981 by a panel of the National Academy of Public Administration.[2] The NAPA Report suitably distinguished a "government enterprise" from a "government corporation." The former was defined as "a Federal instrumentality or program which generates revenue from a commercial type of activity involving the provision of services or goods to the public and which is intended to be substantially self-sustaining. It may or may not be incorporated."[3] A government corporation was defined as "a government entity created as a separate legal person by, or pursuant to, legislation. It can sue and be sued, use and reuse revenues, and own assets; its liability is distinct from that of its officers and directors." The latter definition sets forth clearly the qualities that distinguish government corporations from government bureaus, but it does not capture the corporate variety. The NAPA report implicitly recognized this by describing three types of existing government corporations. These are its words, in part:

Government corporation—a corporation pursuing a government mission assigned in its enabling statute. Financed by appropriations, its assets are owned by the government and controlled by board members or an administrator appointed by the President or a department secretary. Designated in the Government Corporation Control Act as a "wholly owned government corporation."
Mixed public–private corporation—a corporation with both government and private equity; its assets are owned and controlled by board members selected by both the President and private stockholders. It is usually intended for transition to the private sector. Designated in the Government Corporation Control Act as a "mixed-ownership government corporation."

Private corporation—established by federal statute but privately financed and owned, with no government appropriation, loan or
loan guarantee. All or most board members are chosen by private
stockholders.

Even this threefold division does not entirely capture the complexity of the instrument. By one count, there are a dozen federal
government corporations that can be described as belonging in the
third category, but these in turn are evenly divided between nonprofit and profit-seeking corporations.[4] More important, some of
the dozen fail to meet the description given above. It was noted in
1980, for example, that four of the "nonprofits" were wholly dependent on federal financing and gifts, and two of the "for-profits"
were heavily dependent on government funding.[5]

Nor have the classifications found in the statute mentioned
above, the Government Corporation Control Act, been of much assistance in sorting out reality. The NAPA group found that 18 of 35
government corporations responding to its questionnaire do not
come under the Act's jurisdiction.[6] Six of the 18 fall into the private corporation category, which is not even dealt with by the Act.
Nor does the statute contain a procedure that facilitates bringing
new corporations within its compass. In order for a corporation to
be placed under the Act, Congress must specifically so stipulate in
a new corporation's organic statute.

Whatever its classificatory shortcomings, the Government Corporation Control Act embodies Congress' recognition of the legiti-
macy of the corporate form for business-type tasks as well as its
desire for greater uniformity in financial treatment of government
corporations. To achieve effective congressional control, the Act
provided for:

☐ a procedure for considering and acting on contemplated corporate
programs in the form of business-type budgets submitted by the
president
☐ a commercial-type audit and report to the Congress by the comptroller general (who heads the GAO) on corporations' compliance
with congressional directives and restrictions
☐ approval by the secretary of the Treasury of the depositaries, financing, and government security transactions of government corporations.

The budget provisions were to apply only to the wholly owned government corporations; the audit and Treasury provisions were to apply to the mixed- ownership government corporations as well as to those wholly owned by the government.

The picture drawn above of the government-corporation tool can be rounded out with a brief sketch of the organizational framework, using the threefold distinction mentioned above to describe the placement of the corporations, their management, and some governmental strings on them.

Most wholly owned government corporations are supervised by the head of the executive department responsible for the functional area in which the corporation is operating, but some are independent of departments and report directly to the president. Mixed-ownership government corporations have a fairly remote relationship to government, especially if they have reached the stage where any government investment has been largely repaid. The dozen government-sponsored private corporations tend to resemble mixed-ownership corporations in their emphasis on independence, though their individual circumstances have influenced their actual organizational placement.

To help run corporations, boards of directors are almost uniformly employed, but most serve only parttime. Some boards may be composed entirely of government officials in related capacities, others are appointed by government but are a mixture of public officials and private individuals, and still others are selected partly by government and partly by the private sector.

As to personnel arrangements, employees of wholly owned government corporations typically come under the classified civil service; employees of the two other types of corporation do not: two giants, the Tennessee Valley Authority and the U.S. Postal Service, have their own personnel systems. The Office of Management and Budget (OMB) exercises various financial and program controls. Usually, corporations of the first type are subject to more controls than are the others, but there are exceptions to this rule. These corporations are also more likely than others to be included in the government's budget but, again, there are exceptions, as well as instances where a corporation's activities are partly included and partly excluded.

It can be concluded from this recital that, in practice, federal government corporations do not present the sharp, easily identifiable silhouette they have in theory. This fact suggests that policymakers have resorted to government corporations as and when they wished and that the needs of the moment have been thought more important than uniformity or consistency.

Uses

Against this descriptive backdrop, we turn now to a discussion of the uses of the government-corporation tool. What has stimulated the use of government corporations? What purposes have they served?

OCCASIONS FOR USE

Crises in the first half of the 20th century stimulated the use of government corporations on a grand scale. Prior use had been more limited and less permanent. Early in the nation's history, the government had participated with the private sector in two notable corporate enterprises—the First and Second Banks of the United States. Later, it had appointed representatives to serve on the Union Pacific Railroad's board of directors, as a way of rewarding itself for heavy financial support of the first transcontinental railroad.[7] The first 20th century use was in 1904 in connection with the Panama Railroad Company, inherited from the French effort at canal building.[8] Extensive use of government corporations awaited the two world wars and the Great Depression of the 1930s. In both wars corporations were used to mobilize the economy, though their number and scale were much greater in World War II. Franklin Roosevelt's efforts inspired the creation of enduring corporations, such as the Tennessee Valley Authority (TVA), and other less enduring ones, but FDR's Republican predecessor is associated with the creation of the Reconstruction Finance Corporation, which over the years aided a host of private business ventures.

The aftermath of these crises was also significant in characterizing the pattern of corporate development. As a perceptive commentator noted at mid-century, "The system of government corporations has tended to expand markedly in times of military and economic emergency. In the contraction following such crises, a smaller number of government corporations remains to conduct continuing operations for whose performance the corporate device has been more appropriate than an ordinary department."[9] Not surprisingly, corporations created during the economic emergency between the world wars had a better survival rate than those established to mobilize the wartime economy.[10]

The second half of the century has so far witnessed no emergency-inspired ebb-and-flow pattern, but there has been a sharp fluctuation in creating government corporations as well as a considerable reliance on government-sponsored private corporations. In the two decades after 1960, a period of government activism on the domestic front, "approximately 26" government corporations were established.[11] By contrast the Reagan administration, with its philosophy of reducing the size of government, has not established corporations as part of its program, though a few were created because of circumstances to be noted later. Approximately half of the corporations created in the 1960–80 era were private.[12] A precise count is difficult because in some cases only the background documents, not the organic statutes, indicate that the corporation may be listed in that category.

PURPOSES

The present slack time in employing government corporations offers an opportunity to reflect on the instrument and its uses. By identifying the economic areas in which the corporations are clustered, one can perhaps characterize the "normal" uses of the tool. This, in turn, may provide a basis for judging its acceptability in the political system.

The major use of government corporations has been in extending credit. To be sure, this activity is not the exclusive province of government corporations since many regular government agencies extend credit. In 1983, for example, outstanding federal and federally assisted credit consisted of: (1) direct loans of $105 billion "on budget" and $118 billion "off budget," (2) guaranteed and insured loans of $363.8 billion, in addition to (3) government-sponsored enterprise loans of $261.2 billion.[13] But the involvement of government corporations in credit activities is still striking. For example, the Commodity Credit Corporation, whose purpose is to stabilize farm income and prices, employs nonrecourse loans to and purchases from producers as its principal methods. In 1983 it was the largest single credit program in terms of net direct cost to the government.[14] The Government National Mortgage Association purchases mortgage loans guaranteed or insured by two other federal agencies. In the foreign trade area, the Export-Import Bank supplements the private financing market in various ways intended to facilitate exports and imports, such as providing loans and loan guarantees to foreign purchasers of American goods. Also in foreign trade, the Overseas Private Investment Corporation encourages trade relations with developing countries through loans and loan guarantees that aid investment financing. Government-sponsored credit enterprises improve access to credit markets for certain borrowers by serving as intermediaries. They include three that aid housing (Federal Home Loan Mortgage Corporation, Federal National Mortgage Corporation, and Federal Home Loan Banks), three sets of banks that deal with agricultural credit (Federal Land Banks, Federal Intermediate Credit Banks, and Banks for Cooperatives), the Student Loan Marketing Association, and the National Consumer Cooperative Bank. Credit instruments have also been created to provide help to crippled segments of the economy. From the mid–1970s to the mid–1980s, the United States Railway Association provided and monitored the funds made available to the Consolidated Rail Corporation (Conrail) for operating the bankrupt railroads of the Northeast and Midwest, and after the oil-import crisis of the late 1970s, the U.S. Synthetic Fuels Corporation subsidized the effort to develop alternative fuel sources.

Another important area for government corporations has been insurance. Bank deposits are protected by the Federal Deposit Insurance Corporation and the Federal Savings and Loan Insurance Corporation, securities investments by the Securities Investor Protection Corporation. In order to help employees retiring from private firms, the Pension Benefit Guaranty Corporation was established in 1974; its injunction is to administer insurance programs to prevent the loss of benefits to participants if pension plans terminate without sufficient assets. The Federal Crop Insurance Corporation provides a service to farmers that private insurance firms believe is too risky.

In the area of transportation and communications, the U.S. Postal Service and three government-sponsored private corporations— the National Railroad Passenger Corporation (Amtrak), the aforementioned Conrail, and the Communications Satellite Corporation (Comsat)—are well known. Perhaps somewhat less familiar are the Corporation for Public Broadcasting, St. Lawrence Seaway Development Corporation, and Rural Telephone Bank.

Though energy production is largely in private hands, hydroelectric power sites in the Tennessee Valley and the western United States inspired well-known governmental efforts, both corporate (TVA) and noncorporate (Bonneville and Southwestern Power Administrations). The Tennessee Valley Authority produces electric power along with its other efforts at development of the region. The

U.S. Synthetic Fuels Corporation, in addition to extending credit, as noted above, began several joint ventures in coal and oil production with the private sector before the corporation's abolition in 1986.

Traits

From what has been said, it should be clear that the government-corporation tool obviously overlaps with several other policy instruments discussed in this volume. The most obvious are loans and loan guarantees, given the numerous corporations that provide some form of credit. Perhaps less apparent is the overlap with what Christopher Leman, in chapter 3, calls direct government. Utilizing the distinction between direct and indirect delivery mechanisms developed by Lester Salamon in chapter 1, we can note that only a minority of government corporations fall into the first category—essentially involving federal agencies acting without nonfederal actors. It is, however, an important minority, including as it does the several surface transportation services (St. Lawrence Seaway Development Corporation, Amtrak, and Conrail), as well as such behemoths as TVA and the U.S. Postal Service (both of which are mentioned by Leman). A less notable overlap is with the grant-dispensing tool, but it is worth mentioning that the Corporation for Public Broadcasting and the Legal Services Corporation customarily have operated through dispensing grants.

Perhaps the most distinctive characteristic of the government-corporation instrument, however, is its ability, as noted above, to "sue and be sued, use and reuse revenues, and own assets." In seeking to learn what practical difference these qualities make, one is immediately reminded that not all corporations fit this image in every detail. For example, the grant-dispensing corporations do not engage in commercial operations to raise revenue, but simply to dispense funds. (This is not to say that use of the corporate form was inappropriate, on the assumption that Congress was interested in providing a degree of isolation for such politically sensitive actions as government-sponsored radio and television broadcasting and legal aid to the poor.)

When government corporations were asked in 1981 about the advantages and disadvantages of corporate status, 30 respondents cited advantages and only 10, disadvantages.[15] It is, of course, hardly surprising that the beneficiaries of freedom from many government regulations should, in TVA's words, appreciate their "far greater flexibility in budgetary-, financial-, procurement-, and per-

sonnel-related matters."[16] Many respondents cited their ability to
operate in a manner similar to private business as enhancing their
effectiveness, responsiveness, and good relations with the private
sector. Corporations independent of government departments
prized that independence, while those within a department asserted that corporate status gave them more visibility than other
departmental units have. Whether independent or within a department, some corporations complained of being subjected increasingly to governmentwide regulations and, as the St. Lawrence
Seaway Development Corporation put it, "the failure on the part of
a great proportion of Executive and Congressional overseers to
comprehend that there is a difference between government corporations and traditional agencies."[17]

Though corporations have the right to sue and be sued, they do
not always have as free a hand in litigation as this phrase implies.[18]
Corporations wholly owned by the government must often obtain
clearance from the Department of Justice, whereas those classified
as private handle their own litigation, sometimes with outside
counsel. Corporations within departments may well have to clear
suits with departmental counsel.

When statutes label government corporations as private, considerable confusion about legal status may occur. When Comsat, the
first private corporation, was proposed in the early 1960s, members
of Congress challenged the appropriateness of government action to
establish a private corporation and of presidential appointment of
its top officials; even the constitutionality of the latter action was
challenged.[19] The question of how the government's interests might
be represented on the board of a private corporation was also
raised. Should presidentially appointed members of the board represent government interests actively or simply act as communications links for the president of the United States? On Comsat's
board of 15 members, it appears in retrospect that successive in-
cumbents in the three "government" directorships may have done
neither and have had little or no impact on Comsat.[20] In the 1970s,
however, the extent of government representation on the board of
another profitable private corporation became highly controversial.
Disturbed by what she conceived to be an excessive private-sector
orientation by the board of the Federal National Mortgage Association (Fannie Mae), the Carter administration's secretary of Housing
and Urban Development unsuccessfully urged Congress to change
the law to give the government a majority on the board.[21] Uncertainties about legal status undoubtedly helped to fuel both the
Comsat and Fannie Mae debates. A more recent example of uncer-

tain legal status is that of the Federal Assets Disposition Association (FADA), which since 1985 has managed and disposed of assets for the Federal Savings and Loan Insurance Corporation (FSLIC). Chartered under the corporation laws of the state of Colorado as a "private, Federally chartered savings and loan association" by private citizens who had FSLIC blessing, FADA was capitalized at $25 million, with the FSLIC owning 100 percent of the stock and guaranteeing a substantial line of credit. A commentator has raised such questions as the following: if FADA is public, then is it subject to such statutes as the Freedom of Information Act and the Administrative Procedure Act, and to such practices as clearance of legislative proposals by OMB and to review and disallowance of expenditures by GAO? If FADA is private, is it subject to state taxation of corporations, its directors liable for their actions in the same manner as other Colorado corporations, its employees and records protected by Fourth Amendment search and seizure provisions rather than the lesser protections accorded public employees?[22]

What difference does it make to use revenues or borrowed funds as financial resources rather than relying on appropriations? One of the common reasons for establishing corporations is to impose the discipline of the balance sheet on government operations. Applying the concept in practice does not, however, always go smoothly. The history of Amtrak, established (like Comsat and Fannie Mae) as a government-sponsored private, profit-seeking corporation, provides a good illustration of the difficulties.[23] The profitability of Comsat gave great credibility to this version of the government-corporation tool as did Fannie Mae's financial success and growth in size, but the industries in which they operated did not have the acute problems facing passenger rail transportation. Amtrak was created in 1970 via a statute describing it as a "for profit corporation" that was to operate "a basic national rail passenger system." A tension between the conflicting aims of providing service and achieving profitability was built into the statute, and Amtrak skillfully exploited the fear of senators and representatives that passenger trains, a highly visible service in their constituencies, would be eliminated or reduced in number. Though initially there was considerable support for the large annual appropriations necessary to upgrade the system, Amtrak's growing deficit led to a lessening of support in Congress and substantial route reduction. With the prospect of profitability becoming ever more remote, congressional sentiment for eliminating Amtrak's statutory description as a "for profit corporation" grew. Objections to doing so resulted in a compromise, in 1978, by which the phrase "operated and managed as a for profit corporation" replaced the original words. This wording, according to a congressional committee, "'recognizes that Amtrak is not a for-profit corporation' but nevertheless insures that Amtrak is operated as a for-profit corporation even though it may continue to require very substantial operating subsidies."[24] The committee believed, in other words, that the concept of profit seeking for this variety of the government-corporation tool is valuable even when profitability is out of the question. The lawmakers may have been influenced by congressional committee testimony that "a profit test is essential if any discipline is to govern the development of corporate and related public policies."[25]

What of profit-seeking discipline in more conventional government corporations? TVA may be used as an example. Congress directed that TVA's electric power program be self-sufficient, and this fact appears to dominate the Authority's philosophy as thoroughly as the huge power program dominates its other activities. Given "the degree of its independence from the established department structure and political supervision by presidential and congressional staff agencies,"[26] TVA undoubtedly enjoys considerable autonomy. Yet, judging by its replies to specific questions posed by the NAPA panel in 1981,[27] TVA is highly conscious of restraints on its actions. For example, though it has its own personnel system and is not subject to civil service laws, it has, like Amtrak, felt the effects of government limitations on paying its senior staff. The statute that created TVA in 1933 provides that no officer or employee may be paid more than a member of the three-person board of directors. According to TVA,

While this limitation is, in principle, appropriate for activities funded with taxpayer monies, it is creating ever-increasing problems for TVA in offering sufficient salaries and related benefits to keep experienced and competent high-ranking managers in TVA's power-program-related activities from leaving for higher paying positions in the private sector. . . . The continuing loss of such key personnel significantly reduces TVA's ability to effectively operate a power program which is subject to most of the same business-related variables and demands as a private electric utility.[28]

More generally, TVA complained that, throughout its existence,

The imposition on TVA of standardized, Government-wide regulations governing Federal agency activities has actually increased TVA's operating and overhead costs and the number of administrative personnel which TVA must employ without any measurable amount of corresponding benefits. . . . Furthermore, because TVA carries out extensive business-like operations, it has not only become subject to many Government-wide regulations ill suited for the efficient operation of a business entity, but is also subject to many of the same Federal laws, regulations, and paperwork that are imposed on private businesses.[29]

EVALUATING THE GOVERNMENT-CORPORATION TOOL

On the basis of the forgoing description of the instrument and the manner in which it is employed, the government corporation's place in the array of tools available to the government can now be assessed. What influences in the political and economic environment shape its selection for particular tasks? How do these influences impinge on the environment in which the individual corporations operate?

Influences over Instrument Use

Four major influences in the political and economic environment can be identified.

The first is the uneasy attitude of the American public to the government corporation. Of all the alternative tools of government action, the government corporation, especially if it is associated with public enterprise, accords the least with American consensual values. Any modern government, it is reasonable to assume, adapts its instruments to harmonize with the values and perceived needs of society. In choosing economic policy instruments, the American polity seems to prefer indirect to direct tools, presumably because they fit better with the ideals of limited government and free enterprise. These concepts do not preclude using the government corporation as a tool, but they tend to restrict its heavy use to times of emergency (major wars and economic depressions) and, occasionally, to situations where other, preferred instruments have been perceived as inadequate.

In the American setting there usually are congenial substitutes for government corporations. One is government contracts with private enterprise for purchases of goods and services. So extensive has this practice become that more persons are said to work under contract to the national government than are employed by it.[30] Subsidizing elements of the private sector, particularly if it can be done unobtrusively, is usually regarded as preferable to establishing a public enterprise. Furthermore, unlike Western Europe, regulation of privately owned infrastructural industries is typically preferred to government ownership and operation.

The second major influence is the adaptation of the government-corporation tool to the political and economic environment by largely confining its role to supplementing private enterprise. Credit and insurance activities, the most popular, essentially facilitate private efforts in those fields, usually supplanting them only when the private sector finds such activities uneconomical. In the rare cases where government corporations compete with giant private corporations (such as in the fields of transportation and communications), special circumstances are involved. Thus, Conrail was fashioned out of properties formerly owned by the Penn Central Railroad and other bankrupt railroads in the Northeast and Midwest. Significantly, the government sold Conrail to private purchasers in 1987. The energy field provides an instructive example of a different kind. TVA's bold approach to river-basin development included purchasing existing private electric power companies and establishing a vast hydroelectric power generation system; its low electricity rates were touted as a model or yardstick for privately owned utilities. TVA was, in short, confronting the private sector in an unprecedented manner, but one which excited sufficient controversy to prevent similar experiments elsewhere in the country. Congress rejected a proposed Missouri Valley Authority after World War II and authorized unincorporated enterprises for hydroelectric power generation on major rivers. The TVA and Conrail experiences suggest the tenuous hold that public enterprise has on American hearts.

The third influence is the characteristics of the polity and economy that militate against close coordination of either the instrument or the uses to which it is put. Space prevents discussing these features in detail, but they are broadly familiar. Prominent among them are a large and usually vigorous private sector, reinforced by a free-enterprise ideology; reliance on decentralized, pluralistic decision making, which reflects the existence of federalism, separation of powers, weak political parties, powerful interest groups, and a tradition of local autonomy; and repugnance toward national economic planning. As to the last, probably the closest approximation to a planning document is the annual national budget; but even this document is simply the president's proposal to Congress, which adapts the spending plans as it sees fit in translating them into bills for the president's signature or veto.

The final influence is the lack of concerted substantive guidance, which places a heavy burden on organizational and procedural coordination. A cult of autonomy for government corporations flourished in the 1930s, nourished by the establishment of the Tennessee Valley Authority in 1933.[31] The tide turned in the opposite direction in the late 1930s, when government reorganization plans brought most corporations under department direction,[32] and after World War II, when the profusion of wartime corporations stimulated passage of the Government Corporation Control Act of 1945.

The dynamism of the federal government in the postwar era, however, has repeatedly tested the accommodation between flexibility and accountability represented by the 1939 reorganization plans and the 1945 Control Act. "In the new political economy," a commentator noted in 1975, "the traditional distinction between the public and private sectors has become nearly obliterated through the flow of public funds to universities, industry, nonprofit institutions, voluntary hospitals, social welfare agencies, and other quasi-public entities."[33] Catchwords suggest the accompanying confusion: "Twilight zone" organizations proliferated "on the margins of the state," contracting increased vastly, resulting in "the blurred boundaries of public administration."[34]

It is appropriate at this point to ask whether the Reagan administration's deemphasis of the government-corporation tool significantly affected these generalizations. The short answer is that it did not. So limited, so contingent on circumstances is the resort to government corporations in times when neither wars nor depressions are overwhelming threats, that deemphasis of the tool does not affect the generalizations significantly. This is not to minimize the changes proposed by the administration and, in some cases, put into effect. To these we now turn.

Among the "revenue changes" proposed by the Reagan administration in its fiscal year 1988 budget were three that would, if carried out, impinge on the government-corporation tool: "improve the allocation of credit; sell loan assets where appropriate; shift to the private sector the production of certain goods and services."[35] The first "proposes to change the way Federal credit programs are treated in the budget" by charging "the true economic cost of credit—the present value of the subsidy—to any agency making or guaranteeing loans."[36] This proposal expands on earlier ones in previous budgets.[37] The second related proposal contemplates continuing and expanding a pilot program of selling loan assets first proposed in the 1987 budget. Among the 11 agencies from whose portfolios loans would be sold are two government-owned corporations, the Export-Import Bank and the Tennessee Valley Authority. The importance to the administration of the third proposal, involving "privatization," was suggested by the appointment of the President's Commission on Privatization in September 1987, as well as President Reagan's statement, echoing his oft-expressed views, that it would help him "end unfair Government competition and return Government programs and assets to the American people."[38] Building on the sale of Conrail, which was authorized by Congress in 1986 and took place in 1987, the administration proposed a half-dozen privatization initiatives in the 1988 budget. Included was a proposal "to terminate all Amtrak subsidies and dispose of some or all of Amtrak's assets."[39]

The successes of privatization have been mixed. On the plus side, the sale of Conrail and the contracting out of 38,000 government positions between 1981 and 1987 achieved a claimed annual saving of $602 million.[40] On the minus side, the sale of Amtrak facilities received a negative reaction in Congress in 1987. Even the Conrail sale occurred in the context of Congress' rejection of the administration's 1981 plan for the quick sale of segments of the freight railroad.[41]

The Shifting Environment

Implicit in much of what has been said so far is the notion that the milieu is important in judging the government-corporation instrument's performance and even its suitability for a given situation. The purpose of this final subsection is to develop this idea, using examples relating both to the immediate political and economic environment of each corporation and the more general policy-making environment.

THE CORPORATE ENVIRONMENT

TVA furnishes a dramatic example of the influence of the immediate environment, where, to use Avery Leiserson's memorable phrase, "controversiality has been endemic."[42] TVA's extensive involvement with presidential staff agencies, congressional investigations, litigation, critical studies, and the like "all reveal that the board and staff have constantly been obliged to act within political, legal, and administrative constraints."[43] Leiserson argues that

From a system perspective . . . TVA's organizational history may be regarded as a shifting balance on a continuum between formal (legal) autonomy and informal (operating) accountability in an unstable environment of political forces and pressures. From time to time these tensions culminate temporarily in some symbolic, usually legislative act, indicating a modified line of agency development confirming or altering the agency's order of policy priorities.[44]

In support of this analysis, one can speculate that past events help account for the TVA's somewhat defensive tone in its replies (some of which are reported above) in the NAPA report.

It is likely that when a government corporation has a broad and somewhat vague mandate, such as TVA's, the effect is not only to generate controversy, but also to muddy an evaluation of its goal achievement. TVA's precise mission was not stipulated in its statute, permitting it, in its early, bold years, to claim to serve as a "yardstick" for private utilities and as a "grass-roots" democracy. The fallacies in these claims were exploited by critics, but use of the terms had the virtue, from TVA's viewpoint, of dramatizing its mission.[45]

Not only the breadth and vagueness of goals but the extent of obvious conflict among them is likely to affect evaluation of a government corporation's performance. The extended tug-of-war over Amtrak's conflicting goals of service and profitability has already been mentioned. These goals also came into severe conflict within Conrail, the regional freight railroad.[46] Another memorable example of goal conflict is the U.S. Postal Service, which is, technically speaking, not a government corporation but an "independent establishment" within the executive branch. Efficiency was the goal of converting the Post Office Department into the Postal Service. Of five alternative structures considered by a presidential commission dominated by business, a government corporation was recommended because it would give "the most power to the Postmaster General with the least interference from external agents."[47] The premise of the Postal Reorganization Act of 1970 was that "the post office could modernize if it was removed from the political arena, given a corporate form, allowed to borrow money in private financial markets, and encouraged to reward productive managers."[48]

The subsequent history of the Postal Service not only demonstrates the difficulty of attaining efficiency but the risk in overrelying on it. Though patronage became much less of a factor than under the Post Office Department, observers have described a "climate of regulation and political interference that surrounds the postal service, hobbling management's ability to act boldly and effectively."[49] The Postmaster General's reply to the NAPA panel lists 14 "central government oversight bodies" that "review and/or monitor" Postal Service activities.[50] About half of these he judged to be "significantly excessive" in nature.[51] A close observer of the Postal Service argues that, despite such constraints, the Service has achieved a degree of efficiency (for example, in reversing a decline in productivity), though the public, seeing only increasing postage costs, fails to realize that "the price on the face of a stamp represents an out-of-pocket cost where earlier subsidies were hidden in a generalized tax bill."[52] Her conclusion is that "mail service, because of its long history as a government service, is seen as a political right by much of the public, not as an economic product with market-sensitive prices, such as the telephone system."[53]

THE GENERAL ENVIRONMENT

An important part of the general environment facing government corporations is the flexibility Congress exhibits in viewing the corporate instrument. The NAPA Report discerned a trend toward creating corporations that "do not raise revenue by business-type operations," and speculated that they were nevertheless given the corporate form so that they would have "the operational flexibility of corporations."[54] Though Congress departed less drastically from the norm in earlier times, it has displayed inventiveness on various occasions. Forming a government corporation with government capital and gradually, through stock purchases coordinated with transactions, changing to private ownership—as the three dozen agricultural credit banks did—is an example. Another imaginative variation of the tool is the government-sponsored private corporation, whether nonprofit or profit-seeking.

What tends to inspire a departure from orthodoxy? One is a perceived need for compromise among strongly held views when action is thought urgent. It is no exaggeration to say that Comsat, the first private, profit-seeking corporation, was the fruit of policymakers' ingenuity in finding an acceptable formula among widely divergent views at a time when national rivalry with the Soviet Union over communications satellites made some kind of solution seem necessary.[55] Another factor is the raw power of interest group lobbying. The political power of the farm lobby undoubtedly influenced details of the agricultural credit banks' transfer to private ownership. For example, despite objections by the GAO and, later, by the second Hoover Commission, Congress voted to give up any government interest in the banks' surplus and reserves once the government capital—which had helped build these assets—had been retired.[56] In addition, agricultural groups nominate 12 of the 13 presidentially appointed members of the supervisory body for the banks, the Federal Farm Credit Board, and "in practice, the nomination of directors has become the equivalent of election."[57]

In addition to the factors already mentioned, executive-legislative rivalry sometimes skews the use of the government-corporation instrument. Rather than have the Department of Transportation act as the planning and funding medium for Conrail, Congress created the U.S. Railway Association.[58] As another example, the idea behind creation of the Legal Services Corporation in 1974 was to protect legal aid to the poor from political buffeting, but incorporation did not prevent the Reagan administration from repeatedly criticizing the unit and urging Congress to abolish it.

Other things equal, Congress probably has more reasons to favor use of the tool than does the executive branch. Under the Government Corporation Control Act, only Congress can create government corporations, thereby setting the terms of use more specifically than in the typical statute assigning an activity to a government department.[59] Not only is Congress less concerned than the executive branch with hierarchical structures and priorities, but it may be more susceptible to interest group pleas for special treatment. As one government corporation official pointed out, government corporations should be viewed "from the perspective of the creator—i.e., Congress. In that context, one asks what political utility is this organizational structure rather than what organizational utility is this specific structure in the political arena."[60] But this same official acknowledged the stake that the corporations themselves have in the bureaucratic freedom allowed by the corporate form. To place government corporations, especially "single-issue" corporations, within departments or agencies, this official argued, would expose them to "the particular negative bias or lack of priority assigned the specific issue by one or all present departments or agencies."[61]

If proof were needed that practical factors tend to override ideological approaches in the use of the government-corporation tool when adversity threatens, the events of the 1980s provide it. Though neither widespread economic hardship nor a major war face the nation at the moment, there is growing uneasiness over matters such as the perennial unfavorable balance of trade and international payments, high budget deficits, the mounting national debt, a shaky industrial economy, and the persistent farm crisis. Political leaders and interest groups can ignore such signs only at their own peril, as a few illustrations can suggest. In its drive to attain greater competitiveness for American products in world trade, the Reagan administration was brought to revise its approach toward the Export-Import Bank. In the early 1980s, the administration had sought to dismantle the Export-Import Bank because it believed that export financing could be provided more efficiently by the private sector. In 1986, however, the administration asked Congress to approve a $300 million fund to bolster the corporation's ability to counter subsidized foreign credit,[62] and in 1987 President Reagan's State of the Union address cited revamped Bank programs to help competitiveness in international trade.[63]

The farm credit banks, prosperous and privately owned for a generation, have, in the 1980s, encountered farm conditions that have drained their reserves and prompted urgent calls for infusing substantial government funds into the system of banks. Under the terms of the Agricultural Credit Act of 1987, $4 billion in federally guaranteed funds were pumped into the Farm Credit System, and its stockholder-borrowers, directors, and managers were given broad discretion to reorganize the system in response to market pressure. The statute also established the Federal Agricultural Mortgage Corporation ("Farmer Mac") that, à la Fannie Mae, will enable commercial banks to sell off farm loans through a government-backed secondary loan market.[64] Another hard- pressed unit is the Federal Savings and Loan Insurance Corporation, which is beset by the insolvency of about 20 percent of the nation's 3,100 thrift institutions. Once again, Congress came to the rescue (though doubts were expressed about the adequacy of the funds provided). Included in the Competitive Equality Banking Act of 1987 was authority for the FSLIC to borrow up to $10.8 billion dollars over a three-year period for the purpose of paying off depositors in insolvent savings and loans.[65] The Pension Benefit Guaranty Corporation, which insures the pensions of nearly 40 million Americans, announced in May 1987 that it can meet less than half of its commitments to current and future retirees primarily because of vastly increased obligations inherited from bankrupt steel companies.[66]

Amid all this turmoil, it is unlikely that the government-corporation tool will become a nullity in the foreseeable future. Given its history of waxing in perilous times, it may, in fact, play a critical role.

Notes

1. See Congressional Research Service, Library of Congress, "Administering Public Functions at the Margin of Government: The Case of Federal Corporations," by Ronald C. Moe, Report No. 83–236 GOV, December 1, 1983, 65 (hereafter cited as Moe, CRS Report).

2. National Academy of Public Administration (NAPA), *Report on Government Corporations: A Report Based on a Study by a Panel of the National Academy of Public Administration for the Office of Management and Budget,* 2 vols. (Washington, D.C.: NAPA, August 1981) (hereafter cited as NAPA Report).

3. This definition and those that follow are in NAPA Report, vol. 1, second unnumbered page.

4. The former include the Corporation for Public Broadcasting, Legal Services Corporation, National Park Foundation, National Home Ownership Foundation (never activated), Securities Investor Protection Corporation, and the United States Railway Association. The six enterprises in the latter category are the Communications Satellite Corporation, the Consolidated Rail Corporation, the Federal National Mortgage Association, the National Corporation for Housing Partnerships, the National Railroad Passenger Corporation, and the Student Loan Marketing Association. Arguably, the United States Synthetic Fuels Corporation could be added to the latter list. Lloyd D. Musolf, *Uncle Sam's Private, Profitseeking Corporations: Comsat, Fannie Mae, Amtrak, and Conrail* (Lexington, Mass.: Lexington Books, D.C. Heath and Co., 1983).

5. Lloyd D. Musolf and Harold Seidman, "The Blurred Boundaries of Public Administration," *Public Administration Review* 40, no. 2 (March/April 1980), 125.

6. NAPA Report, vol. 1, appendix 2, 2.

7. Lloyd D. Musolf, *Mixed Enterprise: A Developmental Perspective* (Lexington, Mass.: Lexington Books, D.C. Heath and Co., 1972), 53–56.

8. Marshall Dimock, *Government-Operated Enterprises in the Panama Canal Zone* (Chicago: University of Chicago Press, 1934).

9. V.O. Key, Jr., "Government Corporations," in Fritz Morstein Marx, ed., *Elements of Public Administration,* 2nd ed. (Englewood Cliffs, N.J.: Prentice- Hall, Inc., 1959), 224–25.

10. Key, "Government Corporations," 225.

11. NAPA Report, vol. 1, 3. For a list and description of 23 1960–80 corporations, see Musolf and Seidman, "The Blurred Boundaries of Public Administration," 129–30.

12. In two instances where the statute is silent, it nevertheless declares that the corporation's officers and employees "shall not be considered officers and employees of the United States." Musolf and Seidman, "The Blurred Boundaries of the Public Administration," 125.

13. *Budget of the United States Government, Fiscal Year 1985, Special Analyses* (Washington, D.C., 1984), F–6. For further discussion of federal credit activities, see ch. 5.

14. Congressional Budget Office, *Federal Support of U.S. Business* (Washington, D.C., January 1984), 31.

15. NAPA Report, vol. 1, appendix 2, 28.

16. NAPA Report, vol. 2, 10th page of TVA reply to NAPA group questionnaire.

17. NAPA Report, vol. 1, appendix 2, 29.

18. See NAPA Report, vol. 1, appendix 2, 6.

19. See Musolf, *Uncle Sam's Private, Profitseeking Corporations*, 18–24.

20. Ibid., 24.

21. Ibid., 37–41.

22. Ronald C. Moe, "Exploring the Limits of Privatization," *Public Administration Review* 47, no. 6 (November/December 1987): 453–60.

23. See Musolf, *Uncle Sam's Private, Profitseeking Corporations*, 49–70.

24. Ibid., 57.

25. Ibid.

26. Avery Leiserson, "Administrative Management and Political Accountability," in Erwin C. Hargrove and Paul K. Conkin, eds., *TVA: Fifty Years of Grass-Roots Bureaucracy* (Urbana: University of Illinois Press, 1983), 125.

27. NAPA Report, vol. 2 (unpaged). The various corporations' replies are arranged alphabetically.

28. Ibid., 10th page of TVA's statement.

29. Ibid., 16th page of TVA's statement.

30. Ira Sharkansky, "Policy Making and Service Delivery on the Margins of Government: The Case of Contractors," *Public Administration Review* 40, no. 2 (March/April 1980), 117.

31. See Moe, CRS Report, 7–8.

32. Ibid., 8–9.

33. Bruce L.R. Smith, "The Public Use of the Private Sector," in Bruce L.R. Smith, ed., *The New Political Economy: The Public Use of the Private Sector* (New York: John Wiley and Sons, 1975), 8.

34. See, respectively, Harold Seidman, *Politics, Position, and Power: The Dynamics of Federal Organization*, 2d ed. (New York: Oxford University Press, 1975), 279; Ira Sharkansky, *Wither the State: Politics and Public Enterprise in Three Countries* (Chatham, N.J.: Chatham House, 1979), 4–5; and Musolf and Seidman, "The Blurred Boundaries of Public Administration."

35. U.S. Executive Office of the President, *Budget of the United States Government, Fiscal Year 1988* (Washington, D.C., 1987), 2–39.

36. Ibid., 2–42.

37. See, for example, *Budget of the United States Government, Fiscal Year 1984* (Washington, D.C., 1983), 7-11 and 7-12.

38. *New York Times*, September 4, 1987.

39. All quotations are from *Budget of the United States Government, Fiscal Year 1988*, 2-45 to 2-47.

40. *New York Times*, September 4, 1987.

41. Leiserson, "Administrative Management and Political Accountability," 126.

42. Ibid., 127.

43. Ibid.

44. Ibid.

45. For details, see Richard Lowitt, "The TVA, 1933–45," in Hargrove and Conkin, eds., *TVA: Fifty Years of Grass-Roots Bureaucracy*, 56–57.

46. See Musolf, Uncle Sam's Private, Profitseeking Corporations, 78–82.

47. Nicole Woolsey Biggart, "The Creative-Destructive Process of Organizational Change: The Case of the Post Office," *Administrative Science Quarterly* 22 (September 1977), 415.

48. Nicole Woolsey Biggart, "The Post Office as a Business: Ten Years of Postal Reorganization," *Policy Studies Journal* 11 (March 1983), 483.

49. Christopher H. Lovelock and Charles B. Weinberg, "Implementing a Product Market Strategy: The Case of the U.S. Postal Service," in W.T. Stanbury and Fred Thompson, eds., *Managing Public Enterprises* (New York: Praeger Publishing, 1982), 287.

50. Letter dated March 23, 1981, from Postmaster General William F. Bolger to Robert Moot, NAPA, NAPA Report, vol. 2, 5th page of letter.

51. Ibid., 5th and 6th page of letter.

52. Biggart, "The Post Office as a Business," 488.

53. Ibid.

54. NAPA Report, vol. 1, 28. The corporations listed were the Corporation for Public Broadcasting, Inter-American Foundation, Legal Services Corporation, National Park Foundation, Neighborhood Reinvestment Corporation, and U. S. Railway Association.

55. See Musolf, *Uncle Sam's Private, Profitseeking Corporations*, 13–17.

56. See Musolf, *Mixed Enterprise: A Developmental Perspective*, 59–60.

57. Seidman, *Politics, Position, and Power: The Dynamics of Federal Organization*, 243.

58. NAPA, *The Great Railway Crisis: An Administrative History of the United States Railway Association* (Washington, D.C.: NAPA, 1978), 186; processed.

59. The existence of this statute did not, however, prevent the FSLIC from encouraging private citizens to charter FADA. Though it was chartered under the corporation laws of the state of Colorado, the FSLIC cited sec. 406 of the National Housing Act of 1934 as the basis for this encouragement. FADA is said to be referred to as a "406 Corporation." See Moe, "Exploring the Limits of Privatization," 455 and footnote 9.

60. Letter dated August 7, 1981, from Vice President for Policy Analysis James C. Cruse, Export-Import Bank of the United States, to Erasmus H. Kloman, NAPA, commenting on a draft of the NAPA report. NAPA Report, vol. 1, appendix 3.

61. Ibid.

62. *New York Times*, March 20, 1986.

63. Ibid., January 20, 1987.

64. Jonathan Rauch, "After the Bailout," *National Journal*, February 2, 1988, 322–24.

65. *New York Times*, August 5, 1987.

66. Ibid., May 22, 1987.

Part Three

Conclusion

Chapter Nine

CONCLUSION: BEYOND PRIVATIZATION

Lester M. Salamon

A significant transformation has taken place in the basic structure of the public sector in the United States over the past half century or more. This transformation has involved not simply an expansion in the scale and scope of government activity, but more importantly, a significant proliferation in the basic tools the public sector uses to achieve its objectives.

As a consequence of this change, popular conceptions about the nature of modern government and conventional theories of public administration are increasingly out of touch with prevailing realities. The popular stereotype of the government bureaucrat delivering a good or service to a citizen-taxpayer in practice applies only to a small portion of modern government activity. Increasingly, reliance has been placed on other forms of action that involve not the direct provision of goods or services, but the indirect provision of guarantees, payments to other levels of government, outside contracts, regulations, insurance, and a variety of other techniques.

Traditional public administration, with its focus on the management and control of government agencies, has only limited relevance to the operation of many of these newer forms of public action. Where traditional public administration emphasizes the internal dynamics of public agencies, the newer forms of action often involve elaborate partnership arrangements with nongovernmental actors. Where traditional public administration stresses hierarchical lines of authority and the mechanisms of command and control, the newer forms of action utilize decentralized modes of operation and the techniques of bargaining and persuasion.

Beyond this, by shifting the mode of government operations, the proliferation of new tools of public action has significantly altered the foundation of political discourse. Given the new forms of public action, longstanding ideological disputes over the relative merits of public vs. private action have grown increasingly less relevant, Ronald Reagan to the contrary notwithstanding. Rather than having to choose between public and private action, the new tools of government action have made it possible to blend the two in a wide assortment of ways. As Robert Dahl and Charles Lindblom put it more than three decades ago, the proliferation of new tools of public action has effectively displaced ideological competition as the fulcrum of political debate in the western world and, therefore, represents "perhaps the greatest political revolution of our times."[1]

With notable exceptions, however, the implications of this revolution have yet to be incorporated into the design of public programs or the training of public managers. Little systematic knowledge has been accumulated about the underlying characteristics of the various instruments of government action now in widespread use. The distinctive operational requirements and consequences of these instruments has thus remained largely unexplored. Rather than treating various technologies of public action as an appropriate focus for analysis, prevailing paradigms concentrate instead on other units of analysis—individual programs, public agencies, or broad policies. Moreover, prevailing political rhetoric has yet to take full account of the significant change that has occurred.

The recent interest in "privatization" sparked by the Reagan administration's assault on the activist state has begun to alter this situation. By stressing the existence of private alternatives to direct delivery of government service, advocates of privatization have brought the broader topic of alternative tools of public action into the mainstream of policy debate.

As a framework for structuring this debate, however, privatization has serious limitations. For one thing, it remains preoccupied with the distinction between public and private action, thus downplaying or ignoring the many other dimensions in terms of which different instruments of public action can be categorized and assessed. In addition, it tends to take as given that existing government programs are wholly publicly run, thus overlooking the extent to which some of the key features of privatization are already embodied in the existing program structure. Finally, privatization can be a highly loaded term that signals not a search for ways to improve the operation of the public sector, but a way to limit its operations instead.

The *tools approach* that has been the subject of this book provides a potentially more balanced framework for examining the changing shape of the modern public sector. Where privatization focuses attention on only one dimension of public action, the tools approach stresses the existence of multiple dimensions, many of which have cross-cutting effects. Where privatization begins with a decided preference for private as opposed to public action, the tools approach takes a more open view, stressing the variety of criteria by which different instruments of public action can be assessed.

The objective of this book has been to lay the foundation for such a tools approach, and to make some headway in putting this approach into operation. What remains to be done here is to summarize some of the major conclusions that have emerged and identify the next steps that are needed to advance this field of inquiry still further.

MAJOR CONCLUSIONS

Three major conclusions about the tools approach emerge from the chapters of this book. Each has implications not only for the viability and utility of the approach, but also for subsequent work in the field.

The Descriptive and Analytical Challenge

The first of these conclusions concerns the basic description of different tools. A central assumption of the tools approach is that it is possible to distinguish amidst the welter of individual programs a smaller number of distinctive tools or technologies that the individual programs embody.

What the chapters of this book make clear, however, is that the identification of tools of public action is considerably more complicated than might at first appear. While all grants-in-aid involve payments from higher levels of government to lower ones, for example, some leave far more discretion to the implementing government than others. Government corporations take so many different forms that serious questions arise about whether this is a distinctive tool at all. The same is true of loan guarantees, some of which involve partial guarantees and others of which have many of the characteristics of direct loans. What is more, particular programs can embody combinations of tools, as when social regulations are attached to grants-in-aid or interest subsidies appended to loan guarantees.

What this means is that considerable care must be taken in the specification of tools. The nominal categories commonly used to depict tools—grants, regulation, loans, etc.—on closer inspection embrace a variety of different dimensions. Particular programs embodying one of these forms can combine these dimensions in a variety of different ways. The description of tools thus becomes an analytical activity. Only after first clarifying what the critical dimensions are can particular programs and instruments be described in terms of them.

Far from invalidating the tools approach, however, this observation provides further evidence of the need for it. In the absence of clear understanding about the characteristics of the tools the public sector is using, serious problems can arise in the selection of appropriate forms of action and in the management of the programs that result. Greater precision in matching the characteristics of different tools with the particular requirements of the task can thus improve program performance.

The Consequences of Tools

A second conclusion that emerges from the previous chapters is that tools of government action often have consequences that are very different from those that are expected. In other words, a great deal of mythology seems to surround the operation of many of the principal tools of government action.

One of the conventional beliefs in the policy field, for example, is that indirect tools are more efficient than direct ones in getting an ample supply of services out to program recipients. This is supposed to be so because such instruments make use of delivery systems—both public and private—that are already in place, such as the private banking system in the case of loan guarantees; private nonprofit agencies in the case of social service contracts; and state and local governments in the case of grants-in-aid.

The record reviewed here, however, raises significant questions about this belief. Although commercial banks are potentially available to deliver loan guarantees, for example, many banks have little inclination to do so, creating "take-up" problems that reduce the effectiveness of many loan guarantee programs. Similarly, the use of the tax structure often limits the effectiveness of tax expenditure programs because of the Internal Revenue Service's lack of familiarity with the substantive objectives of these programs and the difficulty of influencing the behavior of those taxpayers for whom the tax subsidies have limited impact.

Similar difficulties exist with the use of contracting out. A central premise of this approach is that a competitive market can be created for the provision of public services that will improve the efficiency with which such services are produced. In practice, however, the degree of competition for government contracts has often been quite limited. Robert Bailey found that in New York, for example, the privatization of commercial refuse did not work out as planned because the few private companies in the business formed holding companies and carved up the market among them. Similar developments have been documented in the handling of vocational education and school transportation, as well as in the provision of human services.[2]

What this suggests is that the consequences of using particular tools cannot simply be assumed. They must be subjected to analysis. The results of such analysis can then be used to guide future tool selection as well as to improve the operation of tools already in use. Here again, therefore, an explicit focus on the operating characteristics of alternative tools can improve not only the quality of policy analysis, but also the quality of public services.

Overall Utility of the Approach

All of this leads quite naturally to the third conclusion—that despite its limitations, the tools approach does offer a useful framework for policy analysis and research. In point of fact, there do seem to be commonalities among programs in different fields that can be understood in "tool" terms. What is more, there seem to be generalizations that can be made about the operating characteristics and consequences of different tools. McDaniel's observations about the impact of "tax thinking" on the operation of tax subsidies, Bardach's analysis of the distinctive enforcement dilemmas of regulatory programs, Lund's conclusions about the expectations of private bankers in loan guarantee programs, and Haider's emphasis on federal–state–local tensions in grant programs all provide evidence of this point.

Given the great proliferation of instruments that the public sector uses, and the likelihood that this proliferation will continue as a result of the "privatization" movement and the resource constraints under which government is operating, the development of a body of knowledge that can help guide the selection of tools and instruct program managers about the consequences of these choices seems increasingly worthwhile. By clarifying the characteristics of different tools and identifying more precisely the "spin" that they put on the operation of programs, such knowledge could contribute significantly to both analysis of public activity and management of the public sector.

NEXT STEPS

For the tools approach to make such a contribution, however, additional work will be needed in at least three areas: research, management, and training.

Research Tasks

At this stage of development, the tools approach remains a promising hypothesis rather than a well-developed set of conclusions. As noted above, important questions persist about the basic categories to use in comparing tools, let alone about how different tools compare in relation to them. What is more, suggestive insights into how various tool characteristics affect program operations have yet to be subjected to rigorous empirical analysis.

This situation is not peculiar to the tools approach, of course. Key tenets of public administration—such as the principle of sharp separation between politics and administration, the desirability of limited span of control and grouping of organizational units by like function—were all deeply felt articles of faith well before they were subjected to empirical testing and found wanting.[3] Nevertheless, to have real confidence in the tools approach and what it can reveal, significant research work is still required.

This work can usefully take three different forms. In the first place, we need basic *descriptive work* to identify the distinguishing operating characteristics of some of the major tools now in widespread use. The work performed by the Advisory Commission on Intergovernmental Relations on the operations of the grant-in-aid tool in the late 1960s and 1970s could serve as a model for what needs to be done with respect to other tools as well, such as loan guarantees, direct loans, insurance, contracting out, and even regulation.

In the second place, further *analytical work* is needed on the underlying characteristics to use in comparing and contrasting different tools. The set of characteristics identified in chapter 2 is a start in this direction, but only a start. As we enrich our descriptive knowledge of how various tools operate, new analytical categories for comparing tools will present themselves, and some of these will promise greater explanatory power than those we have outlined to date. Analysts examining individual tools should be alert to such promising underlying tool features and try to identify, at least in theory, how these features might be expected to affect program results.

Finally, *empirical work* is needed to relate the characteristics of tools to actual program operations and outcomes. This is, of course, the ultimate test of the tools framework, but it is also the hardest to achieve. To be done correctly, ideal experimental conditions are necessary. That is, the test must find programs that differ only with respect to a given tool characteristic but that share most other features—for example, mission, substantive field, target population. Any observable difference in program results can then be appropriately attributed to the tool-related difference.

In practice, however, such ideal experimental conditions are hard to achieve. As we have seen, various programs often combine tool characteristics in rather chaotic ways, making it difficult to find a good, much less a perfect, match. Under these circumstances, it may be necessary to relax the verification requirements, to look at the results of broad classes of programs embodying a particular tool or tool characteristic, and to recognize that some of the consequences attributed to tool differences may really result from differences in program purposes. Such analysis can still be productive, however, particularly as data accumulate from a variety of tests of different classes of tools in different policy areas. This certainly appears to be the case in the analysis of regulatory programs, which is one field where the analysis of the consequences of the use of a particular tool is most advanced. Similar work is now needed on other classes of tools and on groups of programs that embody different tool characteristics, such as indirectness or market-type processes.

Management Tasks

While research work on the tools framework goes forward, improvements can be made in government's capacity to manage alternative tools and make choices among them. A first step in this direction must be to sensitize policymakers to the tool-related choices they are making, to the fact that particular programs embody particular types of tools that may have distinctive consequences for the performance of the program. Too often these issues are buried in the policy development process and never surface for explicit attention. Alternative means for carrying out a particular governmental objective are therefore not explicitly assessed. To the contrary, tool choices are often dictated by factors wholly unrelated to a program's purposes—such as a desire to avoid budgetary impact or escape governmental personnel ceilings. A more explicit review of the benefits and drawbacks of alternative approaches would help remedy this and thus gear program operations more closely to program objectives.

Beyond this, more attention needs to be paid to the operating requirements of different tools in the management of the public sector. At present little guidance is available at the federal level about how to design and manage many of the tools now in widespread use. Thus, each agency operating a loan guarantee, or a regulatory program, or a grant-in-aid must develop its own body of doctrine about how to manage this type of tool. The fact that particular tools operate differently from agency to agency and program to program is probably due in substantial part to this situation. For example, the simple question of what constitutes a default on a loan guarantee differs widely from one loan guarantee program to another. Establishing a set of governmentwide standards, even if exceptions were necessary in certain cases, would likely improve the management of many of these tools considerably, and reduce the amount of time and effort each agency must devote to mastering the rudiments of given policy instruments and deciding how to set up their own administrative systems.

Fortunately, some headway has recently been made along these lines with respect to loan guarantee and regulatory instruments, but it is only a beginning. Given the proliferation of tools that has occurred, much more explicit attention to the development of guidelines for the design and management of alternative tools seems called for.

Training Tasks

Over the long run, however, improvement in the management of alternative tools will require alterations in the training of public managers. At present, two bodies of knowledge dominate the training of public sector managers—public administration and policy analysis. Unfortunately, neither of these equips managers with the insights they need to cope adequately with the proliferation of tools of government action that has taken place. Public administration, as chapter 2 noted, tends to take the government agency, not the policy instrument, as its unit of analysis. Students of public administration thus learn about the dynamics of bureaucracies, the techniques of budgeting and personnel management, and the skills of organizational leadership. The basic premise of the field is that the key to success in public management is to learn how to manage a public agency. As we have noted, however, the central characteristics of some of the newer forms of government action is that they bring a set of third parties into the basic operation of public programs. The implementors of the federal government's higher education loan program, therefore, are not employees of the Department of Education, but employees of the Chase Manhattan Bank and other similar financial institutions throughout the nation. The public manager charged with managing this program must thus learn additional skills related to the operation of the private banking system and the functioning of the credit markets. He or she must also learn how to stimulate cooperation from nongovernmental organizations over which government exercises at best only imperfect control. For this, a different set of teaching materials and a different kind of training are needed.

Nor does the new field of "policy analysis" offer much help. Where public administration focuses on the individual government agency, policy analysis tends to focus on the problems public action is supposed to resolve, and on the substance, as opposed to the form of the government response.

To cope with the insights arising from the tools approach will thus require changes in the public policy and public management curricula, to focus explicitly on the characteristics of the different tools the public sector is employing. Public managers need, at a minimum, to understand the substantial operational differences between direct and indirect forms of government action. Beyond this, they should gain some insight into the operational requirements and management challenges associated with some of the major tools, such as regulation, loan guarantees, subcontracting, and the like. As the world of public management has changed, so too must the training of public managers.

CONCLUSIONS

The genius of program design in the public sector has leapt well beyond popular understanding of the nature of modern government, as well as conventional theories of the public sector. Instead of a government composed of bureaucrats who deliver goods or services to citizens, what exists is a complex set of relationships between public and private organizations tied together in a variety of financial and legal arrangements to carry out the public's business. These changes pose fundamental challenges both to our concept of the public sector and to the concrete tasks of managing government programs. Up to now these changes have attracted little explicit attention. Both our prevailing ideologies, which stress conflict between the public and private sectors, and our conventional theories, which stress the importance of hierarchical relations in bureaucratic agencies, have tended to shield these developments from view.

The *tools framework* suggested in this book is an attempt to alter this situation. Instead of downplaying the proliferation of new forms of public action, the tools approach moves it into the center of analytical attention. Instead of assuming that all government programs are roughly similar in basic structure, the tools approach begins with the premise that they often embody strikingly different technologies.

What the chapters in this book suggest is that the tools approach has at the very least a surface plausibility. The challenge now is to translate this plausible line of inquiry into a meaningful body of knowledge and a defensible basis for action.

Notes

1. Robert Dahl and C.E. Lindblom, *Politics, Economics, and Welfare* (New York: Harper and Row, 1953), 8.

2. Robert W. Bailey, "Uses and Misuses of Privatization," in Steve H. Hanke, ed., "Prospects for Privatization," *Proceedings of the Academy of Political Science* 36, no. 3 (1987): 143–47. For evidence of a similar pattern in the contracting-out of human services, see: Ruth Hoogland deHoog, "Human Service Contracting: Environmental, Behavioral and Organizational Conditions," *Administration and Society* 16 (1985): 427–54.

3. For a critique of these notions, see Herbert Simon, *Models of Man* (New York: Wiley Publishers, 1957).

EUGENE BARDACH is professor of Public Policy at the University of California, Berkeley. He is coauthor, with Robert A. Kagan, of *Going By the Book: The Problem of Regulatory Unreasonableness* (Philadelphia: Temple University Press, 1982) and is an expert on policy implementation.

DONALD HAIDER is professor of Public Management at the Kellogg School of Management at Northwestern University. A former deputy assistant secretary of the U.S. Treasury Department, he is author, among other works, of *When Governments Come to Washington* (New York: Free Press, 1974).

CHRISTOPHER K. LEMAN teaches at the Graduate School of Public Affairs, University of Washington. He has written articles and reports on natural resources policy and administration and a book, *The Collapse of Welfare Reform* (Cambridge, Mass.: MIT Press, 1980).

MICHAEL S. LUND is director of the Jennings Randolph Program for Peace, Washington, D. C. He is coeditor, with Lester Salamon, of *The Reagan Presidency and the Governing of America* (Washington, D.C.: Urban Institute Press, 1986).

PAUL R. MCDANIEL, formerly professor of Law at Boston College Law School, is a partner in the law firm of Hill and Barlow, Boston, Mass. He is coauthor, with Stanley Surrey, of *Tax Expenditures* (Cambridge, Mass.: Harvard University Press, 1985).

LLOYD D. MUSOLF is professor of Political Science at the University of California, Davis. He is author, among other works, of *Uncle Sam's Private, Profit-Seeking Corporations* (Lexington, Mass.: Lexington Books, 1983).

LESTER M. SALAMON is director of the Institute for Policy Studies at The Johns Hopkins University. A former deputy associate director of the U. S. Office of Management and Budget, his most recent book is *The Nonprofit Sector and the New Federal Budget* (Washington, D.C.: Urban Institute Press, 1986).